THEY MADE GOOD GREAT

The Story of the 1969-1970 Berrien High School Rebelettes And Their State Championship Season

THEY MADE GOOD GREAT

THE STORY OF THE 1969-1970 BERRIEN HIGH SCHOOL REBELETTES
AND THEIR STATE CHAMPIONSHIP SEASON

SKEETER PARKER AND JIM BARBER

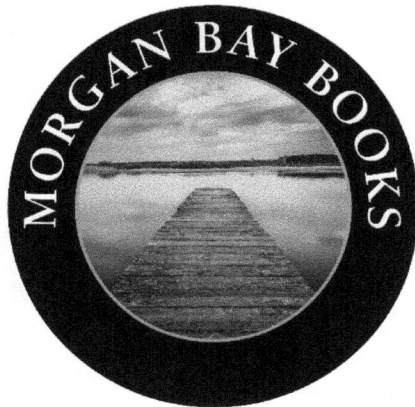

MORGAN BAY BOOKS

In Honor of the

1969-1970 Berrien High School Rebelettes

CONTENTS

ACKNOWLEDGMENTS

The 1969-1970 Berrien Rebelettes were my first heroes. My family moved back to Berrien County from Lowndes County in 1968, just in time for me to start the first grade and my sister to begin high school. It was the next year that I discovered high school sports. The first basketball game I remember was watching Berrien play Cook at the gym in Adel shortly before Christmas in 1969. I didn't really understand the game then (the cheerleaders proved far more interesting), but I knew enough to grasp that Berrien had good basketball teams. And I knew that my cousin, Peggy Barber, played on the team, even though I didn't really know Peggy at the time. We went to a few other games that year, and I kept hearing words like *undefeated, state champions* and my cousin's name, and it all sounded pretty impressive to my 8-year-old self. Somewhere along the way, I began understanding the game as well, and when the season was done and Berrien was crowned state champion, I was starstruck—with the team and the game.

I memorized the stats and scores from that season and collected every article I could find for my own personal scrapbook. It was those newspaper stories that first sparked my desire to become a newspaper reporter, which became my goal in the second grade and led to a journalism career that I thoroughly enjoyed. More importantly, I started playing basketball on the playground at West Berrien Elementary School and fell in love with everything about the game. By the time the 1970-1971 season rolled around, I was a sports fanatic and I understood how the game worked. As much as I loved the 1969-1970 Rebelettes, I loved the 1970-1971 Rebels even better. I saw every one of their home games and remember calling the Nashville police department to get the score when they played Waynesboro for the state championship (my sister actually got to go to all of those state tournaments).

The idea for this book first occurred to me in the 1980s, a short time before what would have been the 20th anniversary of the Rebelettes' first state championship. Of course, work and life got in the way and the idea never came to fruition, but it lingered in my thoughts as a project I would love to pursue. When the opportunity came up to collaborate with Skeeter on this book, I jumped at it.

When you tackle a project of this magnitude, you're usually standing on the shoulders of so many others who poured effort into it long before you got involved. We extend our thanks and appreciation to the following people and organizations: the 1969-1970 Berrien Rebelettes, Coach Dona Gaskins Fields, Betty Jean Simpson, Judy McNabb Walker, Becky Taylor, John Futch, Wenda Gaile Bailey, *The Berrien Press*, the Jamie Connell Photo Collection, Carrie Dorsey Perry Memorial Library and the unnamed and unknown photographers who captured many of the original images in the book, including the late Troy Harsey and Jim Willis. Likewise, we owe a debt of gratitude to the newspapers and sports reporters—especially the *Tifton Gazette* and *Valdosta Daily Times*—who first chronicled this story.

On that note, I can't say enough about my partner in this project. Skeeter Parker loves Berrien County, and he, along with so many others associated with the Berrien Historical Foundation, has invested countless hours in compiling the history of our county, especially the sports history. I have a copy of the notebook Skeeter compiled about Berrien's football program in 1996 and appreciate the memories it evokes when I peruse through those records. His research and compilation of hundreds of newspaper articles made writing the narrative portion of this book not only possible but a true pleasure.

For me, the project was a labor of love. I can't tell you what a joy it was chatting with so many of the women who made up that amazing team and hearing their stories and thoughts about their memorable season. They remain heroes in my eyes.

It's startling to consider that half a century has passed since the events recorded in this book occurred. The memory of it all seems closer somehow. We hope this story will evoke a glimmer of the excitement, drama and magic that captivated Berrien County when a group of high school girls made history and launched a legacy of excellence.

— Jim Barber, March 21, 2020

As we celebrate the 50th anniversary of Berrien High School's first state championship team, I am reminded of the legacy left to Berrien County by the sports teams of my formative years. While I never witnessed a Berrien High athletic event in person until my freshman year of 1981-82, I was keenly aware of the greatness of the school's basketball teams dating back to even before my birth.

From the late 1960s on up through the early 1990s, Berrien High basketball was a mainstay at the state basketball tournament. Growing up in the 1970s, I heard the tales about Berrien's basketball glory everywhere I went, stories both old and new, stories about the players and coaches, and stories about the legend that was BHS hoops. In the 1980s, I was a sophomore during the school year when the Rebelettes won state in both softball and basketball. At some point after graduation, I did various tasks for the teams like running the clock and keeping the scorebook, and in 1990, I was the scorekeeper for the last Rebelette basketball team to win a state championship.

My interest in Berrien County history has always been great and my interest in BHS sports history even greater. Soon after graduating in June 1985, I began a quest to compile the history of the Berrien High football teams. In the intervening years, my search expanded to putting together as much information as possible on all of the school's teams, not just football. There is no telling how many thousands of hours I have spent combing through back issues of *The Nashville Herald* and *The Berrien Press*, not to mention newspapers from other towns.

For many years, 1985-2003, I had a direct involvement with the BHS sports teams, either as a stadium announcer, scoreboard operator, statistician or sportswriter. Some days, it was all four jobs at once. That was a different season in my life, even though I do still do some announcing. I have completed 11 years as the band's halftime announcer, and I announce the Homecoming Courts and Senior Nights.

Besides all the players and coaches who made all the greatness happen, I would like to thank several people who have been instrumental in contributing to all of my documentation of Berrien High School sports. I always like to "blame" my good friend, Coach Ed Pilcher, for getting me involved in keeping statistics back in the fall of 1985, and I probably should blame another good friend, Coach Bart Shuman, for getting me started writing sports for the *Press* in the spring of 1985 when I traveled around with the baseball team.

Then there are all the *Herald* and *Press* sportswriters who came before me and whose work was the basis for everything I have ever been able to compile. I am probably going to leave someone out, but many thanks and kudos to Billy John Hughes, Kenny Drew Fuller, Lee Shearer, Johnny Futch, Tim Moore, Greg Tyson, Jim Barber, Jim Whidden, Dan Taylor and anyone else who has documented sports for our local newspapers.

I have to thank the late, great Dan Taylor again because of all he taught me about keeping statistics and just for being a great person. His daughter Becky is now the sports editor at the *Tifton Gazette*, and I want to thank her for the depths of her research on BHS basketball and basketball in general.

There are so many other people who have shared information and photos with me through the years, and all of them are appreciated more than they ever will know. Thank you from the bottom of my heart for everything that has ever been contributed toward preserving the history of our sports teams.

Go Rebels!

— Skeeter Parker, March 21, 2020

PART 1

THE SEASON

'WE WERE READY TO BE A GREAT TEAM'

AS BASKETBALL TALES GO, they don't get much better than *Hoosiers*, the 1986 film that chronicles a small-town Indiana high school's journey to the state basketball championship.

At first glance—especially in the world we live 50 years after the fact—it might be easy to pick out similarities between the fictional Hickory High School Huskers and the 1969-1970 Berrien High School girls team that earned the first state championship in the history of Berrien County sports. After all, Berrien is one of the smaller schools in Georgia, residing in class AA—now the second smallest of seven classifications in the state—and the Rebels and Lady Rebels have endured their share of disappointment in recent years.

The 1969-70 edition of the Rebelettes (they became the Lady Rebels in the 1990s), however, had more in common with the Milan High School team that won the 1954 Indiana state championship and served as the inspiration for *Hoosiers*.

With an enrollment of 161, Milan was indeed the smallest school ever to win the single-class state tournament in Indiana. But the Milan Indians were never underdogs in their championship season. In the previous season, they had advanced to the state semifinals and entered the 1954 tournament as one of the powerhouse teams with a 19-2 regular season record.

Like Milan, the Berrien High Rebelettes were poised for big things when the 1969-1970 season arrived. Berrien had won region titles

and advanced to the state quarterfinals in the two preceding years. The Rebelettes returned four senior starters from the 1968-69 team that rolled to a 26-3 record, losing 40-35 to Wheeler of Marietta in the AA quarterfinals.

"We knew we were good. We had worked hard and we loved the game," said Lenna Carey Tucker, a starting guard for Berrien who went on to play for the Southern Belles, one of the few women's professional teams playing in an era when sporting opportunities were rare for women, at colleges and especially at the pro level.

"Every year, every game, we expected to win, and we all did our best to do that," Carey Tucker said.

The Rebelettes indeed had high expectations for the 1969-70 season, but perhaps history tempered their belief. Though widely regarded as the most consistently winning team in South Georgia since Coach Stanley "Ramrod" Simpson arrived in 1961, a Berrien girls team had never advanced beyond the quarterfinals of the state tournament.

"Making it to state was the goal, not going undefeated or winning state," recalled Mary Grace Bailey Faircloth, a starting forward on the team. "I didn't think about going undefeated—not because we weren't that good, but because the odds of going that far and not being beaten were not there. We knew we had a pretty good team, and Coach Simpson knew it, too. He pushed us real hard, and we came through."

Unlike tiny Milan, Berrien played in AA, which in those days was the state's *second-largest* classification. Berrien played in the AA classification throughout the 1960 and most of the 1970s, indeed well into the 1980s. With the exception of the nine Region 1-AA teams, scattered across the entirety of the state below Macon, every other AA team in the 1969-1970 season resided north of Macon, most in Atlanta and farther north. Though AA schools were few and far between in South Georgia during those years, Region 1-AA dominated the state tournament, having produced 14 of the previous 18 AA champions.

In a sense, Berrien had failed to uphold the region's honor in the preceding two state tournaments, with their consecutive quarterfinal losses. Various fans recalled feeling like the eternal bridesmaid when tournament time came around.

Berrien entered the 1969-70 season on the heels of eight straight winning campaigns, a period in which they had compiled 158 wins against 42 losses. At home, where the stands came right down to the edge of the court and opposing teams could feel the breath of the Berrien fans, the girls had tallied 28 straight wins, the last loss coming to Northside Warner Robins, a sextet on their way to winning the state AA championship in 1967. Despite all those wins, however, the Rebelettes had little to show for it in their trophy case and had made it to the state tournament just three times in those eight seasons.

Simpson had produced consistently good teams throughout his career, but the 1969-1970 group of girls were the ones who turned good into great.

Throughout the decade, Berrien had seemed to get better and better. One great player on a team gave way to two great players the next year, and the level of talent and experience increased significantly as the decade progressed. As the victories piled up, the desire to play, and win, strengthened with each season.

"I just loved the game; I think everyone of us did," explained Carey Tucker, who had moved from Florida to Enigma when her maternal grandfather was diagnosed with cancer. "We loved the playing, the physical part of it, and the winning. Practices were hard, especially when we lost a game, but we were always challenging ourselves to be better and better."

> "Seldom do you see a team where you have six girls and several others sitting on the bench with that level of potential and talent."
>
> ~ Debra Swain Prince

So, too, did Simpson. Always hard-driving, the coach became even more of a taskmaster in his later years at Berrien, as the talent began to match his expectations, demanding and pushing his teams to ever higher levels of excellence.

No one would admit to it on record, but it appears he pushed none of his teams harder than he did the 1969-1970 edition of the Rebelettes.

It was an experienced, senior-laden team. The four returning starters included three seniors, Carey and fellow guard Peggy Barber, and forward Marla Brown, the team captain. Junior forward Donna Jernigan was the other

1970 ALL·STATE SELECTIONS

Eight members of Coach Stanley Simpson's Berrien High School Rebel and Rebelette basketball teams were selected for All-State honors by members of the press at the 1970 AA State Basketball Tournaments. From Coach Simpson, top center, clockwise, are: Rebel co-captain George Sorrell; Peggy Barber, guard; Donna Jernigan, forward; Brenda Rudeseal, (honorable mention) guard; Andrea Carter, (honorable mention) guard; Lenna Carey, guard; Mary Grace Bailey, forward; captain Marla Brown, forward. The seven Rebelettes were members of the undefeated (30-0) state championship team. Sorrell co-captained the 27-2 Rebels, who advanced to the quarter-finals of the State AA Tournament.

Photo and cutline from the March 26, 1970 edition of the Berrien Press.

returning starter. The other starters were Bailey at forward and Andrea Carter at guard, both of whom received extensive playing time the previous year.

On the bench were three more seniors, Jo Ann Langford, Sandy McMillan and Pat Williams, who would have started in almost any other year at Berrien or on most any other team Berrien played in the 1969-1970 season.

"Seldom do you see a team where you have six girls and several others sitting on the bench with that level of potential and talent," said Debra Swain Prince, a sophomore guard on the team who, in her own words, "collected a lot of splinters" on the bench that year.

"They were exemplary players," continued Swain Prince, who herself would co-captain the 1971-72 team to Berrien's second state championship. "They went above and way beyond what they were called to do. We worked together as a team, all of us. I was a nobody, but we all had the same goal in regard to playing hard, working hard and working as a team. As individuals, those senior girls were just so talented. They had height, experience, everything going for them, and they were leaders, too. They were just extremely good ballplayers, with the commitment and willingness to do the hard work necessary to put it all together."

Judy McNabb Walker, who would co-captain the 1972 state championship team with Swain, played on Berrien's junior varsity team in the 1969-1970 season. She also attended every varsity game that season and came away impressed with "their heart and willingness to give 100 percent to the game."

"There was so much character and drive on that team to give their very best, and I'm thinking about every single one of those girls," McNabb Walker said. "You could feel their sisterhood, whether they were starting or sitting on the bench."

Walker's sentiment was echoed by many of the players on the team, even those who preferred not to be interviewed on record. The player's talent and willingness to work hard, coupled with Simpson's hard-driving ways and demanding expectations, laid the foundation for Berrien's success in the 1969-70 season. But it was the girls' teamwork and close bonds of friendship that propelled them to greatness.

"We got along so well; there was no jealousy between us," Carey Tucker said. "We were ready to be a great team that season."

2

'THERE ARE SO MANY LOST MEMORIES'

ON JULY 20, 1969, Neil Armstrong became the first man to set foot on the moon and uttered the immortal words: "That's one small step for man, one giant leap for mankind." Richard Nixon assumed the presidency that year, with a promise to end the war in Vietnam but not before he expanded the conflict to Cambodia and Laos. Anti-war protests raged all across the country, including one with more than 250,000 people marching in Washington to demand that the U.S. withdraw from Vietnam. The most famous music festival of modern times, Woodstock, took place on a New York farm on August 15th-17th, with more than 400,000 avid fans attending to see the Who, Jimi Hendrix, Crosby Stills Nash and Young and others perform live. The Beatles released their final album, "Abbey Road," and the Doors, Led Zeppelin and Janis Joplin were coming into their own. U.S. Senator Edward Kennedy drove a car off a bridge on Chappaquiddick Island in Massachusetts, killing Mary Jo Kopechne in the process. Hurricane Camille flattened the Mississippi Coast before making its way to the Appalachian Mountains in Virginia, killing more than 259 people in the process. The U.S. Air Force closed its Project Blue Book, concluding there was no evidence of UFOs; *Sesame Street* debuted on PBS; and the first transplant of a human eye occurred—all before school started in Berrien County.

When the basketball season began in 1969, you could buy a gallon of gas for 35 cents, a U.S. postage stamp for 6 cents and a copy of *Sports Illustrated* for 15 cents. The average cost for a new car was $3,270; it was $15,550 for a new house, and the average household income was $9,400 a year. All of those averages were considerably lower in Berrien County.

You could buy a 1-Carat diamond ring for $299; 12 cans of dog food for $1; a bottle of Head and Shoulders shampoo for 79 cents; an 8-track stereo tape player for $38.99; a back-to-college typewriter for $28.88; and a Barbie doll for $4.77. Oh, and a Lava Lamp for $19.95.

The Love Bug, Butch Cassidy and the Sundance Kid, True Grit and *Easy Rider* were popular movies. *Airport* debuted in early March 1970, originating the 1970s disaster film genre just as the Berrien girls were making their final preparations for the state tournament. *Sugar, Sugar* by the Archies and *Age of Aquarius* by the Fifth Dimension topped the music charts in 1969, giving way to Simon and Garfunkel's *Bridge Over Trouble Waters* just as Berrien was winning the Region 1-AA tournament at Crisp County High School in Cordele.

All that history sounds like a long time ago, doesn't it? It was. And in retrospect, one thing seems clear about Berrien's 1969-1970 season. Fifty years was too long to wait to try and capture the feelings, thoughts and memories of that magical season.

"It was incredibly exhilarating winning the state championship, but it was so long ago and there are so many lost memories," said Sandy McMillan Bowen, a senior who scored

41 points as a reserve forward in the 1969-70 season.

Every effort was made to interview each woman who played on the team. Some could not be found; a few preferred not to talk about the experience because it belonged to another time in their life and they want to focus on the here and now; one or two felt shy about being quoted in a book; and even those who happily talked admitted to having forgotten more about that season than they remembered. To a woman, they were all gracious and honorable in the way they reacted.

The story was similar with fans, one of whom recalled the "sheer joy" of watching the Rebelettes play during the 1969-1970 season but could not recall where the state championship was played.

"Was it Atlanta or Cordele?" he asked. "Don't quote me on that!" he added quickly.

What the women do remember is the sense of camaraderie and pride they felt in being the first team from Berrien County to win a state championship trophy.

"What made us successful was Coach and the way he pushed us but also that we were willing to do it," said Peggy Barber Tucker. "Everybody on the team had a part to play and they played it for the better of the team. I am honored to have been part of it."

It's a blessing to have all of these old newspaper articles recounting Berrien's championship season, and Skeeter Parker, a teacher at Berrien High School as well as a staunch advocate for Berrien sports and a loyal recorder of the county's history, has done an

incredible job compiling the records that form the basis of this commemorative book.

Skeeter was just 3 years old when Berrien won the 1969-1970 state championship, but he has logged countless hours digging up the old news clippings and retyping them. It was a true labor of love, and he deserves accolades for the work he has poured into preserving the county's history. Without him, this book would not exist.

> ## "Everybody on the team had a part to play and they played it for the better of the team."
>
> ~ Peggy Barber Tucker

There may be a lot of "lost memories" from Berrien's first state championship season, but John Futch, who began his journalism career covering sports for the *Berrien Press*, perhaps came closest to capturing the team's secret sauce in an article he penned for the *Tifton Gazette* about the state championship game.

Futch, known then as Johnny, was a latecomer to that magical season. He had just returned from serving in Vietnam with the U.S. Army and was stationed at Fort Stewart in Hinesville, Georgia. On weekends when he could, Johnny would make his way to wherever Berrien was playing to watch Simpson's girls and boys as they racked up win after win.

"I know I use it too much, but those seasons were magic," Futch remembered 50 years after the fact. "They helped me get through a difficult period in a backstory, and I owe them a ton for helping me, even though they didn't know it."

Futch's reports, both of the 1969-1970 season and the next year when the Berrien boys captured their state title, may be tinged with a little home cooking, but their swashbuckling style still sings like the swish of nothing but net. Fifty years later, his report on the state championship game for the Tifton newspaper illuminates the magic of that season and lauds the players who made history better than any memories.

"Team captain (Marla) Brown ignored a painful back injury that was supposed to have ended her playing career, scoring 41 points in three games, and coolly quarterbacked the liquid Berrien offense," Futch wrote. "(Mary Grace) Bailey shredded opposing defenses with her driving ability and deadly medium jumper. (Donna) Jernigan, who at 5-4 was a lot closer to the floor than most players, drove, dribbled and shot like a tank-size Pete Maravich, and with a total of 76 points, ran away with high-scoring honors in three of the four tournament games.

"On the other end of the floor, (Lenna) Carey, dominated the boards, setting a school record in the opener against Lakeshore by snaring 12 rebounds and shattering it in the final with 14 on the official books," Futch continued. "(Peggy) Barber, who specialized all season in shutting off hot shooters, did just that against some of the best in the state. The (Brenda) Rudeseal-(Andrea) Carter duo kept opponents off balance with their harassing tactics."

Futch nailed it. His prose told the story without exaggeration.

Five of Berrien's six starters—guards Barber and Carey and forwards Bailey, Brown and Jernigan—were named to the *Atlanta Journal-Constitution* All-State AA Basketball team, voted by a panel of sportswriters and broadcasters. Two others—Carter and Rudeseal, who rotated at the other guard position—received honorable

Aerial view of Nashville circa 1970.

mention recognition. All of those players, plus senior forward Jo Ann Langford, were recognized as the team's most outstanding players at Berrien's annual sports banquet later in the year.

"Coach Simpson had great talent on that team and he kept their feet to the fire as far as a standard of excellence," observed Dona Gaskins Fields, who would succeed Simpson as the girls coach in the 1971-72 season and arguably become Berrien's most successful

coach in just five seasons at the helm. (The Berrien High School gymnasium was named for Fields on January 25, 2020, an acknowledgment of her successful career as a coach, teacher and administrator in Berrien County.)

"They were a good group of girls who didn't mind working hard," Fields continued. "It was also a balanced team, filled with players who were athletic, versatile and capable of doing good things almost anywhere on the court."

3

'RUN, RUN, RUN'

IN THE 1960S, BERRIEN County operated five elementary schools throughout the county—Alapaha, Enigma, Nashville, Ray City and West Berrien. A sixth, East Berrien, consolidated with Nashville Elementary after the 1965-66 school year. There was also Nashville High and Elementary School—which was for black students before full integration occurred with the start of the 1969-1970 school year. It would be two more years, the 1971-72 season, before Vera Wright and Debra Smith became the first black players on a girls basketball team at Berrien.

Lots of girls (and boys) played on those elementary school basketball teams, and the best of the best came together to play on the freshman, junior varsity and varsity teams at the high school. In high school, the girl basketball players became a tight-knit group who genuinely cared about and supported their teammates. Rivalries were reserved for opposing teams.

Mary Grace Bailey Faircloth played on her first basketball team in the eighth grade in Nashville. She made varsity in her sophomore year and recalls being "better at basketball than anything else I tried to do."

"In some sense, it felt like we were ostracized because of being on the basketball team," Bailey Faircloth said. "We stayed together. What little we did outside of basketball, we would do it together."

The 1969-1970 Rebelettes began preparing for their season shortly after they lost a 40-35 heartbreaker to Wheeler of Marietta in the AA state tournament quarterfinals in March 1969. The quarterfinal loss punctuated 26-3 season in which they won the Lowndes Christmas tournament and the 1-AA West Subregion and Region titles.

"I have to say that as seniors, we had nothing else to do," recalled Andrea Carter Hammond, a senior starting guard on the team. "(Most of) our boyfriends had gone to college and we were still in high school. We determined to win the state championship, by practicing all summer, trying to get a starting spot, and to work as hard as we could, including during the Christmas holidays. We practiced every day."

Ultimately, the 1969-1970 sextet would belong to the past in girls basketball, becoming the last of the champions to play the three-on-three half-court game. In those days, girls teams lined up three forwards and three guards on each side of the court. One team's forwards battled the other's guards on one end and vice versa on the other end.

Nationwide, the move was afoot to move girls basketball to full court five-on-five, just like the boys played. In Georgia, school officials decided to transition the game by adopting rovers. In that system, there were two stationary guards on the defensive end of the court, two stationary forwards on the offensive end, and two rovers who could cross the half-court line to play both offense and defense.

In the lead-up to the 1969-1970 season, it appeared Georgia would transition to the rover

Andrea Carter, right, and Peggy Barber put the pressure on an Appling County forward during Berrien's 46-28 win in the first round of the region tournament in Cordele.

system, but at the last minute, officials backed off the decision and kept the traditional three-on-three format at both ends of the court.

Coach Simpson worked the girls hard. They ran suicides on court; they ran up and down the gym stairs and around the full gymnasium, even in the lounge area. They did countless crabs, crouched low to the ground, shuffling from side to side and up and back. They did leg lifts and push-ups, all geared toward getting them into top physical shape.

"We thought we were going to the rover system and we practiced for that," Bailey Faircloth said. "Run, run, run—it was constant. We practiced right after school and on weekends, and we were in the best shape of any team around us."

"We had closed practices a lot because you never knew how long and how much we would practice, over and over," Carter Hammond remembered. "Coach Simpson was rabid to have a state championship. We were too."

Sometimes, Simpson played music when the team practiced. He loved country music, and Willie Nelson was one of his favorites for practice, players recalled. He often played against the girls to teach them specific techniques.

Judy McNabb Walker, the junior varsity guard that year, said her favorite memory from that magical season occurred during one of the rare open practice sessions that she attended. "Coach Simpson was really working them hard

Donna Jernigan shoots over a Waycross guard in the state championship game at Northeast Atlanta High School.

and the girls were so tired," she recalled. "He was standing in the middle of the top section of the old gym and told them, 'Okay, girls. You can have a rest and sit down until I make a basket from up here.' The girls thought they had it made in the shade, and then he wound up making his very first shot. When the ball went through the basket, everybody almost had a heart attack. And it was back to work."

Following tryouts, the varsity team included eight seniors, forwards Marla Brown, Mary

Grace Bailey, Jo Ann Langford, Sandy McMillan and Pat Williams, and guards Peggy Barber, Lenna Carey and Andrea Carter; two juniors, forward Donna Jernigan and guard Brenda Rudeseal; sophomore guard Debra Swain; and two freshmen, forward Donna Bennett and guard Debbie Harrell.

Debra Swain Prince, who today is a retired nurse and lives in Metter, Georgia, with her husband, said she felt blessed to have made that 1969-1970 team as a sophomore. A guard,

Swain Prince felt a special bond with all of her fellow guards but especially Carey.

"Lenna called me Swain-ey bird and took me under her wing," Swain Prince recalled. "I have always loved her for that. She had so much talent, was tall, in great physical condition, and her attitude was incredible. She was relentless, but then, all of the guards, Peggy Barber and Andrea Carter, too, were the same way. They wanted to win badly. I learned a lot from watching them."

McNabb Walker, Swain's co-captain on the 1971-1972 state championship team, appreciated the work ethic she learned from watching the girls practice during the 1969-1970 season. McNabb Walker, who moved to Florida after graduating from high school and has since retired as the deputy elections supervisor in Winter Haven, especially admired Marla Brown for her leadership and support, even after Brown had graduated from high school and gone to college.

Brown's leadership on and off the court resulted in her being named captain of the 1969-1970 team. In addition to making the *Atlanta Journal-Constitution's* all-state team that year, Brown would earn the most valuable player award on the *Tifton Gazette's* seventh annual Tiftarea all-star team.

"She is the most dedicated ballplayer I have ever coached," Simpson told the *Gazette* when Brown won the MVP award. "Marla Brown has put in over 1,150 individual work hours on basketball during the past three years. Her leadership ability has been above and beyond the call of duty. Her on and off the floor leadership for the past two years has played one tremendous role toward making our record what it is."

As the intensity of practices increased and the season opener drew near, the team's confidence grew. They understood their strengths and how to overcome any weaknesses, even the momentary dips in play that can be the difference between a win and a loss.

> ## "Coach Simpson was rabid to have a state championship. We were too."
>
> ~ Andrea Carter Hammond

"I think what made us good was that we each had a specialty, something that we did well and it completed each other," Bailey Faircloth recalled. "Lenna Carey, for instance, could have played forward or guard, but she did better at guard and having her there made us a better team.

"But one person can't win a basketball game," Bailey Faircloth said. "You need a team effort and that's what we had from the very beginning. Our bench was deep, too. They could come in and replace either one of us in a heartbeat."

If the girls were confident prior to the season opener, Simpson was less enthusiastic. He complained about "a general lack of hustle and lack of offensive consistency" to the *Berrien Press*. He told the *Tifton Gazette* another winning season seemed likely but "to do so, we are going to have to get a much better effort out of the girls than we have been getting in the preceding practices."

"Untrue!" quipped Lenna Carey Tucker when reminded of Simpson's concerns prior to the season opener against Tift County. "It was just his psychology. He was a good coach, and he wanted to make sure we were ready."

'A LOT OF IMPROVING TO DO'

COACH SIMPSON CALLED IT "Berrien's toughest opening week in history," and he wasn't exaggerating by much. Over a four-day period, the Rebelettes would play three of the toughest teams on their schedule in Tift County, Lowndes and Bainbridge. Tift and Lowndes were AAA schools and traditional rivals for the Rebelettes. The Tift Angels, led by Coach Sandra Withrow, "come after you from start to finish," Simpson told the *Berrien Press*, and Lowndes featured 6-2 forward Kay Price "who hooks with either hand," the newspaper reported. Bainbridge was said to have one of the best forwards in the state.

Tough competition was waiting, and Simpson's concerns mounted when Marla Brown hurt her ankle a few days before the opening game. The injury would linger throughout the season.

"I don't recall any low points during the season, except for Marla's injuries," Lenna Carey Tucker said. "That worried us because she was our captain and we looked to her for leadership."

The 1969-1970 season started oddly, on a Wednesday night, December 3rd, even though high school games, then and now, are traditionally played on Tuesdays, Fridays and Saturdays. Berrien made the 28-mile trip from Nashville to Tifton, and the game tipped off at 7 p.m.

Carey won the opening jump-off, but no one recalls who grabbed the ball and got first offensive dibs. Indeed, no one remembers who scored the game's opening points, but Tift raced to an early 6-2 lead, despite playing without their top scorer, Juanita Dickens, who was out sick.

> "I don't recall any low points during the season, except for Marla's injuries. That worried us because she was our captain and we looked to her for leadership."
>
> ~ Lenna Carey Tucker

The Rebelettes quickly righted the ship, and their stifling defensive trio of Carey, Peggy Barber and Andrea Carter held Tifton scoreless through the remainder of the first quarter and the entirety of the second. Berrien led 17-6 at halftime.

The defense kept up their relentless pressure in the second half, limiting the Angels to 10 points through the remaining two

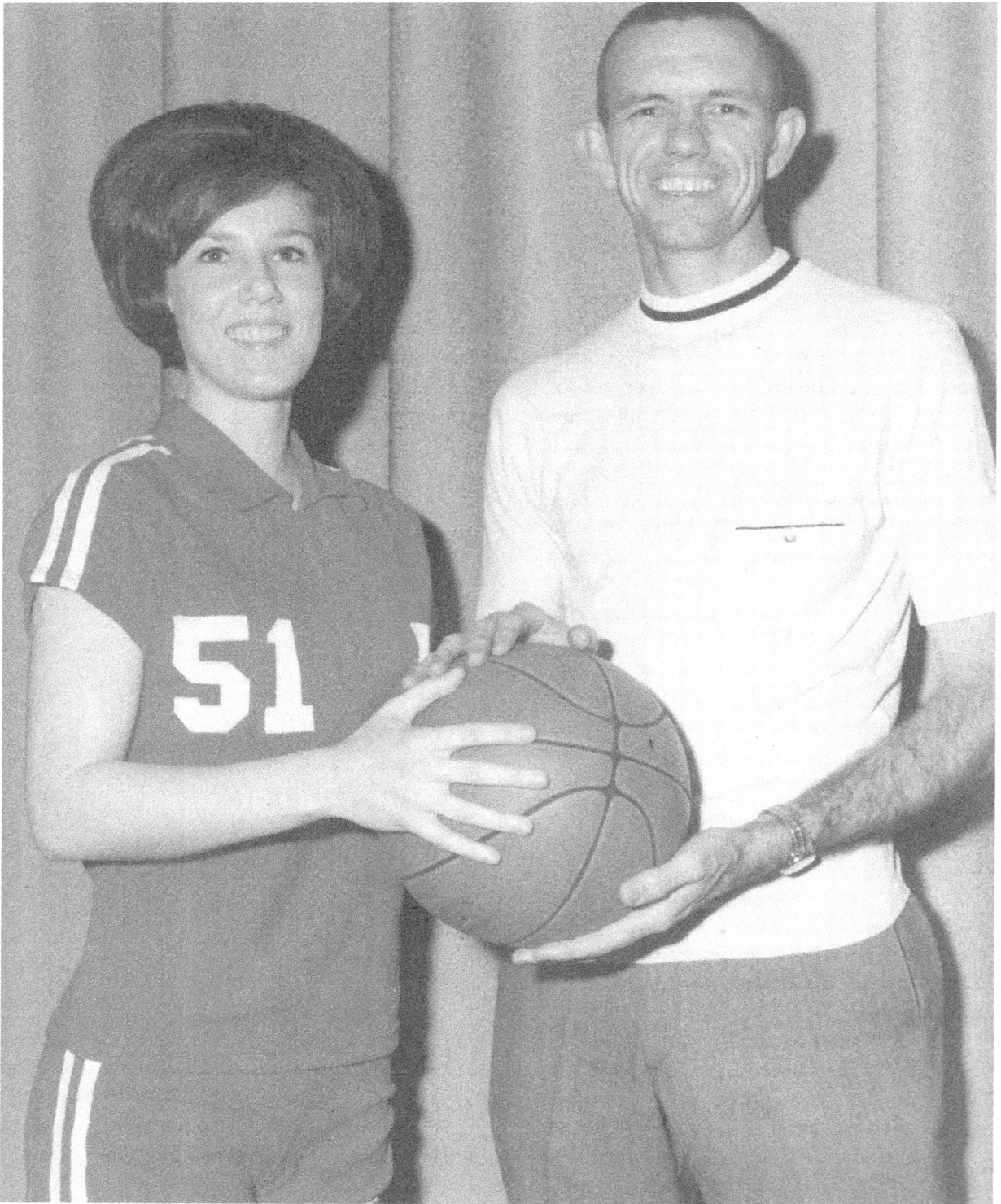

Marla Brown captained the 1969-1970 team. Brown battled injuries throughout the season, first an ankle, then a serious back problem that left her in jeopardy for the state tournament. Despite the setbacks, she racked up 503 points for the offense. Teammates praised her leadership, and Coach Simpson called Brown "the most dedicated ballplayer I have ever coached."

quarters, while the offense found some punch in the third quarter. Berrien won the opener 40-16, as Donna Jernigan dropped in19 points and Brown shrugged off the ankle injury to tally 17. The girls were on their way.

It may have been a sluggish start in many ways, but it was win, something the boys could not muster on this night. The Rebels went cold in the second half and the Blue Devils rallied from an 11-point third-quarter deficit to upset Berrien 46-45. The Rebels would not lose again until they fell 70-60 to Carver of Atlanta in the quarterfinals of the state AA tournament.

Lowndes brought a perfect 2-0 mark to Nashville two nights later, Friday, December 5th, as Berrien kicked off their slate of home games. The Vikettes matched Berrien point for point, with the score knotted at 11-11 after a tough opening period. But Berrien broke open the game in the second quarter, outscoring Lowndes 14-6 for a 25-17 lead at halftime. Kay Price used her hook shots to score 16 points on the night for Lowndes, but no other Vikette came close to double figures against the Berrien defense. In the fourth quarter, the Rebelette offense racked up 18 points, their best showing yet in the young season. Jernigan finished with 19 points, and Brown added 13, as Berrien roared to a 51-30 win, handing Lowndes their first loss of the season.

The next night, Saturday, December 6th, Bainbridge made the long drive to Nashville only to see Berrien put together their best

HOME OPENER – The Berrien High Rebelettes opened the home court season with a 51-30 win over the Lowndes County Vikings. Marta Brown in white shoots for another score as Jo Ann Langford comes in for a backup.

This is a picture of a photo that appeared in the December 11, 1969, edition of the Berrien Press *following Berrien's first home game of the season. The actual photo could not be located.*

performance of the season. It was the first subregion game for both teams, and Berrien served notice they were primed to win a third straight title. The girls led 14-6 after the first quarter and 32-13 at halftime. Still nursing the ankle injury, Brown scored only 3 points in limited playing time, but the Berrien offense finally shook off the early-season doldrums. Jernigan tossed in 31 points, Mary Grace Bailey added 14, and Berrien nailed 13 of 16 from the free throw line as the Rebelettes romped 63-32 to finish their opening week at 3-0.

Simpson was proud of the girls after that first week, but he told the *Berrien Press* they "had a lot of improving to do before he would call them a good ball club."

'OUR KIDS WORKED HARD AND WE WERE LUCKY'

AFTER A HECTIC OPENING week, three games in four nights, Berrien played only one game in the second week of the season. On Tuesday, December 9th, they traveled to Lakeland to line up against neighboring Lanier County, who played in Class C, the state's smallest classification. Berrien simply overpowered the Bulldogettes 59-27. The Rebelettes led 18-3 at the end of the first period, 33-11 at halftime and 49-19 at the end of the third quarter. Almost every player on the team saw action. Mary Grace Bailey pumped in 27 points to lead all scorers, with Marla Brown scoring 14 and Donna Jernigan 13. The Rebelettes were 4-0 and the early wins were coming easy.

"Some nights are better than others for everyone at some point, and we knew how to get the ball to the right person, especially when one of us wasn't at our best," Mary Grace Bailey Faircloth recalled. "There were a few times when I would be the high scorer and wouldn't even know it until we saw the stats."

One week later, Tuesday, December 16th, Berrien made the 13-mile trip from Nashville to Adel to meet rival Cook. The Wasps were winless in seven starts and overmatched against Berrien's well-balanced attack. Berrien led 33-19 at halftime and outscored Cook 20-5 in the third period to put the game on ice. Brown led the way with 26 points, while Jernigan and Bailey added 18 and 17 points, respectively. The final score was 63-33 and the Rebelettes were 5-0.

On Friday, December 19th, Berrien hosted Worth County to close out their pre-Christmas part of the season. The Rebelettes were clicking on all cylinders offensively and Worth caved against the defensive pressure of Lenna Carey, Peggy Barber, Andrea Carter and Brenda Rudeseal. Berrien led 14-3 at the end of the first period, 27-5 at halftime and 40-10 after three quarters. The final score was 56-15. Jernigan dropped in 21 points, followed by Brown with 19 and Bailey with 12. Berrien was 6-0 and would enter the Lowndes Christmas tournament as the top seed and two-time defending champion.

The Lowndes Christmas tournament dated back to 1952 and drew strong fields year after year, mixing up schools from all sizes, from class C to AAA. The tournament had been held in Hahira during its first 15 years before moving to Lowndes when those two schools were consolidated to become the new Lowndes High School, which opened in 1967. As recently as 1966, Manor High School, a class B school that no longer exists, won the girls tournament, with Atkinson County, another Class B team, having won the boys title in 1965. The Berrien girls had won the tournament in 1958, and both Berrien teams had swept the titles over the past two years when the tournament settled at Lowndes

Mary Grace Bailey rattled defenses with her patented drives and medium-range jumpers.

High School. In 1969, Berrien would be going for a tourney first, a third consecutive sweep of both titles.

As the top seed, the Rebelettes received a first-round bye in the seven-team tournament and then found themselves playing rival Tift County in the semifinals. The occasion marked the first time Berrien had played a team twice in the young season.

This time, the Tift Angels had their top scorer, Juanita Dickens, on hand for the game. She had missed the season opener with illness. Dickens would rip the nets for 21 points on this night, outscoring the rest of the Tift team combined. It would not be nearly enough to keep the game close, although the Angels did just that throughout the first half.

Berrien outscored Tift 13-10 in both quarters to take a 26-20 halftime lead, as their strong physical conditioning began to exert itself in the game. Tift was spent by the second half and kept falling further behind on the scoreboard as guards Barber, Carey and Carter stuck to their forwards like glue. The Berrien forwards found the nets with regularity in the second half, and the Rebelettes raced to a 57-36 win, bringing their record to 7-0. Bailey poured in 24 points to lead all scorers, while Jernigan hit for 18 and Brown 15.

In the final, on Tuesday, December 30th, Berrien matched up for the second time of the season against Lowndes, this time on the Vikettes' home court. When the Berrien sextet jumped to a 9-0 lead early in the opening stanza, it looked like the game would be a repeat of the 51-30 rout they had administered to Lowndes in the second game of the season. But Lowndes rallied. Berrien led 13-5 at the end of the first quarter before Lowndes began climbing back in the game behind 6-2 forward Kay Price's lethal shooting.

"I remember the tall girl from Lowndes County," said Bailey Faircloth, who watched the Berrien guards battle Price on the defensive end of the court. "Our guards had a hard time

with her. She could just stand there and have the ball up so high that even Lenna couldn't jump high enough to defend it."

> ## "We knew how to get the ball to the right person."
>
> ~ Mary Grace Bailey Faircloth

The guards on both teams kept the pressure on all night. Price finished with just 16 points, as Berrien broke open the game in the third quarter, outscoring Lowndes 9-4 for a 33-23 lead going into the final quarter. The Vikettes refused to give up, outscoring Berrien in the final period, but never really getting close to making the game tight. Berrien captured their third straight Lowndes Christmas tournament title with the 44-37 win over the hosts. Jernigan ripped the nets for 26 points to lead all scorers, while Brown added 14. It was the eighth straight win for Berrien as they earned the first of four new pieces of hardware that would be added to their trophy case throughout the season.

"Our kids worked hard and we were lucky," Coach Simpson told the *Valdosta Daily Times* after his Rebels had completed a sweep of the tournament for Berrien with a 48-37 win over Lowndes to run their record to 8-1.

Sammy Glassman, the *Times* sports editor, acknowledged it helps to have a little luck in sports, but he also saw clearly what everyone else was feeling about the Berrien teams.

"Simpson is one of those do-it-then-brag coaches, so you won't catch him climbing out on any limbs," Glassman wrote in his New Year's Day column for the Valdosta paper. "But both the Rebs and Rebelettes must be rated as title contenders in both divisions of Region 1-AA. It just may be both will be making state tourney appearances this year."

'The Wins Just Stacked Up'

THE CHRISTMAS HOLIDAYS MAY have given Berrien's basketball teams a break from their schoolwork, but not from basketball practice. The hard work continued through the break to ensure they would stay sharp and not lose any physical conditioning for their upcoming games. It was necessary because the second half of the season started just three days after they lifted the Lowndes Christmas tournament trophies.

On Friday, January 2, 1970, perennial power Cairo came to Nashville. The Syrupmaids brought an 8-2 record to the game. Berrien led 13-8 after the first quarter, and that was close as it got. Marla Brown outscored the entire Cairo team with her 29-point effort and Berrien won 55-28 for their ninth straight win and their second in the 1-AA West subregion.

On Saturday night, January 3rd, Berrien traveled to Valdosta to play their second game against Lowndes in five days and for the third and final time that season. It proved to be a tough outing.

The lead changed hands four times on the way to a 7-7 deadlock before Marla Brown sank two quick baskets to put Berrien on top 11-7 at the end of the first period. Neither team could muster any offense in the second quarter, and the half ended with Berrien leading 13-9. Berrien built their lead to five points in the second half, but tall Kay Price brought the Vikettes back to a 24-24 tie at the end of the third quarter. A battle to the finish seemed at hand, but Berrien struck quickly in the fourth quarter. Donna Jernigan and Mary Grace Bailey each netted both a field goal and two free throws to put Berrien on top for good at 32-24. The eight-point lead held and the Rebelettes won 37-29 to move to 10-0. Brown and Jernigan paced the scoring with 14 and 13 points, respectively. The Vikettes—9-4 on the season at that point, with three losses to Berrien—had given the Rebelettes their toughest test of the season, and it's probably safe to say both teams were glad to be finished with each other for the year.

Three days later, Tuesday, January 6th, Valdosta High School came to Nashville. Berrien remained sluggish on the offensive end of the court, but the defensive group of Peggy Barber, Lenna Carey, Andrea Carter and Brenda Rudeseal—as they had done all season—continued to make scoring difficult for their opponents. The stingy defense never allowed Valdosta to reach double-digit scoring in any single quarter, and Berrien ripped the Kittens 42-20 behind Brown's 21 points.

Lenna Carey Tucker attributed the team's strong defensive play to their years of practice and play together. "We could almost read each other's minds," she said. "We could feel where the other people were on court, especially because we played three on three. I always

Lenna Carey terrorized opposing offenses with her height and steely concentration.

knew where Peggy was going, where Andrea was going. Someone was always there wherever we needed to be."

———

"The more we won, the more we realized there was a possibility that we could go undefeated. I know Ramrod beat that into their heads. He encouraged them and built them up to believe they could go undefeated."

~ Debra Swain Prince

On Friday night, January 9th, Berrien made the long drive up Interstate 75 to play Crisp County, another 1-AA West subregion foe. It was truly a battle of Rebelettes, the nickname for both teams in those days, although Crisp is now known as the Cougars.

Crisp, 5-4 on the season, played Berrien tough at the outset, leading 8-7 at end of the first period. But the Berrien Rebelettes shook off the slow start and rebounded for a 24-16 halftime lead. The defensive trio of Carey, Barber and Rudeseal (Carter missed the game because of illness) allowed Crisp only 10 points in the second half, and Berrien finished the game on top 42-26. Jernigan led the Berrien offense with 17 points and Brown added 14 as the girls moved to 12-0. Simpson played his reserves throughout the second half, giving valuable court time to guards Debra Swain (Prince) and Debbie Harrell and freshman forward Donna Bennett.

"I'm not sure you ever expect to go all the way, but one game built upon another game," said Swain Prince. "The wins just stacked up. The more we won, the more we realized there was a possibility that we could go undefeated. I know Ramrod (Coach Simpson) beat that into their heads. He encouraged them and built them up to believe they could go undefeated."

'THEY WANTED IT AS BAD AS WE DID'

THROUGHOUT THE 1960S AND 1970s, well into the 1980s, fans packed the stands whenever and wherever Berrien played. The teams were known for smooth offenses, pressuring defenses and their willingness to run at full tilt. This style of play made them a popular attraction. As both teams chalked up win after win in the 1969-1970 season, it was not uncommon for the visiting Berrien team to pack a gym with more fans than the home team.

In sports, when you're on top, you have a target on your back, even if you don't realize it. As the Berrien girls stacked up win after win, fans and sportswriters weren't the only people taking notice. So, too, were their opponents. And, for a brief stretch, chinks appeared in the armor and the Rebelettes began to struggle.

"The best I can remember is that they were just tough teams," Mary Grace Bailey Faircloth said, recalling that tough stretch. "I don't remember how far into the season it was, but there came a point where I personally think we were recognized as the team to beat and they wanted us bad. We felt like we had to work hard in all of our games. There were several struggles where we had to get down to the nitty gritty to pull it out."

Fresh off their victory against Crisp County the previous night, Berrien hosted rival Tift County on Saturday, January 10th. At 3-6, the AAA Angels were having a poor season. Berrien had routed the Angels twice already, by

24 points in the season opener in Tifton and then by 21 points in the Lowndes Christmas tournament. The teams were rivals on the basketball court, but no one really expected Tift to mount a serious challenge. And, frankly, attention that night was riveted on the boys game, where the Rebels would bring a 12-game winning streak into their rematch with the Blue Devils, who had upset Berrien 46-45 to start the season.

The Berrien girls got off to yet another slow start, but their reliable defense made it tough on the Angels. Berrien led 7-4 after the first period. And then the wheels fell off, offensively and even defensively. In one of their worst quarters of the season, Berrien was outscored 12-3 in the second quarter and found themselves trailing 16-10 at halftime.

Simpson railed at the girls during intermission, and Berrien came out determined and focused in the third quarter, even though their offense remained sluggish. The Rebelettes outscored Tift 7-2 in the third period and headed into the fourth quarter trailing by one at 18-17—by far the most anemic performance by the offense all season.

Sandra Withrow, the Angels' coach, called it "the best team effort so far" for the season and she was particularly happy with the tough play of her guards against the Berrien forwards. Finally, after having chipped away at Tift's lead throughout the third quarter, the Rebelettes found their footing in the final period. Still, Tift refused to yield and the lead changed hands

The 1969-1970 Berrien High School Rebelettes—Front row, left to right: Debbie Harrell, Sandy McMillan, Donna Jernigan and Donna Bennett. Middle row, left to right, Team Manager Gloria Mathis, Peggy Barber, Pat Williams, Debra Swain and Team Manager Cynthia Bailey. Back row, left to right: Coach Stanley Simpson, Andrea Carter, Marla Brown, Jo Ann Langford, Mary Grace Bailey, Lenna Carey and Brenda Rudeseal.

several times throughout the final stanza before Berrien pulled away for 32-27 win. Donna Jernigan and Marla Brown led Berrien's offense, scoring 14 and 12 points, respectively.

One reason Berrien struggled was poor free throw shooting, which was usually one of the team's strengths. Against Tift that night, they hit only eight of 15 attempts. The Angels only had two attempts from the free throw line all night, which helped secure Berrien's 13th straight win.

"They wanted it as bad as we did, but we just did a little better when it mattered," recalled Bailey Faircloth, discussing that tough stretch of games for the Rebelettes. "We never let our guard down."

———

Frankly, the letdown and struggle against Tift County could have been the result of plain-old tiredness. After all, Berrien had played seven games over a 10-day stretch, more than half of them against opponents they had already matched up against earlier in the season. If not physically tired, it stands to reason they were at least mentally exhausted by the crammed schedule. And by their third match-ups against Lowndes and Tift, their opponents knew what to expect from Berrien and they had revenge on their minds as well.

Following the struggle with Tift, Berrien enjoyed a six-day rest from game play. But they continued to practice hard, and Simpson made sure they stayed in shape with plenty of running.

On Friday, January 16th, they returned to action, hosting Thomasville, another 1-AA

West subregion foe. At 9-2, Thomasville was no pushover and Berrien expected a tough battle.

The Bulldogettes came out strong, their forwards pushing hard against the Berrien guards, and led 16-14 after the first period. Berrien bounced back strong in the second quarter, however, outscoring Thomasville 16-5 to take a 30-21 lead into the locker room at intermission. In the first half, the Berrien girls hit 13 of 18 shots from the field for a torrid 72 percent. Both teams scored 11 points in the third quarter and Berrien appeared poised for an easy win, leading 41-32 as the final stanza began. But then things unraveled. Behind the shooting of Anne Rumble and Joyce Alligood, Thomasville began to find the basket while their defensive trio clogged up the middle to slow down the Berrien forwards. The Bulldogettes steadily chipped away at the deficit, but time ran out on their rally and Berrien emerged with a hard-fought 49-47 win. Brown and Jernigan each dropped in 21 points to pace the winners, still unblemished after 14 games. Rumble scored 24 points for Thomasville, the best showing of any forward against the Berrien defense to that point in the season.

"I just don't remember the details of the games, but I know they were tough teams to beat," Lenna Carey Tucker said. "They had strong girls who were ready to play and they had a reputation for winning teams. We knew we had our work cut out for us. We were proud to be undefeated and wanted to stay that way—that's what I remember."

The Thomasville game was physically and mentally exhausting, and Berrien had to follow it the next night with a long road trip to Cairo. The Rebelettes had routed Cairo by 27 points two weeks earlier at home in their first game of the new year. In that game, Rita Ponder had scored just five of Cairo's 28 points.

LEADER -- Pacing the Berrien Rebelette too-close-for-comfort 49-47 victory over Thomasville were Donna Jernigan (shooting) and Marla Brown. Backing up this shot was Mary Grace Bailey (42).

Picture from the January 22, 1970, edition of the Berrien Press.

On this Saturday night, January 17th, Ponder ripped the nets for 31 points and the Syrupmaids, who entered the game at 8-6, had Berrien on the ropes throughout the night. The Rebelettes had a solid start, taking a 15-11 lead after the first quarter. But then things fell apart.

Ponder was hot for Cairo, and the vaunted Berrien guards struggled to stop her. Cairo outscored Berrien 18-9 in the second quarter to take a 29-24 lead at halftime. When they had trailed Tift County at halftime a week earlier—the only other time they were down at the midpoint all season—Berrien had used a solid third quarter to narrow the gap. That was not the case on this night. Cairo matched Berrien point for point in the third quarter and entered the final period with a 41-36 lead.

"We let ourselves down because we knew we could do better than that. Coach Simpson let us have it. But it was not a low point; it was just a time to reboot, get ourselves back together and do what we knew we were capable of doing."

~ Mary Grace Bailey Faircloth

WITH LANIER -- The Berrien Rebelette offensive had to work hard against a stout Lanier defense for a 54-46 victory. Grace Bailey (42) and Marla Brown (50) tangle with the Bull-dogettes for the ball as Donna Jernigan anticipates a pass.

The Rebelettes had several struggles throughout the season in their run to the state title. This is a picture of a photo that appeared in the February 5, 1970, edition of the Berrien Press.

The records are unclear as to precisely how the game unfolded, but at one point in the second half, Cairo built an 11-point lead, either late in the third or early in the fourth period. Just when their unbeaten season seemed likely to end, however, Berrien took charge with a 16-1 run to gain the lead sometime in the fourth quarter. It's unclear exactly when Berrien took the lead, but news reports suggest once they got it, they never let it go. The final 48-47 win was too close for comfort, but it was a win. Brown scored 26 points, Jernigan added 15, and Berrien made the long, late-night trip back to Nashville with a 15-0 mark.

"We let ourselves down because we knew we could do better than that," Bailey Faircloth said. "Coach Simpson let us have it. But it was not a low point; it was just a time to reboot, get ourselves back together and do what we knew we were capable of doing."

DEFENSE - Key to the Berrien High Rebelette success is good defense, provided here by Brenda Rudeseal, Lenna Carey and Peggy Barber, in the white suits from left to right.

This is a picture of photo that appeared in the January 8, 1970, edition of the Berrien Press.

8

'THEY ARE PROBABLY THE BEST IN SOUTH GEORGIA'

WITH THAT TOUGH THREE-game stretch behind them, the wins really started piling up for the Berrien girls and they came easily. As Mary Grace Bailey Faircloth said, the Rebelettes knew what they were capable of doing it and they did it.

On the Tuesday night, January 20th, after the Cairo game, rival Cook came to Nashville. Berrien led 19-13 after the first period, but the defense limited Cook to just eight points in the final three periods, including a shutout in the final stanza. Donna Jernigan led Berrien with 20 points, while reserve forward Jo Ann Langford, subbing for Bailey who missed the game with an ankle injury, scored 18. Marla Brown added 17 as Berrien ran away with the game, 56-21, to move to 16-0.

Next, Saturday, January 24th, they traveled to Thomasville to play the Thomasville Central Jackettes. Berrien outscored Thomasville Central in every quarter. The Rebelettes led 28-10 at halftime and finished with a 55-23 waltz. Brown, Bailey and Jernigan scored 16, 15 and 12 points, respectively, in what the *Tifton Gazette* described as "balance at its best."

Lanier made the short trip to Nashville from Lakeland on Tuesday, January 27th, and the game was not nearly as close as the final 54-46 score suggested. Berrien led 31-20 at halftime and extended their lead to 12 points in the fourth quarter before Lanier rallied to close the gap in the final minutes. Brown dropped in 28 points to lead the Rebelettes, while Jernigan and Bailey added 12 and 10

points, respectively. The win raised Berrien's record to 18-0.

On Friday night, January 30th, the outstanding group of seniors played their final game in the Berrien gymnasium. The result was never in doubt. Berrien led Crisp County 24-11 at halftime, and as was becoming the custom, outscored their opponents in all four quarters. Berrien closed out their home campaign with a 48-27 win, their 28th straight at home dating back to 1968. Brown and Jernigan finished with 15 points each and Bailey added 14.

The next night, Saturday, January 31st, Berrien made their longest road trip of the season to face the Bainbridge Bear Kittens for the second time. Bainbridge's Jackie Williamson had scored 22 points against Berrien in their first meeting and was considered one of the state's premier forwards. Williamson got another 22 points on this night as Bainbridge played Berrien close in the first half. The game was tied 10-10 after the first period and Berrien led 17-15 at halftime. But while Williamson was piling up points, the Berrien defense held the other two Bainbridge forwards to just two points each all night. Meanwhile, Berrien's increasingly balanced offense outscored Bainbridge 25-11 in the second half for a 42-26 win. Brown scored 17 points while Jernigan and Bailey dropped in 14 and 11, respectively.

Simpson was cautiously optimistic after watching his undefeated Rebelettes net their 20th consecutive win of the season. "We

Just how deep were the Berrien girls in their championship season? Brenda Rudeseal, a junior reserve guard, made honorable mention on the Atlanta Journal-Constitution's *All-State AA Team.*

"Berrien keeps the ball until they get the open shot," Sullivan explained. "They usually shoot above 50 percent. Berrien has great outside shooters, but their offense is centered around clearing out the middle and driving for a good shot."

As for the Berrien guards, "They are probably the best in South Georgia," Sullivan said.

Praise aside for Berrien, the Thomasville coach liked his team's chances in the upcoming rematch with the Rebelettes. "We have to control the ball to beat Berrien," Sullivan said. "We have three girls that can score on any guards. But we can't force anything on the Berrien girls. We will have to keep the turnovers down and not miss any scoring chances.

"It's just a case of who has the best guards and shooters," Sullivan concluded.

The rematch came Friday night, February 6th, in the Thomasville gym. The Bulldogettes kept the game tight in the opening stanza. Berrien led just 12-10 after the first quarter before pulling away for a 25-17 halftime lead.

In their first meeting. Berrien had led by nine points at halftime and heading into the fourth quarter before Thomasville mounted their big rally and made it a close game. This time, the Rebelettes applied the pressure early in the third period and built their lead to 33-22 with four minutes remaining in the quarter. When Thomasville sliced that lead to six, 33-27, it appeared another comeback might be in the offing. A quick goal and a free throw in the final 45 seconds of the period brought Berrien's lead back to nine at 36-27 heading into the final stanza. This time, there would be no rally. Thomasville could never get any closer than nine and Berrien finished with a 50-38 win to move within one game of an undefeated regular season.

Free throws provided the winning margin for Berrien on this night. The Rebelettes

thought here lately we could perform a little better than we have," he told the *Tifton Gazette.* "We've played in streaks ... look good for a few minutes and then look bad ... Experience has carried us ... five seniors in the starting lineup."

After six days off, Berrien went on the road again for another bout with Thomasville, which had come within two points of the upset when the teams played three weeks earlier in Nashville. Prior to the game, Thomasville Coach Guy Sullivan told the *Thomasville Times-Enterprise* why Berrien was such a formidable foe.

Lenna Carey blocks a shot from the Waycross forward in the 1970 region championship game, as Brenda Rudeseal positions herself to snatch up the loose ball.

connected on 18 free throws as the Thomasville guards stayed in foul trouble throughout the contest. Thomasville scored just eight free throws on eight fouls from the Berrien guards. Jernigan ripped the nets for 25 points and Brown tossed in 22 to provide the bulk of Berrien's offense in the win.

Valdosta presented the final hurdle in Berrien's quest for an undefeated regular season. Berrien had routed the Kittens 42-20 in the teams' first meeting a month earlier in Nashville. But pressure has a way of creating tension and causing athletes to perform well below their capabilities.

"The term 'choke' is commonly used to describe when an athlete's performance suffers greatly under pressure, their well-planned strategy goes out the window, they struggle to do things they've practiced hundreds or thousands of times before; sometimes their mind just goes blank when they most need to think on their feet," explains Simon Boulter, a British trainer, fitness expert and the author of *Unleash The Champion Within: An Athlete's Guide to Mental Toughness, Peak Performances and Achieving Greatness.* "It's one thing to perform a little below your capabilities under pressure, but choking and performing significantly below what you're capable of is another. Skills that they can easily perform in nonpressure situations can become extremely difficult for an athlete when choking under pressure, at a time when they want to do their best."

Okay, maybe that's a little overkill to explain what happened when Berrien, 21-0, and Valdosta, 9-10, met on Tuesday night, February 10th, before a packed crowd in the Valdosta gym. No matter how you analyzed it, the game was ugly. The Rebelettes felt the unwanted tension of trying to finish unbeaten and made mistakes, especially on the offensive side of the court. And, too, the Valdosta girls rose to the occasion.

Sammy Glassman, sports editor for the *Valdosta Daily Times*, explained the outcome this way in his report on the game. "Last night's girls game saw some brilliant defensive play by the Kittens' and the Rebelettes' guard corps. It was primarily the work of VHS' Nita Brantley, Evelyn Graham and Debbie Stephenson and Berrien's Lenna Carey, Peggy Barber and Andrea Carter, which accounted for the low score."

The Kittens took the early lead and stayed in front by one to four points throughout the contest. Valdosta led 9-7 at the end of the first quarter and 15-13 at halftime. Depending on the point of view, the third period was either a defensive dream or an offensive nightmare, as both teams combined for a grand total of three points over the seven minutes of play. Valdosta led 16-15 heading into the final stanza.

None of the women interviewed recalled what Simpson told them during the break between quarters. In fact, 50 years after the fact, none even remembered the closeness of that game with Valdosta.

The Kittens refused to fold and maintained their lead until 42 seconds left in the game when a Valdosta guard fouled Berrien forward Marla Brown. Valdosta led 21-20 at that point.

"I didn't think for a while it was meant to be."

~ Coach Stanley Simpson

Brown walked to the foul line, bounced the ball and calmly drained the first shot to tie the game at 21-21. The scene quickly replayed and Berrien led for the first time all night at 22-21.

With the lead in hand, Berrien shook off the night's pressure and attacked the final 42 seconds with a champion's confidence. Brown hit a field goal to push the score to 24-21 and Jernigan nailed two free throws following a quick Berrien steal and a desperation foul by the Kittens. The game ended with Berrien on top 26-21 and the Rebelettes had become the first team in Berrien's hoops history to go undefeated in regular season play. Captain Brown scored 15 of Berrien's 26 points for the sluggish offense, and Berrien was headed to postseason play with a 22-0 mark.

"I didn't think for a while it was meant to be," Coach Simpson told the *Tifton Gazette* after the game. "We didn't play well, but we won."

9

'IT WAS JUST GAME TO GAME AND KNOWING WE COULD DO IT'

BERRIEN ROLLED INTO THE 1-AA West Subregion tournament in Thomasville as the top-seed and heavy favorite. Nine days passed between the Rebelettes' last game against Valdosta and the tournament tipoff. The time off gave the girls an opportunity to catch their breath from the mental strain of trying to finish the season unbeaten. Not having games to play also allowed them to recover physically, but Simpson continued to train them hard in anticipation of the tournament. Now was not the time to let anything slip.

Simpson, too, had a method to his madness, according to John Futch, the returning Vietnam War veteran turned sports reporter, who spent countless hours talking with the coach during the 1969-1970 and 1970-1971 seasons. "Rod told me a number of times that he did not want his teams to get too comfortable too early," Futch recalled. "He wanted them to peak at the end of the season, not in the middle. The end was where it counted. That was the carrot on the stick."

The girls drew a first-round subregion game with Bainbridge. Berrien had won their first two meetings with Bainbridge by 31 and 16 points and the Bear Kittens had struggled all season, finishing at 7-14. Nevertheless, Berrien would not take the Bainbridge girls for granted. Their senior forward Jackie Williamson was averaging over 30 points per game and considered one of the best in the state.

The Berrien-Bainbridge bout kicked off the tournament at 7 p.m. on Thursday night,

February 19th. Bainbridge played their best game of the season. The Bear Kittens led throughout most of the first quarter, as Berrien shook off the rust from their nine-day break in play. With 14 seconds remaining, Mary Grace Bailey hit a short jump shot to knot the game

Junior forward Donna Jernigan led the Berrien offense, scoring 511 points, or 17 per game, and nabbing 93 rebounds in 30 games.

at 13-13. Undaunted and confident, the Bear Kittens inbounded the ball, pushed it past half court and Williamson added one last basket to put Bainbridge on top 15-13 as the quarter ended. How good was Williamson on this night? She scored all of Bainbridge's first-quarter points and a total of 22 in the first half.

Bainbridge maintained the pressure in the second quarter, never trailing until they built a 26-22 lead with three minutes remaining in the half. At that point, Simpson called a timeout and reminded the Berrien sextet to believe in themselves. When they returned to the court, Marla Brown and Bailey promptly drained two field goals to tie the game at 26-26. Donna Jernigan followed with two more shots to put Berrien on top 30-26, and then Brown hit a free throw and a long set shot with 10 seconds left in the half. Brown's basket completed an 11-point run for the Rebelettes and gave them a 33-26 lead.

Again, though, Bainbridge refused to yield. Shaking off the momentum shift, they quickly moved the ball down court and Pam Long hit a field goal as the buzzer sounded to cut Berrien's lead to 33-28 at halftime.

In the third quarter, Williamson pumped in seven more points, and Bainbridge outscored Berrien 14-13, leaving the Rebelettes with a slender 46-42 lead as the final period began. Berrien finally asserted their superior talent in the fourth quarter. Carey shut down the high-scoring Williamson, limiting her to a single basket the entire period, and the Berrien forwards drove relentlessly toward the goal, forcing the Bear Kittens to foul. Bailey, Brown and Jernigan combined to hit 12 of 14 free throws in the final stanza and Berrien outscored Bainbridge 17-4.

Williamson led all scorers with 31 points on the night, but the balanced attack and depth from the Berrien forwards made the difference. Brown led Berrien with 26 points, followed by Jernigan with 22 and Bailey with 15. The Rebelettes drained 75 percent of their free throws on the way to a 63-46 win and a berth in the final.

"Bainbridge was tall, but they weren't fast," Mary Grace Bailey Faircloth remembered half a century after the game was played. "We did a great job of going around them to the basket."

The subregion final pitted Berrien against another familiar and tough foe, tourney host Thomasville. The Bulldogettes had romped past Crisp County 54-39 to reach the final, and Thomasville Coach Guy Sullivan was confident about his team's chances against Berrien based on their two previous encounters.

> "The pressure on that team was almost insurmountable with every game they played. The more they won, the more that was expected out of them, with no exceptions."
>
> ~Judy McNabb Walker

"It's the first subregion game to my knowledge that a Thomasville girls team has ever won," Sullivan told the *Thomasville Times Enterprise*. "And, we have a good chance to win tonight."

In their two previous bouts, Thomasville forward Anne Rumble had scorched Berrien

Mary Grace Bailey provided offensive versatility with her medium-range jump shots and willingness to take the ball to the basket. She scored 317 points for the Rebelettes, including 133 field goals.

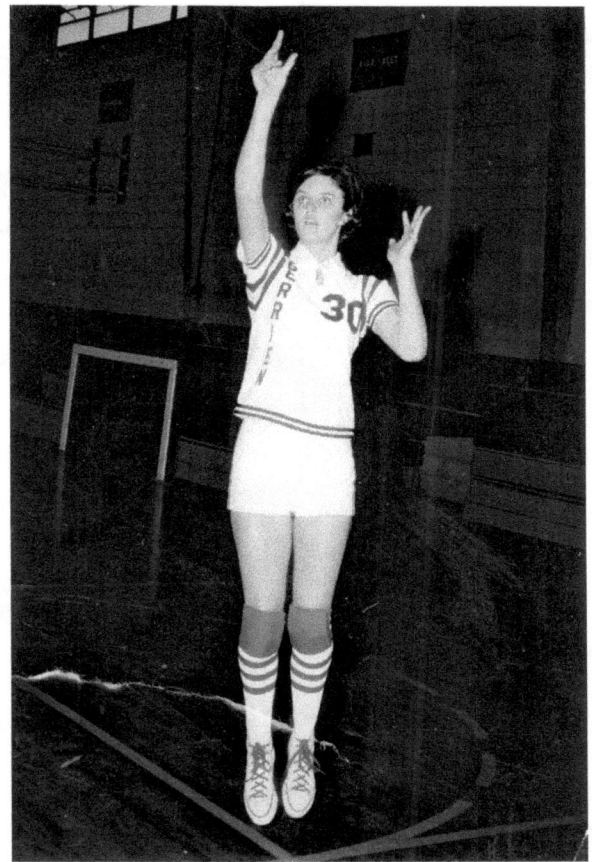

Senior reserve forward Jo Ann Langford would have been a starter on virtually any other team in Georgia in the 1969-1970 season. She was one of eight girls honored at the team banquet as "most outstanding."

with 24 and 25 points. But Rumble had been out for two weeks—first sick with the flu and then on a student exchange program to South Dakota. Still, she had led Thomasville's attack the previous night with 23 points in the win over Crisp County.

The game began at 7 p.m. on Saturday, February 21st, and Berrien jumped to a 4-1 lead. Rumble and the high-powered Thomasville forwards attacked the Berrien defense and drew multiple fouls, scoring all of their points on free throws to tie the game at 6-6. Marla Brown responded with six straight points to put Berrien on top 12-6 at the end of the first quarter and the Rebelettes never looked back.

Carey clamped down on Rumble, holding the high-scoring forward to just five points for the entire night, and Peggy Barber and Brenda Rudeseal played a tenacious man-to-man defense against the other Thomasville forwards. Thomasville managed just two fields in the entire first half, shooting a miserable 8 percent from the field, while the Berrien forwards connected on 61 percent of their shots from the floor. The Rebelettes led 32-14 at halftime, and every player on the team saw action as Berrien rolled to their third consecutive subregion title with a 53-27 rout over the tournament hosts.

Brown outscored the entire Thomasville team, slashing the nets for 29 points, including

Debra Swain made the 1969-1970 team as a sophomore. A guard, she "collected a lot of splinters" on the bench but appreciated the learning opportunity from her more experienced teammates.

Andrea Carter earned a starting position on the powerful Berrien defense in her senior season and was rewarded with an honorable mention on the Atlanta Journal-Constitution's *All-State AA team.*

a perfect nine for nine from the free throw line. Jernigan added 12 and Bailey 10 as Berrien moved to 24-0 on the season.

Judy McNabb Walker, the 1969-70 junior varsity guard who would co-captain the Berrien girls to a second state championship two years later, recalled the growing belief and confidence among fans, students and her fellow players about the varsity team's chances as the wins mounted up.

"They knew they had a solid team from the outset, but I don't think the team expected to go undefeated or that they would win a state championship," McNabb Walker said. "As the season progressed, that's when the

expectation that they could win state became a reality. The pressure on that team was almost insurmountable with every game they played. The more they won, the more that was expected out of them, with no exceptions."

McNabb Walker's assessment was spot on. Simpson's unbeaten girls were feeling the pressure, but their confidence was pushing it down and they believed in themselves and their teammates.

"There was no big defining moment for us as a team," Bailey Faircloth explained. "It was just game to game and knowing we could do it."

10

'How defense is supposed to be played'

BERRIEN DREW APPLING COUNTY in the opening round of the Region 1-AA finals, which were played at Crisp County High School in Cordele. Appling, 16-5, had lost the 1-AA East subregion final to Waycross.

Playing on Thursday night, February 26th, the Rebelettes got off to their usual slow start and trailed Appling 12-7 after the first period. Then the defensive trio of Peggy Barber, Lenna Carey and Brenda Rudeseal took over the game, holding the Lady Pirates scoreless in the second period as the first half ended with Berrien on top 18-12. In the second half, Berrien simply took over the game, maintaining the pressure on defense and finding the basket with increasing accuracy from the field. Berrien outscored Appling 16-8 in the third period and 12-8 in the fourth period on their way to a 46-28 win. Donna Jernigan paced the Rebelettes with 20 points, while Marla Brown and Mary Grace Bailey added 13 each.

In the region final, Berrien faced Waycross, the Region 1-AA East champion. Waycross, 20-3, had routed Thomasville 52-35 in their semifinal.

The scouting report showed the Waycross girls played a strong man-to-man defense led by guards Dale Baker, 5-11, and Ava Williams, 5-9. The Waycross forwards, all seniors in the starting positions, were led by 5-6 Vicki Cason's 22.9 points per game, and strong outside shooting from Christine Garner and

Gail Baker, both 5-8. Against Thomasville, Cason had scored half of her team's points, bombing in long-range set shots to give Waycross the easy win.

A near-capacity crowd filled the gym in Cordele for the 7 p.m. tip-off on Saturday, February 28th. Waycross came out determined to shut down Brown and Jernigan, and their guards played the Berrien forwards tight. Indeed, Brown was held scoreless throughout the first half. The lead changed hands several times in the first quarter. With Berrien on top 8-7, Cason and Gale Baker each scored late in stanza to give the Bulldogettes' an 11-8 lead after the first period.

In the second quarter, the Rebelettes struck quickly. Jernigan scored and then Mary Grace Bailey found the basket for two more and Berrien moved on top 12-11. For good measure, Jernigan and Bailey matched their previous baskets and the lead widened to 16-11.

On the other end of the court, meanwhile, the Berrien defense was in the process of showing "how defense is supposed to be played," the *Waycross Journal-Herald* reported in their wrap-up of the game.

"Lenna Carey, Peggy Barber and Brenda Rudeseal of Berrien threw up a defense that stymied Waycross' offense," the newspaper wrote in their March 2, 1970, edition. "Miss Barber turned in one of the finest individual defensive exhibitions seen in South Georgia in many years, sticking like a leach to Vicki Cason all evening."

Mary Grace Bailey goes over Waycross' 5-11 guard Dale Baker for two of her game-leading 24 points in Berrien's 41-35 win in the Region 1-AA final played in Cordele.

Cason would finish with just 15 points, well below her season average, as the Waycross forwards connected on just 15 of 45 shots, 33.3 percent, from the field.

While Waycross succeeded in holding down Brown and Jernigan, Bailey opened up the scoring with deadly short jumpers and wide-open layups. Berrien outscored Waycross 13-3 in the second quarter to grab a 21-14 halftime lead. The Rebelettes widened their lead to 32-21 by the end of the third quarter. Waycross rallied in the final quarter,

pulling to within 39-33 with 1:21 left in the game. Bailey responded with the last of her 24 points and Waycross scored late as Berrien garnered a 41-35 win. Jernigan managed 12 points, and the Rebelettes were on their way to state with 26-0 mark.

"Our defensive people ... particularly Peggy Barber and Lenna Carey ... did a tremendous job," Coach Simpson told the *Tifton Gazette* after the game. "Grace Bailey took hold on the offensive end ... They played Brown and Jernigan real tough."

11

'HE WORKED US LIKE WE WERE UNDERDOGS BEFORE EVERY GAME'

A SCHEDULING QUIRK IN the 1969-1970 basketball season meant the state-bound girls AA basketball teams had two weeks off between the region finals and the beginning of the state tournament. For the Berrien girls, the "time off" translated into more grueling practices to ensure they stayed sharp and in great shape for the games to come. It also meant watching the boys team compete in the state tournament, which was held in the second week of the layoff.

After their opening-game loss to Tift County by a single point, the Rebels had rolled right along with the girls team, winning every game they played, including the subregion and region titles. In the state sectionals—the name given back then to the first round of the state tournament when the region champions and runners-up played against each other—Berrien overcame an eight-point deficit in the first half to beat Lakeshore of College Park 57-46. The game was played in Cordele at Crisp County High School, where the Berrien teams had swept the Region 1-AA titles a week earlier. Led by senior Richard Tucker and juniors George Sorrell, Charles Wright, Roger Guess and Bobby Taylor, the Rebels had compiled a 27-1 record and served notice they were a team on the rise. But their championship moment had not yet arrived.

In the quarterfinals—played Thursday afternoon, March 12th, at Georgia Tech's Alexander Memorial Coliseum—the Rebels faced Carver of Atlanta. Berrien entered the tournament with the best record of any team, but Carver was the defending state champions. Carver came into the game averaging more than 80 points and had throttled Murphy of Atlanta 114-77 in the first round. The strong Berrien defense, which had limited opponents to 38.9 points per game, held the run-and-gun Carver offense well below their season average, and the Rebels led 27-24 at halftime. But foul trouble—three starters had three fouls at halftime—and 40 turnovers doomed Berrien as Carver roared back in the second half. The Panthers built their lead to 20 points early in the fourth quarter and then coasted home to a 70-60 win. Now it was the Rebels' turn to watch and learn (maybe yearn) from the way the Berrien girls would handle their role as the pre-tourney favorites.

With their 26-0 record—the only unbeaten team in the field—Berrien rated as the team to beat when the AA girls state basketball tournament began. The Rebelettes were averaging 48.9 points per game coming into the tournament while holding their opponents to just 30.5. Coach Simpson continued to work the girls hard, including a Saturday practice on the day after his boys were eliminated in the quarterfinals.

"Coach wouldn't let us get cocky or big heads," Lenna Carey Tucker recalled. "He worked us like we were underdogs before every game, even before the state tournament. He

Peggy Barber battles a Lakeshore forward for a jump ball. Berrien beat the team from College Park 43-26 in the first round of the state tournament.

was a good psychologist. He knew how we could get the big head or go off and think we were better than we were. He made us work hard the entire year."

Still, the Berrien team was confident about their chances as they practiced and waited for the tournament to begin. Then matters took an ominous term. Marla Brown, the team captain and leading scorer, had struggled with an ankle injury throughout much of the season. In the week before the tournament began, she sustained a serious back injury that sent her to an orthopedic specialist and sidelined her for the first game of the tournament.

The state sectional game pitted Berrien against Lakeshore of College Park, the runner-up from Region 2-AA, with an 18-9 record. The game tipped off at 8 p.m. Monday, March 16th, at Vienna High School, and the outcome was never in doubt. Playing without their captain, the Rebelettes came out in top gear and led from start to finish. Berrien led 16-8 after the first period, 28-15 at halftime, and 34-18 at the end of the third quarter. In the final stanza, Simpson substituted freely and Berrien rolled to a 43-26 win over the Lancerettes.

Donna Jernigan led the Berrien attack with 20 points and also used her ball handling skills to make sharp passes to the open forwards. Senior Jo Ann Langford, substituting for

> "Coach wouldn't let us get cocky or big heads. ... He was a good psychologist."
>
> ~ Lenna Carey Tucker

Brown, scored 11 points and Mary Grace Bailey added 10 for the Rebelettes.

"Defensively, we did an outstanding job," Simpson told the *Tifton Gazette* after the game. "We thought the forwards, considering they had to adjust some things at the last minute, did all right."

With their 27th consecutive win in the books, the girls returned to school for two days and prepared for the trip to Atlanta. Brown's back injury continued to be a source of concern but by Wednesday—just before the girls boarded the bus for the almost four-hour trip to Atlanta—there was good news from Simpson.

"If Brown is ready, our chances are probably better (than any other team), he told the *Gazette*. "It looks as though she'll play some."

12

'THERE'S ALWAYS PRESSURE GOING INTO THE STATE TOURNAMENT'

THE BERRIEN GIRLS WERE unbeaten and confident about their chances in Atlanta. By this point, the girls knew they were a topnotch team but then again, they were also going up against the best of the best from all over the state. Plus, they had to overcome history. Three times before—the preceding two years and in 1962, Simpson's first year at the helm in Nashville—the Rebelettes had advanced to the quarterfinals only to lose each time. The previous year, they had been vanquished by Wheeler of Marietta, 40-35, and the Wheeler girls were back to defend their title.

"There's always pressure going into the state tournament because you're going into the unknown as far as the other teams are concerned," Mary Grace Bailey Faircloth said. "All we had to go on was what Coach told us about them and what we learned from watching film. But there again, we knew by that time that we were capable of doing it and good enough to come out on top."

Berrien's quarterfinal opponent was Okeefe of Atlanta, the Region 6-AA champion. The fighting Irish brought an 18-10 mark to the contest, and were clearly overmatched from the start.

Played at Northside High School in

The Rebelettes were vying for the first state championship trophy in the school's history.

Atlanta, the game tipped off the tournament at 4:30 p.m. on Thursday, March 19th. Typically, Berrien started slowly. Still, when Bailey hit a medium jumper to put the Rebelettes on top 6-0 with 2:15 left in the first period, it looked like smooth sailing. Then, the Irish fought back, tying the game at 6-6 with three quick baskets. Captain Marla Brown was playing, despite the crippling back injury, and she propelled Berrien's attack. In rapid succession, the Rebelettes reeled off seven straight points and the defensive trio of Peggy Barber, Lenna Carey and Andrea Carter shut down the O'Keefe forwards to end the first period with a 13-6 lead. For all practical purposes, it was over.

Donna Jernigan started the second period by rolling down the middle to hit three easy shots and Berrien expanded their lead to 25-13 at halftime. In the third quarter, the Berrien guards stifled the O'Keefe offense while Brown, Bailey and Jernigan tossed in six points each to build the lead to 43-16 heading into the final period. At that point, Simpson pulled his starters and let reserves Jo Ann Lanford, Sandy McMillan and Pat Williams play the forward positions while Brenda Rudeseal, Debra Swain and Debbie Harrell rested the guards.

In their outstanding, if somewhat limited action, Carey and Barber hauled down eight rebounds each as Berrien dominated the boards, 38-20. Brown, despite the bad back, poured in 20 points to lead the balanced offense, while Jernigan and Bailey tossed in 17 and 14 points, respectively.

"Irish eyes stopped smiling in the third quarter as guards Lenna Carey, Peggy Barber and Andrea Carter shut down the O'Keefe offense and the Brown-Bailey-Jernigan combo contributed six points each to outscore the Atlantans 18-3 and blow O'Keefe out of the gym," John Futch wrote in a report for the *Tifton Gazette*.

The 53-28 win made them the first Berrien girls team to advance to the state semifinals and pushed their unblemished record to 28-0. More importantly, it cemented in their minds that they were the

> ## "We were confident by then—not overconfident—but sure of ourselves and what we could do."
>
> ~Mary Grace Bailey Faircloth

team to beat and the worst pressure they could expect would come as much from themselves as their opponents.

"I don't have specific memories of the actual games in Atlanta, but I never felt like we would lose a game in the state tournament," Bailey Faircloth recalled. "We were confident by then—not overconfident—but sure of ourselves and what we could do. Everything was one step at a time, taking care of the game at hand. Really, it was like that through the whole season."

In the remaining quarterfinal bouts that Thursday evening, Forsyth County beat St. Pius X of Atlanta, 79-68; defending champ Wheeler edged Franklin County 59-51; and Waycross, the runners-up to Berrien in the Region 1-AA final, routed East Atlanta, 47-19.

———

The semifinals paired Berrien against Forsyth County from Cumming, Georgia, at 7 p.m. on Friday, March 20th. In addition to Brown's bad back, Carey came up lame with an ankle injury, but both girls were primed and ready to play regardless of the pain.

The Bulldogettes were a solid team, one of the best Berrien faced all year, and they proved tough at the outset. Behind the shooting of forward Joyce Gravitt, Forsyth eased out to a 12-10 first quarter lead "as the Berrien defenders had difficulty adjusting to the attack," John Futch wrote in his report for the *Tifton Gazette*.

Forsyth added another quick goal in the second period before Bailey connected on a short jumper to tie the game at 14-14. With 5:13 left in the half, Brown struck for two and Berrien led 16-14, "the last time the game was close," Futch reported. Berrien outscored Forsyth 16-5 over the next five minutes and strolled into the locker room at intermission with a 32-21 lead. Nothing changed in the second half, as foul troubles plagued Forsyth. Berrien connected on 20 free throws, expanding their lead to 40-28 at the end of the third period. The 12-point margin held up through the final quarter as Berrien rolled into the final with a 54-42 win. Jernigan paced the Berrien attack with 24 points, while Bailey added 21.

"The (girls) decided at the beginning of the year they were not going to be denied," Coach Simpson told the *Tifton Gazette*. "They said practically every day of the season they were going to win the state championship."

Now, the Rebelettes, 29-0, were within one game of their goal. And waiting in the final was a familiar foe in Waycross.

Foul trouble plagued Berrien's semifinal opponent, Forsyth County. Mary Grace Bailey is on the receiving end of one of 20 fouls called against Forsyth.

Waycross had denied Wheeler a rematch with Berrien and a chance for a second consecutive state crown with a 55-51 overtime win. The Bulldogettes led throughout the game until a late Wheeler rally knotted the score at 51-51 at the end of regulation play. In the two-minute overtime, Waycross connected on four free throws and held Wheeler scoreless for the win, improving their record to 23-4.

"What was advertised as the State AA Girls championship will be an instant replay as the Pine Flats' playoffs when Berrien meets Waycross for the Georgia title (tonight at 8:30)," Futch wrote the next day in his report for the Tifton newspaper.

13

'IT WAS MORE OF A CORONATION THAN A GAME'

RAIN FELL ALMOST NONSTOP in Atlanta throughout the weekend of the state finals. Nevertheless, the stands in the Northside High School gymnasium were packed and the crowd roared almost from start to finish as Berrien and Waycross collided in the title game on Saturday night, March 21st.

"It was an amazing atmosphere and so exciting to be there," remembered Judy McNabb Walker, the sophomore guard on the junior varsity team who watched every game the varsity played in the 1969-1970 season. "I don't really remember the game that much, but the fans were enthralled."

Walker is not alone in her recall of the game itself. The women who played it don't remember much about the state championship game either.

"I don't remember much about the tournament period, but the state championship game stands out," Lenna Carey Tucker said. "I can't remember details, but I do remember the pure excitement of it. We were so proud of each other, proud to win the game, happy for Coach Simpson. I don't think we were surprised to win; we knew we could do it."

Fortunately, plenty of news reporters watched the game and recorded the details. For the record, here's how the night unfolded.

Mary Grace Bailey opened the game with a layup on Berrien's first possession to put the Rebelettes on top 2-0. She followed with a short jumper to make it 4-0, as the Berrien defense was smothering the

> "It was an amazing atmosphere and so exciting to be there. I don't really remember the game that much, but the fans were enthralled."
>
> ~ Judy McNabb Walker

shorter Waycross forwards. The Bulldogettes missed their first four shots before their sharp-shooting forwards, Vicki Cason and Gale Baker, both connected from outside to tie the game at 4-4. Seconds later, Marla Brown struck from long to put Berrien on top 6-4. And that was all in the first 82 seconds.

Donna Jernigan hits two of her game-leading 15 points for Berrien in the final against Waycross. At 5-4, Jernigan was the shortest Berrien forward, but the junior led the team's offense in both scoring and rebounding for the season.

"The remaining 26 minutes and 38 seconds just made things official," John Futch wrote in a report for the *Tifton Gazette*.

When Bailey hit a free throw to make it 7-4, Waycross would never get any closer. The patient Berrien forwards connected on six of nine field goal attempts in the first period on their way to a 14-6 lead. In the second period, Carey, Peggy Barber and Andrea Carter "kept the Waycross forwards off balance and shooting hurriedly," the *Waycross Journal-Herald* reported, and Berrien connected on half of their shots to build the lead to 23-12 at halftime.

"I can't remember how the score went, or even what the final score was," Carey Tucker said. "We were just in it moment by moment, trying to do everything Coach said and 100 percent focused on the game. I do remember Mary Grace did an awesome job in the championship game."

Throughout much of the second half, Berrien led by as many as 12 points in a display of "astounding accuracy from the field," according to the Waycross newspaper. For the night, the deliberate Berrien forwards connected on 15 of 24 shots from the field for a sizzling 62.5 shooting percentage. Meanwhile, the intense pressure from Carter, Carey, Barber and Brenda Rudeseal kept the Waycross sharpshooters, Cason and Baker,

cold on their end of the court. The Bulldogettes hit just 13 of 45 attempts for a miserable 28.8 percent from the field.

"Cason, used to hitting in the 30s, was baffled by Barber and could hit only 16," Futch wrote in his game report. "Baker, named with Cason to the All-State first team, had 14."

Berrien led 32-22 at the end of the third period. Waycross did outscore the Rebelettes 10-5 in the last stanza, but the outcome was never in doubt and the game never as close as the final 37-32 score suggests. Throughout the final minutes, the Rebelettes stalled the ball as Berrien fans roared, "We're No. 1."

Berrien's intense pressure on the defensive end of the court frustrated their opponents all season.

Mary Grace Bailey races around the Waycross guard for a left-handed layup, scoring the opening points in Berrien's 37-32 win over Waycross in the championship game. Special Berrien Press *tourney photo by Jim Willis.*

"The state championship game was never in question," John Futch recalled 50 years after the game was played. "It was more of a coronation than a game.

"An image that lingers is the state championship trophy sitting on the scorer's table," Futch continued in a conversation from his home today in Phnom Penh, Cambodia, where he retired following a long career in journalism. "This was still the half-court days and when the offense would go down and score, they came back to midcourt to sneak a peek at it. The defensive players did the same."

BERRIEN COUNTY:
HOME OF 1970 AA
STATE CHAMPIONS
IN GIRLS' BASKETBALL

BERRIEN COUNTY:
HOME OF 1970 AA
STATE CHAMPIONS
IN GIRLS' BASKETBALL

The Berrien Press

"Of The People, By The People, For The People Of Berrien County"

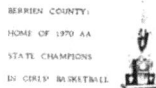

OFFICIAL ORGAN OF BERRIEN COUNTY $4.00 A YEAR   NASHVILLE, BERRIEN COUNTY, GEORGIA 31639   SINGLE COPY 10¢   VOL. 11, NO. 43 - MAR. 26, 1970

Simpson Builds Character Along With Champions

ALL-STATE SELECTIONS

The Long-Awaited Happy Moment As The Trophy Was Presented

Car Wash

1st Annual Steer Show And Sale Set For April 21

Sing Sunday

BERRIEN HIGH REBELETTES WIN STATE AA BASKETBALL TITLE

Piney Woods Rooter Says...

City Invites Bids For Hall

W. L. Lanier Farm Bureau Pres. Resigns

Stock Car Races

Berrien County Fans Jammed The Stadium To Support The Rebelettes In The Title Game

(Continued on Page)

14

'I CAN CLOSE MY EYES AND STILL REMEMBER SEEING THE SMILE ON HER FACE'

THE BERRIEN GIRLS JUMPED for joy and hugged each other when the buzzer sounded to end the state championship game. Fans swarmed the court. And Jimmy J. Powell, an executive committee member of the Georgia High School Association and a former resident of Berrien County, presented the trophy to the Rebelettes. It was truly a crowning moment for the girls, for Coach Stanley Simpson and Berrien County. Never before had a sports team of any kind from Berrien County reached such lofty heights, posting a perfect 30-0 season and winning the state championship.

"All of us were thrilled, but we tried to be cool," Andrea Carter Hammond recalled. "Also, we were grateful for the pulling together that had occurred as a team."

"I don't remember the final very well," Mary Grace Bailey Faircloth said a few weeks before this book was published. "It was like a whirlwind, kind of surreal. I do remember coming home on the bus afterwards, and everything was really quiet and it was like, 'Wow! We did it.'"

They did it, indeed.

"They were just fabulous, each and every one of them," Coach Stanley

"Ramrod" Simpson, who was named AA coach of the year by the *Atlanta Journal-Constitution*, said after the victory. "I'm proud of them all."

For Simpson, it was the realization of a dream to coach a state championship team and the reward for all the hard work and hard-driving effort he had put into the program and demanded from teams since arriving in Nashville nine years earlier.

"It just wouldn't have been right for this area's most successful high school basketball season in more than a decade to end without a state championship being added to the list of honors," Sammy Glassman, sports editor for the *Valdosta Daily Times*, wrote in an article recapping the basketball season in South Georgia.

There had been a few close calls and the occasional sloppy play, but the Rebelettes never faltered when it really mattered. They handled the tough teams, the expectations, the pressure and the demands from their coach and themselves.

"I think the only time we felt any pressure was in the subregion tournament (at Thomasville)," Simpson told the *Tifton Gazette*. "I thought in the state tournament

The crowning moment:
Jimmy Powell, a former Berrien County resident and executive committee member of the Georgia High School Association, presents the AA state championship trophy to the Rebelettes and Coach Stanley Simpson.

they were as loose as any group I've had … loose as a goose."

The Berrien girls had succeeded with four guards—Peggy Barber, Lenna Carey, Andrea Carter and Brenda Rudeseal—that the *Valdosta Daily Times* "rated as one of the all-time great defensive combos to turn up on a girls team in this or any other part of the state." The forwards—Captain Marla Brown, Mary Grace Bailey and Donna Jernigan— "offered an attack that was well-balanced and very potent," the newspaper wrote.

John Futch, who had watched and chronicled the ascendancy of Berrien's basketball program through the years, perhaps summed up the story best in an article about the state championship tournament in the *Berrien Press*.

"No team in recent years has so totally dominated a tournament like Berrien, a fact underscored by sportswriters and broadcasters when they named seven Rebelettes for All-State honors," Futch wrote.

Mary Grace Bailey Faircloth remembers being on court when the state championship game ended, but she can't recall the specifics or emotions of the night. But half a century later, one special memory remains etched in her mind.

Bailey Faircloth was the youngest of four children, born six and a half years after her three brothers. Because of her father's work schedule, her parents never attended any games.

"I didn't know it until the end of the game, but my mama and daddy went up there (to Atlanta) just to see their baby girl play the final," Bailey Faircloth recalled in a voice tinged with emotion. "After the game, we were in the dressing room trying to gather up as a team, and there were all these people from the stands coming to us. I looked up and saw Mama. I remember her smiling at me, and I was surprised to see her. I said, 'Hey, Mama,' but didn't get to talk to her because Coach was calling us back. I look back and wish I had taken a moment to say a little more to her then because she passed away the next year.

"Winning the state championship was just awesome, but that moment with my

> ## "Everything else—as great as it was, as well as we did—was just taking care of business, but that moment with my mom stands out to me."
>
> ~ Mary Grace Bailey Faircloth

mom was truly outstanding," Bailey Faircloth continued. "Everything else—as great as it was, as well as we did—was just taking care of business, but that moment with my mom stands out to me. I can close my eyes and still remember seeing the smile on her face standing there."

FACES AT STATE

Johnny Futch recorded with camera some impressions of the faces in Atlanta at the State AA basketball finals Saturday, starting at bottom left and continuing clockwise: Ramrod checks the press coverage . . coach Wayne Harris was caught by a print as well as a slippery road . . Peggy Barber is pleased about something . . Andrea Carter reads too . . Cynthia Bailey isn't missing this . . Mary Grace Bailey was almost caught unawares . . and Debra Swain wonders about that . . but Marla Brown is taking it all in . . as well as Jo Ann Langford . . as it gets sleepy time for Donna Jernigan and in the center Lenna Carey pensively watches.

Photo reproduction from an original March 26, 1970, edition of the Berrien Press.

15

'THEY HELPED US SEE WHAT IT TAKES TO MAKE GOOD GREAT'

FIFTY YEARS HAVE PASSED since that magical 1969-1970 season for the Berrien High School Rebelettes. A few memories linger; more have been lost. One outcome shines bright and clear: The girls on that team did not become women who live in the past. Rather, they took what they learned from that time and applied it to their futures.

To this day, Andrea Carter Hammond appreciates the determination of her teammates to give their very best to that championship season. It meant hard work, sacrifice and even suffering to some extent, but the effort yielded a result that has paid dividends throughout her life. After high school, Carter Hammond eventually wound up in Atlanta where she carved out a successful career in real estate until retiring to raise her son. Today, she lives in Hilton Head Island, South Carolina.

"Winning that state championship, going undefeated, was a defining moment in my life—to work toward a goal with my teammates and have it come to fruition," Carter Hammond said. "I loved all of them and felt my teammates' support, many times in hard times. I think all of us went into life with confidence, determination to do well, and the ability to bond with others in preparing for goals in all kinds of endeavors. It was a milestone of excellence for all of us."

Basketball taught Lenna Carey Tucker "to work hard and give my best, especially if it's something you love, to just give it your all."

"Because I was long and lanky and very self-conscious about it, basketball gave me confidence," Carey Tucker said a few days after Christmas in 2019. "I knew I could run; I could jump and play. And I felt I was good at it, which gave me a sense of self-confidence."

After graduating from high school, Carey Tucker played one year with the Southern Belles, a women's professional basketball team based in Carraway, Arkansas. The experience allowed her to travel the United States and create more friendships like those she enjoyed with her fellow Rebelettes.

"I loved it," she said. "I thought it would be a great opportunity to play and it would be more like a pro team where my skills would improve. I played one year, then came home and got married."

Lenna Carey played one year for the Southern Belles professional basketball team before returning home to Berrien County to marry her high school sweetheart, Richard Tucker.

She married Richard Tucker, who was captain of the 1969-1970 boys team, in 1971 and they have two children and several grandchildren. For the past 40 years, she has owned and operated Carey Antiques in Tifton.

One of her sisters-in-law is former teammate and fellow guard, Peggy Barber Tucker, who married Richard's older brother, Raymond, who graduated from Berrien in 1968 and went on to play basketball at both Brewton-Parker College and Columbus State College. Another teammate, Donna Jernigan Barber, is also Peggy's sister-in-law. Jernigan Barber coached the Berrien girls varsity team during the 1976-1977 season.

"Richard and I think about those years and basketball sometimes, especially with the aches and pains we have now from it," Carey Tucker said with a laugh. "I have missed it from time to time. It's so funny. I don't often do it now, but several years ago, I would go into a locker room and just the smells would bring back the memories. It's so easy to remember running up and down that wooden floor. Even going to high school games now, you want to go out there and play."

Carey Tucker actually coached the Enigma Elementary School basketball team for several seasons before Berrien County consolidated all of its schools.

"I found myself trying to coach like Simpson did," she said. "Focus on ball handling, fundamentals and to act both on and off the court in a way that you could hold your head up."

The Southern Belles also called Mary Grace Bailey a couple of times to ask her

Lenna Carey Tucker's Southern Belles played a game in Nashville during the year she played on the professional team. Carey Tucker later coached the Enigma Elementary School basketball team in Berrien County and has operated Carey Antiques in Tifton for more than 40 years.

to join their team, but she never followed through on the requests. She had made up her mind, however, "to go play with them if they called again," but then she met John Faircloth. "When the Southern Belles called the next time, we were already serious about getting married," she said.

Bailey Faircloth graduated with a degree in bookkeeping and accounting from Val Tech in 1971 and married Faircloth later in the year. They have a son and daughter, three grandchildren and two great-grandsons. The Faircloths live in Sparks, Georgia, and she helps her husband run a used pallet business.

"As far as legacies go, the only thing I can say is that we got it done," Bailey

Faircloth said in December 2019. "We were the first to go 30-0 and win the state championship. We never thought of ourselves as superior or anybody's heroes. We were just people who played basketball well and played well together. I'm thankful for the experience because it gave me one of the best memories of my life and some incredible friendships with people I know cared about me."

In a way, the 1969-1970 team stood on the cusp between the past and present. They were the last of the teams who played three on three on both ends of the court, and given their ability, accomplishments and the way sports evolve, it's quite possible they were the best ever to play that particular style of girls basketball in Georgia. The game changed the next year, and girls played four on four on each end of the court, with two rovers having the ability to play both offense and defense. In 1975, girls in Georgia began playing five on five.

On a more personal note, the girls on that team missed out on the possibilities that would soon be available to women with the passage in 1972 of Title IX, the landmark civil rights law that prohibited discrimination in education and paved the way for increased athletic opportunities for women.

Dona Gaskins Fields, who played for the Rebelettes in the late 1950s and is still the all-time leading scorer for Berrien, played at Florida State University in the early 1960s, but those opportunities were few and far between for women in those days. In fact, the first national collegiate basketball championship for women was not played until 1972 when it was won by tiny Immaculata College from Pennsylvania, a journey that is chronicled in the movie, *The Mighty Macs*.

Had they played and won in today's world, every member of the 1969-1970 Berrien Rebelettes would likely have had the chance to continue their basketball careers in college. It's a testament to their character and focus on the here and now that none of the women expressed any regret about what they might have missed.

> "That 1969-70 team set the stage for girls basketball at Berrien High School, for seeing what could be attained. In the eyes of other girls not on that team, there became a feeling of 'We can do it, too.'"
>
> ~ Dona Gaskins Fields

Like the players from that 1969-70 team, the fans, too, are getting older. But they still remember and care about what the team accomplished. Engage in

On January 25, 2020, the Berrien High School gymnasium was named after Dona Gaskins Fields, who succeeded Stanley Simpson as head coach of the Rebelettes and added two more state championship trophies in her five-year varsity coaching career. Fields, who played for Berrien in the late 1950s, remains the school's all-time leading scorer. Many of her former players returned for the occasion. Photo by Wenda Gaile Bailey.

conversations with people who watched the games, and while they may cannot recall specific memories, they're quick to toss around phrases like "best ever," "They were awesome to watch play," or "Now, there's a group who knew how to play ball." The team is remembered not only for going undefeated and being the first to win state, but for setting a standard of excellence that ran through the Berrien program for the next two decades to come.

"That 1969-70 team set the stage for girls basketball at Berrien High School, for seeing what could be attained," said Coach Fields, who succeeded Simpson in the

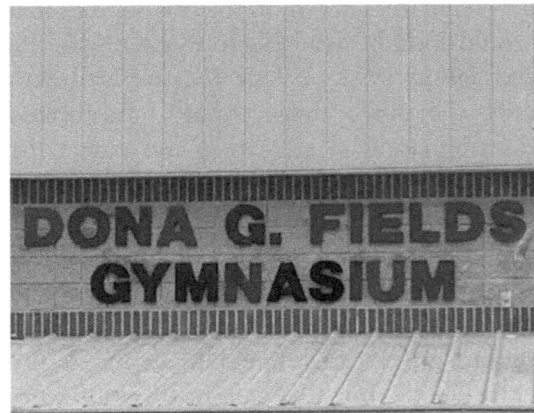

Dona Gaskins Fields was a great player and coach for Berrien, but it was also her accomplishments as a teacher, principal and encourager that influenced the decision to name the current Berrien High School gym in her honor.

One of two freshmen on the team, Debbie Harrell helped Berrien win a second state championship in 1972 and reach another tournament final in 1973, her senior year. After high school, she married and raised a family before passing away from cancer at age 40. In recognition of her commitment to youth sports, Berrien County named a softball complex after her—the Debby Browning Fields.

Judy McNabb Walker regards members of the first state championship team as "my heroes." She co-captained the 1971-1972 team to Berrien's second state championship. After graduating from high school, McNabb Walker moved to Winter Haven, Florida, where she married, raised a family and eventually retired as deputy elections supervisor for the county.

1971-1972 season and promptly added a second state title to the team's trophy case. "In the eyes of other girls not on that team, there became a feeling of 'We can do it, too.'"

Fields won a state title in her first year at the helm in 1971-1972 and again in 1975, the first year the girls played the traditional five-on-five game. In addition, her teams lost a final in 1973 and twice made it the quarterfinals of the tournament before she left coaching to move into school administration. Berrien's girls also would win state tournaments in 1979, 1983 and 1990.

"Berrien took girls basketball seriously in an era that not many did," said Becky Taylor, a Berrien County native and the current sports editor of the *Tifton Gazette*. "There were only a handful of truly competitive teams at the state level each year, and Berrien was always consistent, always a threat in the Simpson years and for many years after that as well."

Judy McNabb Walker, the co-captain of the 1971-1972 state championship team, has given a lot of thought about the legacy of the basketball program and spearheaded the campaign to get Berrien High School's current gymnasium named after Fields. She regards members of the first state championship team as "my heroes."

Years after graduating from high school, McNabb Walker came to understand how

Berrien County Fans Jammed The Stadium To Support The Rebelettes In The Title Game

Donna Jernigan gets off a free throw, with Marla Brown (with back to camera) and Mary Grace Bailey set for the rebound. Jim Willis caught this expectant moment for The Berrien Press at the State AA finals Saturday night.

This photo from the March 26, 1970, issue of the Berrien Press shows how much fans appreciated and respected what the 1969-1970 team accomplished. Their undefeated season and first state championship title meant a lot to Berrien County—then and now. (Photo reproduction from original newspaper)

legacies perpetuate themselves when a young woman from Alapaha told her that watching the team win state in 1972 inspired her to play basketball.

"I know we (the 1972 team) became something people looked up to, and I know I looked up to that (1969-1970) team," McNabb Walker said. "They became a benchmark for me, to strive to be their caliber. They were always held to a high standard and it made me hold myself to a higher standard. But their impact on my life was not just a basketball lesson I learned but a life lesson to see how you can accomplish the impossible when you don't give up, when you work together, keep doing your very best and working your hardest. That's the legacy they left."

Her thoughts were echoed by her co-captain on the 1971-1972 team, Debra Swain Prince. Swain Prince played on that first state championship team as a sophomore, and acknowledges that it was an incredible opportunity to see potential morph into greatness. "That first team to win state set a precedent, an example for us girls who were following closely behind them," she said. "They showed us hard work could pay off, and they were encouragers. They helped us see what it takes to make good great, and it made us believe we could do it, too."

Make no mistake: The women who won that first state championship for Berrien feel a huge sense of pride in their accomplishment, even all these years later. There's something special about being remembered for the achievement, especially half a century after the fact. It was indeed a magical time and a special moment in their lives, even for those who remember it as hard work and something that wasn't always fun. But they are humble heroes, too. And like those girls who followed them, they know they stand on the shoulders of others who came before them and played alongside them.

"If I could tell my teammates something from those years, I would tell them how much I enjoyed playing with them and how much I loved them," Carey Tucker said. "I would thank them for being dedicated and working as hard as we did together. I'd say that to even the teams before that senior year, because they played a role in our success, too. It was a building process over several years. We were always there for each other, always helping each other out, not just in the classroom, but in life. We knew someone was there for us."

"For me, it's humbling to hear words like a *magical season* or *hero*," Faircloth said in a reflective moment near the end of her interview. "I know that I—and I'm sure the others, too—thought of ourselves as just a team of basketball players and friends trying to do our best at what we loved."

She paused, then gave jolly laugh and said:

"Guess we pulled it off pretty good!"

> "If I could tell my teammates something from those years, I would tell them how much I enjoyed playing with them and how much I loved them. I would thank them for being dedicated and working as hard as we did together."
>
> ~ Lenna Carey Tucker

PART 2

THE COACH

16

'A DESIRE TO ACCOMPLISH GREAT THINGS'

"MARY GRACE BAILEY, MARLA Brown, Peggy Barber, Lenna Carey, Donna Jernigan, Andrea Carter."

Betty Jean Simpson rattles off the names of the six starters when asked to recall her memories from the 1969-1970 state championship season.

"Mary Grace came through when it mattered. She peaked at tournament time that year," the 81-year-old widow of Stan Simpson continues in a litany of memory.

"Marla was the number one player as far as leadership. She was self-motivated. Stan expected a lot of her and she always answered the call.

"It was the same with Peggy Barber. Peggy tried to be the best you could be.

"Lenna wanted it as much as any of the girls and her love for the game was amazing. There was talent there to be sure, but it was Lenna's want and love for the game that made her a great player."

Fifty years removed from that first state championship, Betty Jean still thinks of those girls—and the girls and boys who came before and after them—as her "children." She has a soft spot for the group of girls who gave her husband his first state championship season.

"They were just doggone good, talented, talented players," Betty Jean said. "They practiced all the time and they were dedicated to the game. Stan would be so hard on them. Today, if you were as hard on them as he was, they'd probably run you out of town. His expectations were too much at times, and I stayed on him for being too hard on them at times. But he loved his players and wanted them to do their best, and they wanted to please him.

"Winning that first state championship (in 1970) and then winning again the next year with the boys—there's no way to describe how good it was," she continued. "That was the ultimate goal and the reward for so much hard work by Stan and so many players for so long."

Back to the beginning

Born June 14, 1937, and raised in then-rural Buford, Georgia—now a growing suburb in northeastern Atlanta—Stanley "Ramrod" Simpson loved basketball from an early age, even though his first and greatest love was baseball. He played both sports in high school, which is also where he got the nickname "Ramrod."

"The nickname came from a book his class had to read when he was in high school," Betty Jean explained. "He told me what the name of it was, but I just can't remember. Anyway, his friends started calling him that and it stuck."

After graduating from high school, Simpson first attended North Georgia College and eventually Georgia Southern College in Statesboro in the 1950s. He would ultimately earn a master's degree in education from Middle Tennessee State University, where he maintained a 4.0 grade point average to rank number one in his class.

"Somewhere along the way when he was in college, he decided to drop out of school and his mother put him to work, so he decided to go back," Betty Jean said. "He finished up with two degrees—one in education and, I like to joke, one in playing."

Betty Jean grew up in Wheeler County and met Stan in an English class at Georgia Southern. They married in 1958.

Simpson's worst defeat as a coach actually occurred when he was coaching the girls junior varsity team at Montgomery County in Mount Vernon, Georgia. In December 1960, the Montgomery County JV squad was scheduled to play the neighboring Wheeler County team from Alamo, which happened to be coached by Betty Jean Simpson.

The wife's team routed the husband's team 56-12 in that meeting, the first and only time they were opposing coaches.

"She didn't pull her first string. She left them in the whole game … It was 33-3 at one point," Stan told a reporter from the *Tifton Gazette* in March 1970, on the eve of the state championship tournament. *(The full story is available in the newspaper archive of this book.)*

That was Stanley's version of the debacle. Betty Jean remembers it a little differently. "I just did a better coaching job than he did," she laughed, recalling the game played almost 60 years earlier to the date.

It was shortly after that shellacking the Simpsons learned of two job vacancies in Berrien County. They packed up their belongings and headed to Nashville to begin teaching—him at the high school and her at the elementary school in Nashville—when classes resumed after the Christmas vacation.

> "When Ramrod Simpson came to Berrien High School fresh out of Georgia Southern, basketball was awash in the doldrums of averageness."
>
> ~ John Futch

When the new school year started in the fall of 1961, Simpson was named head coach for both the boys and the girls teams.

"We started with nothing there, not even a gym," Betty Jean recalled. "But when you're young, you think you can conquer the world. And Stan had a desire to accomplish great things."

Stanley Simpson's first order of business in Nashville was to get a home gym built for his Berrien High School Rebels and Rebelettes. He then proceeded to build one of Georgia's preeminent basketball programs, culminating with successive state championships for the girls and boys teams, respectively, in his final two years at the school.

The new gym was built for the 1962-1963 season and it would prove to be a daunting challenge for opposing teams. Simpson's boys and girls teams lost very few home games during his decade at Berrien. The boys in fact would win their last 60-plus home games in the Simpson year's, their last loss coming in December 1965 against Madison County.

Very few pictures exist of the old Berrien High School gymnasium, which was torn down in 2015, and this one does not even show the entrance to the building. The stands came right down to the court, and a Crisp County coach once compared playing in the Berrien gym to taking a steam bath. On occasion, Simpson would turn up the heat during pregame warmups and opposing teams would practically melt on the court.

Building the program

"When Ramrod Simpson came to Berrien High School fresh out of Georgia Southern, basketball was awash in the doldrums of averageness." That's how sports reporter Johnny Futch, who grew up in Berrien County, started *The Simpson Years*, a book he wrote about the school's basketball program.

Futch, who went on to have a distinguished journalism career, wrote the book in 1969 shortly after he returned from a tour of duty in the Vietnam War. One of his specific memories is a moment he shared with Simpson in the Berrien gym one Friday night after the girls had edged Thomasville 49-47 and the boys had routed the Bulldogs 55-28.

"Everyone was gone except me and Rod," said Futch, now 74 and living in

Cambodia. "He was using a push broom in the hall above the court and finally stopped, leaning on the broom. 'Johnny,' he said, 'I want to die here.'"

Read through old newspapers and it's clear Berrien had some decent teams in the decades preceding Simson's arrival in Nashville. Dona Gaskins Fields, who would succeed Simpson as the girls coach in the 1971-72 season, set scoring records in the late 1950s and was playing college ball at Florida State University when Simpson took on the coaching duties at Berrien.

But the program's lack of tradition was underscored by the fact that Berrien did not even have a home gymnasium when Simpson came to Nashville.

In his first two seasons at Berrien, Simpson's teams played their home games at the elementary school gymnasiums in Alapaha and Ray City.

Success did not come overnight. Simpson had a rough start with the boys team, posting a 2-20 campaign in the 1960-61 season, described by the *Berrien Press* as a "homeless traveling circus." The Rebelettes fared significantly better, going 16-5 and reaching the quarterfinals of the state tournament.

"Ramrod was a tough taskmaster; his focus was laser-like, and he expected the same from his players," Futch said when asked how Simpson built the Berrien program into a state powerhouse, basically from scratch. "That approach none of us had seen before and I am sure it was uncomfortable to some, but the payoff came against Waycross (in the 1970 state championship game) after a perfect season run-up."

Simpson himself summed up his approach to the game, and life in general, even more succinctly: "My philosophy of

life is: If you work hard and sacrifice a lot, success will come your way," he said.

Simpson was a "great communicator," according to multiple sources, and it was these skills that persuaded county officials to bite the bullet and find the dollars to build a new gymnasium.

"He could tell stories and keep you entertained and he had a way of making believers in what we were trying to accomplish," Betty Jean said. "It started when we didn't have a gym, but he kept pulling and pushing for the game and the highest levels of achievement. It helped to build a crowd that followed the game and it created a tradition of excellence."

"My philosophy of life is: If you work hard and sacrifice a lot, success will come your way."

~ Stan Simpson

With the arrival of the 1962-63 season, Berrien had its new gym and the Rebels and Rebelettes had a home. In that first year, the 1-AA West subregion honored the school by allowing Berrien to host the subregion tournament in their new digs.

Coming into the tournament after fair-to-middling seasons, both teams caught fire and outclassed the favorites to win the subregion tournaments that year. It was the beginning of a love affair with the gym for the Berrien teams, where long winning streaks would stack up over multiple seasons during the next 25 years of excellence.

Berrien would not be asked to host another basketball tournament of any kind until 1994, after the wins and state tournament appearances had stopped coming with regularity for both the girls and boys teams.

Secrets of success

Basketball was Stan Simpson's life and he was driven to succeed. And, he drove his players to succeed. Even if they didn't always like him, his players respected Simpson's commitment to excellence.

"He was tough, tough," recalled Mary Grace Bailey Faircloth. "I liked him most of the time, but he was tough on us. But then he had to be. He did what he had to do to make us the champions we were."

Discipline was Simpson's trademark, coupled with a relentless work ethic and exacting expectations. From the very beginning, he made no secret about his desire to coach at the college level. He told his players they needed to win games—lots of games—for him to have that opportunity. And he was the first to admit his high expectations exacted a price on his teams.

"I just don't believe another coach could have coached these boys any harder than I did," Simpson said after his Rebels won the state AA tournament in the 1970-1971 season. "When they go to college, no coach will work them anywhere near as hard as I did. I ran them until they couldn't run anymore, then we ran some more."

Simpson had a fun side and a great sense of humor, but he could be hard and harsh when players failed to live up to his expectations. He demanded a total commitment to the game from his players, and his strict expectations carried over to literally every phase of their lives—from the classroom to 10 p.m. curfews every night during the season to a ban on ugly language, drinking or smoking.

"The worst part was if we broke curfew, even if it was an innocent thing like going to church with someone and getting back late," said Lenna Carey Tucker. "He also used to tell us that we weren't safe unless we dated one of his basketball boys. They had a curfew, too, and would make sure we got home on time."

Fifty years after that magical season, Carey Tucker still remembers the lessons she learned from Simpson, even the hard ones, and tries to apply them. For example, she expects the kids in her Sunday school class to look her in the eye when she's teaching or talking to them—a lesson Simpson hammered into his players.

Carey Tucker also appreciates the emphasis Simpson put on making sure his players studied hard. Five members of the 1969-1970 team were selected to the *Atlanta Journal-Constitution's* all-state team, and two others were honorable mention—quite an achievement to have seven players recognized at such a high level when only six girls could play on the court at one time.

"It says a lot about the talent on our team," Lenna said. "But you know we also had five girls who were academic honor graduates and recognized for that, too, in the newspapers. That says a lot about the character of who we were and what was expected of us."

Shortly before the state tournament, the *Tifton Gazette* named Pat Williams, Andrea Carter, Peggy Barber, Sandy McMillan and Jo Ann Langford to their All-Academic

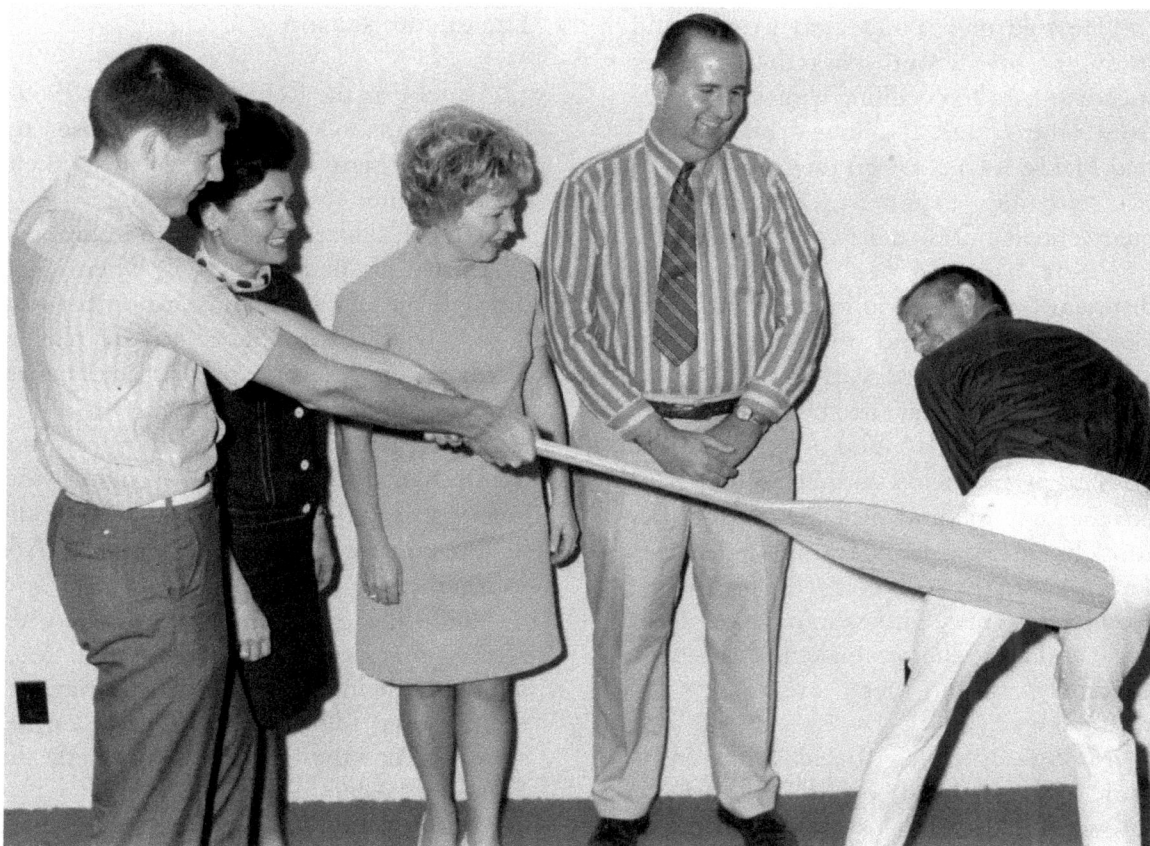

Stanley Simpson had a great sense of humor and certainly didn't mind being the butt of jokes or taking one for the team! Left to right: Roger Guess, a member of the 1970-1971 state championship boys team, Betty Ann Simpson, and Elna and AT Bragdon.

Tiftarea basketball team, which honored seniors who maintained a 90 average over their four years of high school. Berrien placed five of the eight girls honored, with Pat Williams having the highest average at 96. Carey, Bailey and Brown received honorable mention recognition in the list.

On the court

Simpson was a great tactician and an astute observer of the game, but it was his focus on the fundamentals that laid the foundation for success. His teams succeeded with a give-and-go offense, nothing flashy or tricky, a stifling defense and superb physical conditioning.

"As good as those (1969-1970) girls were playing just half court, three on three, I would have loved to have seen them play five-on-five, full court," John Futch said. "They would have wiped the court with every team they played. They were that much stronger than every other team out there."

Dona Fields, who succeeded Simpson as head coach of the Rebelettes in 1971, called Simpson a "scholar of the game."

"He told me, 'You've got to read and study a lot about basketball to be successful, go to coaching clinics and learn from others,' and I followed his advice," said Fields, who coached the Rebelettes to two state titles, a runner-up finish and two quarterfinals during her five-year career.

Fields had her own coaching style, different from Simpson in many ways, but like him, she found that success was attained through hard work.

"That's what it takes to build a program. You don't skip a day. You practice and you go hard at it," Fields said. "I used to have coaches call me and pick my brain—they thought we had a magic formula at Berrien. I always told them, 'No, it's just hard work. You have to have girls who have the heart for it and are willing to make the sacrifices, especially when there are a lot of distractions."

Multiple players labeled Simpson as "one of the smartest coaches" they've ever known and praised his ability to size up their opponents. They credited his unique ability to help them use their strengths to exploit opponents' weaknesses.

"I won't ever forget a game in my junior year," said Judy McNabb Walker, referring to the 1970-1971 season, Simpson's last at Berrien. "We always played man to man and Coach told me to stand on this particular girl's left side. Usually, we would play shoulder to shoulder, but he told me, 'I don't want to see you to the right of her. If she goes right, you let her go. But I want you glued to her left arm and leg.' That girl was the high scorer on their team, but turns out, if she could not go left, she could not score. We held her to the lowest score she ever had in a game."

The encore season

As good as the Rebelettes were in 1969-1970, Simpson's boys came close to matching them. The Rebels lost their season opener 46-45 to Tift County.

After the upset loss, Simpson quipped, "We'll have a better ball club when I get through putting some mustard on my hot dogs." It was a reference to the team's youth and propensity to entertain fans at the expense of solid play.

Simpson got the mustard right, and the Rebels racked up 27 straight wins before losing 70-60 to Carver of Atlanta in the quarterfinals of the state AA tournament.

While the girls team was loaded with seniors that year, the Rebels started four juniors in their 27-2 season. Doug Hawley, then sports editor of the *Tifton Gazette*, summed up the situation succinctly in February 1970.

"Almost any coach would have to be considered a success with a 20-1 basketball record," Hawley wrote. "Yet, the Berrien boys must win in self-defense.

"After all, the Berrien girls are rolling along with an evenly slightly better record. They've compiled a perfect 20-0 mark."

When the 1970-1971 season rolled around, the Berrien girls and boys found themselves in reverse positions from the previous year. Graduations had left the girls team short on height and experience, while the Rebels entered the year with a highly talented group of seniors who had learned their lessons well from the previous year.

Despite their shortcomings, senior Donna Jernigan—one of the five who made the all-state team the previous year— and the young Rebelettes continued their winning ways into February 1971, stretching their winning streak to 47 before a tall Tift County team staged a dramatic finish to beat them 30-29 on a Tuesday night in Nashville. The team went on to capture the 1-AA East Subregion and Region titles before losing 31-25 to Telfair County in the first round of the state tournament to end the season with a 25-2 mark. Meanwhile, Simpson's Rebels ran roughshod over every team they played, rolling to a perfect 30-0 season and the state AA championship. The Rebels—led by George Sorrell, Charles Wright, Roger Guess, Bobby Taylor and Wayne Taylor—capped their dominant season by dismantling Waynesboro 62-29 in the championship game at Georgia Tech's Alexander Coliseum in Atlanta. For the effort, Simpson was named Basketball Coach of the Year by the Georgia Coaches Association.

"The first year Coach Simpson was there (1961-62), the girls got into the state playoffs and that was unprecedented. It was a gradual upswing from that point," recalled Wynn Hancock, a Berrien County native who was a freshman when Simpson arrived on the Berrien campus and later served as the timekeeper during the school's long tradition of winning basketball teams.

"That first state championship was the culmination of a lot of work that went into the program," said Hancock, a longtime teacher and principal in Berrien County. "Coach Simpson had a super team with those girls and then the next year (1970-71), his boys team went undefeated and won state, too, and it was the final building block. He put the Berrien High School basketball program on the map."

Photo and caption from the front page of the March 12, 1970, edition of the Berrien Press. *CALENDAR BOY FOR MARCH – Finally, by public demand,* The Berrien Press *has relented and brings the first, and probably last, Calendar Boy for March, Coach Stanley (Ramrod) Simpson. Clowning over a Rebelette as Calendar Girl posing with a map, Coach Simpson was looking for Atlanta for the Rebels' encounter today.*

"When people come into the county now, I talk to them and tell them, 'Look, there was a time if we weren't in the state playoffs, then it was a bad year.'"

Life after Berrien

In 10 seasons coaching both the girls and boys teams at Berrien, Simpson compiled a record of 412-105—213-44 with the girls and 199-61 with the boys. Simpson's girls never had a losing season. They won six subregion titles, three region titles and four Lowndes High Christmas tournaments, and made the state AA quarterfinals four times prior to the 1970 state championship. After the 2-20 record the first year, Simpson's boys reeled off nine straight winning seasons. Their trophy haul included four subregion tournaments, three region titles and four Lowndes Christmas tournaments. In Simpson's last three years, the boys finished third in the state in 1969 and reached the quarterfinals in 1970 before winning the 1971 title and being widely regarded as the best team in the state regardless of classification.

While he had suggested he would leave Berrien only to coach at the college level, Simpson relented after the 1970-1971 school year and accepted a job to coach the boys team at Druid Hills High School, a AAA team in Atlanta. It was the beginning of an incredibly chaotic transition period in his and Betty Jean's lives.

Simpson departed Berrien without any specific plans, although there were significant rumors of potential assistant coaching jobs at various colleges and head coaching roles at other high schools. He finally accepted the Druid Hills offer.

The rough period began when Simpson was coaching the South Georgia Cage team to victory in the annual Georgia High School Association all-star game in Macon in August 1971. Simpson, 34, experienced several blackouts during the practice sessions. Doctors concluded he was suffering from physical exhaustion—an unsurprising diagnosis for someone whose work week sometimes stretched to 100 hours—and advised him to stay away from the coaching ranks until after Christmas.

Simpson never coached at Druid Hills. He resigned and took a very brief assignment as an assistant coach at Oglethorpe University in Atlanta. Within a few weeks, he departed Oglethorpe for the head coaching job at Shorter College in Rome. And then, before even coaching a game at Shorter, he accepted an offer at Middle Tennessee State University.

> "He put the Berrien high school basketball program on the map. When people come into the county now, I talk to them and tell them, 'Look, there was a time if we weren't in the state playoffs, then it was a bad year.'"
>
> ~ Wynn Hancock

Simpson started as an assistant coach at Middle Tennessee before serving as the head coach from 1979 to 1984. Over five seasons, Simpson compiled an 81-76 record at Middle Tennessee. Those 81 wins, however, included the biggest one in the school's history—a 50-44 stunner over Kentucky in the opening round of the NCAA tournament in 1982 at Nashville, Tennessee.

"We didn't have any choice but to win," quipped Simpson after the game, ever the king of one-liners. "I didn't have a ticket for Saturday's game."

After he retired from Middle Tennessee, the Simpsons returned to Berrien County, which they had come to consider home, in 1985. Simpson took a job with Life of the South insurance company.

Around 1995, he was diagnosed with multiple myeloma, a type of cancer that attacks the bone marrow. Simpson waged a four-year fight against the disease with the same fierce determination that made him a great coach. He died October 24th, 1999, at age 62 in his and Betty Jean's home in Nashville.

"His commitment to the game made him successful first of all, but he wanted more out the players than just basketball," Betty Jean said. "He was very much into life skills, about what is happening after basketball and to you as a person when you go out into the world. He was like a father figure in that respect. If you misbehaved, you got punished. I think his players knew how much he loved them, though."

The following photo appeared in the April 9, 1970, issue of the Berrien Press: *CONGRATULATIONS – Luther Webb, left, commander of Veterans of Foreign Wars, Berrien County Post 5978, presents a photo of the Rebelettes, AA State Champions to coach Stanley Simpson and looking on are captain Marla Brown of the Rebelettes and the Rebel co-captains Richard Tucker and George Sorrell. The VFW honored the coaches and teams with a steak supper.*

PART 3

Newspaper Scrapbook

THE FOLLOWING IS A compilation newspaper articles from various sources around the state. It includes photos that were available from the *Berrien Press* and the Jamie Connell Collection. In some instances, the same article appeared in multiple newspapers. Where possible, we have simply noted the duplications without reprinting them in the scrapbook. In addition, we have deleted multiple copies of the box scores to conserve space. You will also note photo captions without photos. We included the captions, even though the photos themselves could not be successfully reproduced. Likewise, the articles have been reconstructed to appear as they appeared in the newspapers, including misspelled words and unusual styles. For example, you will see

Berrien junior guard Brenda Rudeseal's name spelled in a myriad of ways. On various occasions, Donna Jernigan is referred to as Frances Jernigan and our favorite, Donnie Jernifer. In addition, you will see many different variations on *girls basketball* and *girls team*—which is the Associated Press style used in the narrative portion of this book. In the following articles, you will see girl's basketball, girls' basketball and girls basketball, the way it was originally written in the publications. We are greatly appreciative, and indebted, to the *Berrien Press, Tifton Gazette, Valdosta Daily Times, Thomasville Times-Enterprise, Moultrie Observer* and *Waycross Journal-Herald* for the outstanding coverage they provided to their communities.

November 1969

The Berrien Press, front page, October 30, 1969

Calendar Girl For November
A reminder of the Nashville Elementary School Halloween Carnival tonight, 6 to 10, is given by Andrea Carter, The Berrien Press Calendar Girl for November. A costume contest is to be held for age groups up to sixth grade on the courthouse square at 5 p.m. Besides carving pumpkins, Andrea plays basketball at Berrien High where she is a senior, member of Beta Club, Tri-Hi-Y, B Club and Pep Club. Daughter of Dr. and Mrs. Frank Carter of Nashville, she attended the 8th District Honors Program last summer.

The Berrien Press, front page, November 20, 1969

Berrien High Basketball Season Opens Dec. 3

By TIM MOORE

Basketball drills for the Berrien High Rebels and Rebelettes are going full speed in preparation for the 1969-70 season which opens on Wednesday, Dec. 3 in Tifton.

Coach Stanley Simpson who begins his ninth year at the helm of the boys and girls teams of Berrien reports that practice action must pick-up somewhat if the two teams are ready for what he calls, "Berrien's toughest opening week in history." He is not just talking through his crewcut when he calls the opening week tough because the teams face three of their four toughest opponents during the first four days of the season.

The Rebelettes return four of six starters from last year's team which finished 26-3 and placed three trophies in the case of Berrien High.

Joanna Smith, last year's leading scorer, graduated from the forward corps and finding someone to fill her shoes has been something more than desired.

Judy Rowan, all-state guard, also graduated, but this vacancy seems to have been filled although Rowan will be missed by the Rebelettes. A general lack of hustle and lack of offensive consistency are the main worries for Simpson as the season approaches for the girls. When asked to comment on the Rebelettes, Simpson related that the Rebelettes had a long, long way to go before they can compare with last year's group.

The Rebels had a good "rebuilding" season last year to the tune of 18-5 and return three of five starters. Charles Dieas, David Connell are the departed starters. Also gone via the graduation route are Donnie Roberson, Larry Ray, Dorman Benefield and Don Gaskins. Drills for the boys have been highlighted by excellent quickness and fine shooting but a lack of rebounding. Simpson states that the Rebels must improve on defense greatly if they are to compete in 1-AA.

In addition to the above-mentioned starters lost from last year's girls team: replacements must be found for Barbara Polk, Patty Harvey, Nancy Futch, and Joyce Harpe. So with the opening of bounceball less than two weeks away, a few old faces and a few new ones will take to the floor in the name of the Berrien Rebels and Rebelettes to defend and continue in the winning tradition, but as Coach Simpson says, "things must pick-up."

The Berrien Press will carry complete rosters and schedules along with another team articles in next week's edition.

December 1969

The Berrien Press, front page, November 27, 1969

Calendar Girl For December
Right after turkey time comes basketball season for the teams in Berrien County. Tifton there on Dec. 3 is the first opponent for the Berrien High School Rebels and Rebelettes, reminds Mary Grace Bailey, The Berrien Press Calendar Girl for December. She is a senior, in her fourth year as forward with the Rebelettes and a member of the B Club, Pep Club and Senior Tri-Hi-Y. She is the daughter of Mr. and Mrs. E.M. Bailey of Nashville. The turkey floral arrangement was at Hughes Flower & Gift Shop where the theme turns to Christmas at the annual open house Sunday.

The Berrien Press, front page, November 27, 1969

Berrien High Basketball Season Opens Dec. 3
By Tim Moore

The 1969-70 basketball season for the Berrien High Rebels and Rebelettes will tip-off on Wednesday, Dec. 3, when they pay a visit to Tifton High School and battle the 1-AAA Devils and Angels.

With opening day just a week away, the Rebels and Rebelettes are beginning to smooth their offensive and defensive attacks in preparation for what is expected to be two hotly contested opening games. Although not playing in the same region, Tifton and Berrien have always been big rivals and both schools look on their meetings as big games.

The Rebelettes of Coach Stanley Simpson will probably take the floor with Captain Marla Brown, Mary Grace Bailey and Donna Jernigan starting at the forward positions and Lenna Carey, Peggy Barber and Andrea Carter getting the call at guard. Coach Simpson expects Tift to give the Rebelettes a stern test in the opening game. "We must be ready to put our every effort into every move we make against Tift"; "they not only have a fine group of girls, but they also come after you from start to finish," stated Simpson.

The Rebels will be meeting a group of Tifton boys, who have worked harder to prepare for an opening game than any Tift team in recent years. "They will be ready to go," expressed Simpson as he watched his own Rebels take the practice floor in preparation for the Tift game. George

Sorrell, Richard Tucker, Bobby Taylor, Wayne Taylor, Roger Guess, David Harnage and Bobby Conway seemed to be fighting it out for starting positions.

The Rebels and Rebelettes will stage a pre-season scrimmage this Saturday evening at 7:00 and 8:15 p.m. The admission is free and the public is urged to come and give the teams some crowd experience before they open the season.

BERRIEN HIGH BASKETBALL SCHEDULE 1969-1970
NICKNAME: Rebels & Rebelettes   COACH: Stanley Simpson
COLORS: Red & Gray

Wed., Dec. 3	Tifton	There
Fri., Dec. 5	Lowndes	Here
Sat., Dec. 6	Bainbridge	Here
Tues., Dec. 9	Lanier County	There
Tues., Dec. 16	Cook	There
Fri., Dec. 19	Worth County	Here
Fri., Jan. 2	Cairo	Here
Sat., Jan. 3	Lowndes	There
Tues., Jan. 6	Valdosta	Here
Fri., Jan. 9	Crisp	There
Sat., Jan. 10	Tifton	Here
Fri., Jan. 16	Thomasville	Here
Sat., Jan. 17	Cairo	There
Tues., Jan. 20	Cook	Here
Sat., Jan. 24	Thomasville Central	There
Tues., Jan. 27	Lanier	Here
Fri., Jan. 30	Crisp	Here
Sat., Jan. 31	Bainbridge	There
Fri., Feb. 6	Thomasville	There
Tues., Feb. 10	Valdosta	There

Dec. 26, 27, 29 & 30 - LO-HI Xmas Tourney
Feb. 19, 20 & 21 - 1-AA West at Thomasville
Feb. 26, 27 & 28 - 1-AA at Crisp County

The Tifton Gazette, page 3, December 1, 1969

Berrien Rebels, Rebelettes Again Look Like Sure-Shooting Winners

(This article on Berrien County High's basketball teams, who open their season Wednesday night against Tift County in Tifton, is the first in a seven-part series about Tiftarea prep cage squads).
By Johnny Martin
Gazette Staff Writer

NASHVILLE – Chalk up another one for Coach Stanley (Ramrod) Simpson, coach of Berrien County. Another winning season for the Rebels and Rebelettes, that is.

Sure as shootin' Coach Simpson will turn his ninth coaching season into his ninth straight winning season for his boys and the eighth for his girls.

Ramrod has compiled an outstanding record for both teams. Altogether, the Rebelettes have 158 wins and 42 losses, while the Rebels have compiled a 142-65 record.

Speaking about his Rebelettes, Simpson said, "All indications are that we should have another good winning season, but in order to do so, we are going to have to get a much better effort out of the girls than we have been getting in the preceding practices."

In returning four of six starters on the Rebelettes, the old Ramrod should make plenty of headway again this year. Last year, the girls secured 26 wins, and only lost three for the season.

Five of the first seven of the Rebels of last year are back for another crack at the Region 1-AA crown. This includes three of five starters from last year. "We have experience," said Simpson, "and are probably a bit quicker than we have been in the past.

"Last year we lost Charles Dieas, our strong rebounder, to Abraham Baldwin College. He's one very hard to find a replacement for," said Simpson.

"We also lost Judy Rowan, our starter for last year on the girls' squad, along with Joanna Smith, the leading scorer. Her shoes are going to be something else to fill," said Simpson.

The Rebels and Rebelettes will still be in there tossing, turning and fighting all the way, despite their serious losses last year of several fine players.

Probable starters for the Rebels will be: guards, Wayne Taylor, (5-10 soph.) and Roger Guess, (6-0 jr.); forwards, Richard Tucker (6-2 sr.), and Bobby Taylor (6-0 jr.); center, George Sorrell (6-4 jr.). The top reserves are Carl Howell (6-3 jr.), Charles Wright (6-5 jr.) and Bobby Conway (6-0 jr.)

Starters for the Rebelettes figure to be: guards, Andrea Carter (5-6 sr.), Peggy Barber (5-7 sr.), and Lenna Carey (5-10, sr.); forwards, Marla Brown (5-9 sr.), Mary Grace Bailey (5-10 sr.), and Donna Jernigan (5-4 jr.). Leading reserves include Brenda Rudeseal (5-8 jr.), Donna Bennett (5-3 fr.) and Joann Langford (5-8 sr.).

Berrien's schedule includes: Dec. 3 – Tift Co., there; Dec. 5 – Lowndes, here; Dec. 6 – Bainbridge, here; Dec. 9 – Lanier Co., there; Dec. 16 – Cook Co., there; Dec. 19 – Worth Co., here; Dec. 26-30 – Lowndes Christmas Tournament; Jan. 2 – Cairo, here; Jan. 3 – Lowndes, there; Jan. 6 – Valdosta, here; Jan. 9 – Crisp Co., there; Jan. 10 – Tift Co., here; Jan. 16 – Thomasville, here; Jan. 17 – Cairo, there; Jan. 20 – Cook Co., here; Jan. 24 – Central of Thomasville, there; Jan. 27 – Lanier, here; Jan. 30 – Crisp Co., here; Jan. 31 – Bainbridge, there; Feb. 6 – Thomasville, there; Feb. 10 – Valdosta, there; Feb. 19-21 – Region 1-AA West Tournament (Thomasville); Feb. 26-28 – Region 1-AA Playoffs (Cordele).

Photo caption:
BERRIEN BASKETBALL GATHERING – This Berrien County basketball gathering includes (from left), George Sorrell, Coach Stanley Simpson and Marla Brown. (Staff Photo).

The Tifton Gazette, page 4, December 3, 1969
Tift Squads Host Berrien In Opening Action Tonight
By Staff Writer

Tift County High's basketball teams begin 1969-70 play tonight, and they could hardly have found tougher opening competition than Tiftarea foe Berrien County.

Coach Stanley Simpson, who guides both the Berrien varsity boys and girls, returns numerous veterans from last year's squads which compiled 18-5 and 26-3 records, respectively.

The girls' varsity game is slated for 7 p.m. The boys' varsities tangle at 8:30 p.m.

A girls' B-team contest begins the activity at 4 p.m. Then there's a 5:30 p.m. boys' B-team skirmish.

Arthur Otwell, the new head coach of the Tift boys' team, will be seeking to improve on last year's 5-12 record. Already, misfortune has struck his squad in the form of a hunting accident which eliminated 6-6 center Edd Dorminey for some six weeks – suffering from a hand and upper portion of the arm wound.

Dorminey's starting assignment will go to one of three, namely Robert Hodge (6-1), Ray Henderson (6-0) or Kenny Luke (6-1). The remainder of the Blue Devils' starting quintet figures to include Riley Cates (6-0) and Larry Mims (5-7), guards; John Thompson (6-1) and Glenn Parkman (5-11), forwards.

Mrs. Sandra Withrow, the Angels' headmaster, says that her tentative starters include Juanita Dickens (5-6½), Bonnie Evans (5-2), and Patty Cole (5-5), forwards; Sherri Whittington (5-7½), Kathy Evans (5-2½) and Jerry Crowley (5-9) or Bonnie Tucker (5-5).

The boys' probable starters for Simpson are Wayne Taylor (5-10) and Roger Guess (6-0), guards; Richard Tucker (6-2) and Bobby Taylor (6-0), forwards; George Sorrell (6-4), center.

The girls' likely starters include Marla Brown (5-9), Mary Grace Bailey (5-10) and Donna Jernigan (5-4), forwards; Andrea Carter (5-6), Peggy Barber (5-7) and Lenna Carey (5-10), guards.

Tift's squads host Moultrie in Friday night action. Then, they travel to Albany for Saturday night play against Dougherty County.

Berrien undergoes home play Friday and Saturday against Lowndes and Bainbridge, respectively.

The Berrien Press, front page, December 4, 1969
BHS Basketball Teams Open Home Game
By TIM MOORE

The Berrien High Rebels and Rebelettes of Coach Stanley Simpson open their home basketball season on Friday of this week when they play host to the Lowndes High Vikings and Vikettes of Valdosta. Home action continues on Saturday evening when Region 1AA opponent Bainbridge comes to town to battle the local clubs.

The Rebels are reported well and ready to battle two of the toughest teams in head-to-head competition this weekend. Lowndes has a few new players who have already started to contribute to the success of the Vikings. Bainbridge comes to town with all five starters returning from last year's winning club and have two additional boys who are expected to win starting berths on this year's team. The starting five for Berrien will come from a group of the following boys: George Sorrell, Richard Tucker, David Harnage, Wayne Taylor, Bobby Taylor, Roger Guess and Bobby Conway.

The Rebelettes opened the season on Wednesday in Tifton with captain Marla Brown on the doubtful list. Brown injured her ankle in drills last week and will be slowed or out of action for at least a week. This did not help an already weak-in-depth offense. The Rebelettes must really be ready to give an all-out effort against two of the toughest teams on their schedule. The Lowndes girls are led by 6-2 forward Kay Price who hooks with either hand. The Bainbridge girls feature one of the best forwards in the state in Jackie Williamson. The last time she faced the Rebelettes she scored 35. Berrien will start Lenna Carey, Peggy Barber, Andrea Carter at guard and Donna Jernigan, Joann Langford, Mary Grace Bailey at forward depending on the condition of Brown.

The junior varsity teams will play on Thursday and Friday afternoon here in the local high school gym.

The Tifton Gazette, page 3, December 4, 1969

Devils Surprise Berrien

By Doug Hawley
Gazette Sports Editor

For the first time in most people's memories, the Tift County High varsity boys' basketball team has captured its season opener.

Coach Arthur Otwell's Blue Devils staged a spirited second half comeback to upset highly-regarded Berrien County, 46-45 Wednesday night at Tift High gymnasium before a vociferous, near-capacity audience.

Meanwhile, the Tift varsity girls were not as fortunate, Berrien gaining a convincing 40-16 verdict.

Berrien captured both preliminary B-team contests. The boys triumphed, 46-30, and the girls won, 25-21.

In the exciting boys' varsity duel, Tift trailed during the early part of the third quarter by 11 points, 30-19. Heading down the home stretch, the Blue Devils were still seven off the pace, 39-32, after narrowing the gap to two, 34-32.

With 4:14 remaining, Kenny Luke sacked back-to-back free throws to knot the count, 41-41. Then, Charles Wright put the Rebels ahead with a fielder.

Here, Luke registered a gratis toss and followed that with a fielder. Larry Mims potted back-to-back free throws for a three-point lead, 46-43, 30 seconds showing.

Only 13 seconds remained as David Harnage pitched in two consecutive free throws for the visitors. To say that the crowd was loud in those dying seconds would be putting it mildly.

"You can't come from behind without that kind of support," Otwell said after the smoke had cleared. "I just hope that they'll back us like that all year. ... I was real pleased that we came back. The fact that we had such a good floor game made the difference. Larry Mims (guard) just took over."

With 6-6 center Edd Dorminey on the injury lest, the Blue Devils were outrebounded decisively, 43-25. However, they showed only nine turnovers as compared to the invaders' 20.

"That's the best I've seen Tifton play in five or six years," personable Berrien Coach Stanley Simpson praised. "We'll have a better ballclub when I get through putting some mustard on my hot dogs (reference to players)."

Riley Cates and Luke were the Blue Devils' leading point producers with 17 and 13, respectively. Bobby Taylor and George Sorrell got nine apiece for the Rebels.

Like the Blue Devils, the Angels had to play without their top scorer, Juanita Dickens, who came up sick. The local squad, which held an early 6-2 lead, went scoreless in the second period against Simpson's heralded girls' squad.

"I think she (Dickens) means 20 more points to my ballclub," Angels' coach Mrs. Sandra Withrow pointed out. "Overall, when you put our inexperience against their experience, our guards did all right ... especially the sophomores."

Donna Jernigan sparked the winning girls with 19 points, while Marla Brown tossed in 17. Nobody for the Angels gained double figures.

The Tift squads entertain Region 1-AAA foe Moultrie in Friday night action. Then, they visit league foe Dougherty County for Saturday night play.

Berrien, a Region 1-AA affiliate, is at home to league team Lowndes and Bainbridge for Friday and Saturday skirmishes, respectively.

Eddie Sims paced the Berrien boys' B-Team with 17 points. Tifton's Vance Kennedy garnered 10.

In the girls' tilt, Cathy Watson scored 19 for Berrien, Karen Jones tallied 12 in a losing effort.

BOX SCORES
Girls' Game

Berrien

	Fg	Ft	Pf	Pts.
* Brown	6	5-5	2	17
* Bailey	0	0-1	0	0
* Jernigan	7	5-6	2	19
* Carey	0	0-0	1	0
* Barber	0	0-0	1	0
* Carter	0	0-0	0	0
Rudeseal	0	0-0	1	0
Swain	0	0-0	2	0
Swain	0	0-0	2	0
Langford	1	0-0	0	2
Bennett	0	0-2	0	0
McMillan	0	0-0	0	0
Williams	1	0-0	0	2
TOTALS	15	10-14	9	40

Tift

	Fg	Ft	Pf	Pts.
* B. Evans	2	1-3	0	5
* Cole	3	1-4	1	7
* Conner	1	0-0	0	2
* Whittington	0	0-0	5	0
* K Evans	0	0-0	0	0
* Crowley	0	0-0	5	0
Haman	1	0-1	0	2
Fordham	0	0-0	0	0
Hawkins	0	0-0	0	0
Tucker	0	0-0	1	0
Bruce	0	0-2	0	0
TOTALS	7	2-10	12	16

Score by Quarters

Berrien	9	8	15	8 –	40
Tift	6	0	5	5 –	16

Boys' Game

Berrien

	Fg	Ft	Pf.	Pts.
* W. Taylor	2	4-5	0	8
* B. Taylor	4	1-1	5	9
* Harnage	1	2-3	0	4
* Tucker	2	3-4	0	7
* Sorrell	4	1-2	5	9
Wright	2	0-2	3	4
Guess	1	2-3	4	4
Slaughter	0	0-1	0	0
TOTALS	16	13-21	17	45

Tift

	Fg	Ft	Pf	Pts.
* Cates	8	1-3	4	17
* Thompson	0	2-4	3	2
* Parkman	2	1-2	3	5
* Luke	5	3-3	4	13
* Mims	2	3-3	1	7
Henderson	1	0-3	2	2
Hodge	0	0-0	0	0
TOTALS	18	10-18	17	46

Score by Quarters

Berrien	14	14	11	6 --	45
Tift	12	7	13	14 --	46

* -Denotes starters.

The Valdosta Daily Times, page 25, December 4, 1969

Area Hoop Outlook Bright This Time

By Sammy Glassman
Times Sports Editor

The early indications are that the area is going to have more than a fair share of talented boys basketball teams this season.

Earlier in the week we mentioned coach Jon Hazelip's Georgia Christian School Generals down at Dasher. This small, but very talented team has a perfect 6-0 record right now.

The Generals campaign in Region 1-C and another area team, coach Billy Pafford's Lanier County (Lakeland) Bulldogs, also belong to this circuit and they're off to a very fast start.

The Bulldogs are 4-0 and Pafford is already singing the praise of 6-5 senior Drew Dickson.

"Drew's got to be the most improved player on our team," Pafford said. "He's played only about a half in each of our first four games, but he's averaging better than 25 points. We're hoping he can keep it up, but what we're really counting on is balance and team effort to pull us through. You can't win consistently without that."

Over at Homerville, coach Austin DeLoach's Clinch Panthers are rolling along with a 3-0 record, and they can look forward to lots and lots of traveling this winter.

Since a state fire marshal has ruled the Clinch High gym can no longer be used for the Panther's home games, DeLoach's charges will have to play all of their contests on the road.

Brooks County's Tigers are 2-1 so far and Cook's Hornets are 1-2. Both are handicapped by a lack of experience this time out.

At the time this was written coach Stanley Simpson's Berrien (Nashville, Ga.) Rebels hadn't begun play. But the word is that Berrien could be a title contender in Region 1-AA. The Rebs have a measure of height, experience and what Simpson describes as "a lot of quickness."

Too Early

After just a couple of games it's too early to get a definite line on coach Charles Cooper's Lowndes Vikings. They are currently 1-1.

The Vikes are having to go without Terry Wilkes, their top gun last season and one of the best players in this or any other section of the state.

In their last game, Lowndes went with a starting lineup of Curtis Jones (6-4, sr.), Martin Hendrix (5-9, sr.), Henry Otis Register (6-0, sr.), Jerome Register (6-1, sr.) and Jerry Whiddon (5-7, sr.).

Jones, who was a regular at Westside High last season, looked quite impressive in the one game in which I saw him play. He has ability as both a scorer and a rebounder.

"We really aren't far enough along to tell just how things will go for us," Cooper said.

Have Potential

Although Valdosta High is still involved in the football playoffs, coach Joe Wilson's cage 'Cats got their season underway Tuesday night with a triumph over Thomasville.

The starters were Roger Rome (6-5, jr.), Don Golden (6-4, sr.), Benjie Webb (6-3, sr.), Willie Jones (5-11, sr.) and Warrick Taylor (5-5, sr.).

Golden and Webb are returning starters from VHS' 1968-69 team, while Rome, Jones and Taylor were all front line performers for Pinevale High last winter.

"I feel that we have potential," Wilson says, "but we won't know for sure about our team until the football playoffs are over and we can devote full time to basketball."

Considering all things, the cage 'Cats looked good against T'ville. I'd also have to tag them as a team with potential.

I think the Lowndes Vikings and Valdosta Wildcats are going to play an exciting brand of basketball this season and so are other quintets in the area. It should be an interesting season all the way.

The Valdosta Daily Times, page 26, December 4, 1969

Lowndes Cagers to Face Berrien

By Times Staff Writer

Lowndes High's Vikings and Vikettes are scheduled to go against their third opponent, Berrien's Rebels and Rebelettes, in a high school basketball doubleheader in Nashville Friday night to head a list of 10 twin-bills to be played in the area this weekend.

The Vikettes of coach Steve Kebler won both of their first two games, while coach Charles Cooper's Vikings are now 1-1. The Rebels and Rebelettes of coach Stanley Simpson opened their season against Tift County Wednesday night. This will be their second game.

Other basketball action Friday will see Baker County (Newton) at Echols County (Statenville), Cook (Adel) at Thomasville, Lanier County (Lakeland) at Doerun, Turner County (Ashburn) at

Brooks County (Quitman) and Clinch County (Homerville) at Wilcox Central (Rochelle). Saturday Wayne County (Jesup) will be at Lowndes and Bainbridge at Berrien.

Both coach Billy Pafford's Lanier Bulldogs and coach Angie DeVivo's Bulldogettes will put perfect 4-0 records on the line when they meet Doerun.

Coach Austin DeLoach's Clinch Panthers have a perfect 3-0 record to crow about.

The Valdosta Daily Times, page 27, December 4, 1969
Tift Boys Trip Up Berrien
Special to the Times

TIFTON – Tift County's Blue Devils got together to ruin the Berrien Rebels' season opener, but the Angels did little to slow down the Rebelettes as the two schools split a high school basketball doubleheader here Wednesday night.

The Rebels took a quick lead and managed to stay well ahead of the Imps until three minutes were left in the game. Then Tift took the lead and went on to defeat Berrien, 46-45. The girls game was no match with the Rebelettes rolling past the Angels, 40-16.

Bobby Taylor paced the Rebels with 11 points. Riley Cates and Charles Luke led the Imps with 17 and 15 points respectively.

Donna Jernigan and Marla Brown led the scoring for the Rebelettes, hitting for 19 and 17 points respectively. High pointmaker for the Angels was Patty Cole with 7.

The game opened the season for coach Stanley Simpson's teams. They are scheduled to see action again Friday when they host Lowndes in a double-header in Nashville, Ga.

(Box Scores Omitted)

The Tifton Gazette, page 3, December 6, 1969
Berrien Gets Cage Sweep Over Lowndes
Special to Gazette

NASHVILLE – Berrien County High's varsity basketball squads swept a pair from visiting Lowndes here Friday night. The boys triumphed, 58-40, and the girls triumphed, 51-30.

Roger Guess, George Sorrell and Charles Wright bagged 22, 18 and 14 points, respectively, for the victorious boys. Jerome Register had 15 in a losing cause.

In the girls' contest, Donna Jernigan got 29 points for the winners. Kay Price had 16 to pace the losers.

The Berrien girls now stand 2-0 and the boys 1-1.

The Valdosta Daily Times, page 11, December 6, 1969
Lowndes' Cagers Bow to Berrien
Special to The Times

NASHVILLE, Ga. – Berrien's Rebels and Rebelettes used strong defensive play to take the basketball measure of Lowndes Vikings and Vikettes here Friday night.

Coach Stanley Simpson's Rebels trimmed coach Charles Cooper's Vikings, 58-40. Simpson's Rebelettes defeated coach Steve Kebler's Vikettes, 51-30. It was the low point total for both Lowndes teams this season.

The Vikes are now 1-2 and the Vikettes have a 2-1 chart. The Rebs are 1-1 and the Berrien girls have a 2-0 record.

Lowndes is to return to action tonight. It will host Region 1-AAA foe Wayne County (Jesup) in a doubleheader at Valdosta. Berrien is to meet 1-AA opponent Bainbridge in a twin-bill here tonight.

Donna Jernigan got 29 points to lead the Rebelettes' attack in last night's game. Kay Price, with 16 points, was the Lowndes girls top scorer.

In the boys outing, the Rebs' Roger Guess, 22; George Sorrell, 18, and Charles Wright, 14, led the way on offense.

The Vikings' leading scorers were Jerome Register, with 15 points, and Henry Otis Register, who got 10.

GIRLS				
Berrien	11	25	33	51
Lowndes	11	17	21	30

BERRIEN (51) – Jernigan 29, Brown 13, Bailey 5, Langford 2, Bennett 2, Swain, Carter, Barber, L. Carey, Williams. Team totals: field goals 20, free throws 11 of 15, fouls 8.

LOWNDES (30) – Price 16, Wilkins 6, Passmore 5, Shaw 2, P. Dawkins 1, Webb, Lumley, Wheeler, May, Mitchell. Team totals: field goals 12, free throws 6 of 10, fouls 12.

BOYS				
Berrien	12	26	40	58
Lowndes	11	21	35	40

BERRIEN (58) – Guess 22, Sorrell 18, Wright 14, Tucker 2, Taylor 2, Harnage. Team totals: field goals 26, free throws 6 of 14, fouls 5.

LOWNDES (40) – Register 15, H. Register 10, Jones 5, Hendrix 4, Haynes 2, Whidden 4, Thomas, Saengerhauser. Team totals: field goals 18, free throws 4 of 7, fouls 11.

The Tifton Gazette, page 5, December 8, 1969

Berrien Teams Beat Bainbridge

NASHVILLE – Berrien County's basketball teams captured two games from invading Bainbridge here Saturday night with the Rebels winning 49-32 and the Rebelettes coming out on top, 63-32.

The Rebelettes built up a 21-point lead in the three quarters and held on behind the shooting of Donna Jernigan, who finished the night with 31 points – high in the game. Grace Bailey added 14 more points for the Berrien girls.

George Sorrell turned in a fantastic performance for the Rebels as they broke open a relatively close game in the fourth quarter. Sorrell netted 25 points and snared 24 rebounds.

(Box Scores Omitted)

The Valdosta Daily Times, page 19, December 8, 1969

Region Foe Cut Down By Berrien

Special to the Times

NASHVILLE, Ga. – Berrien's defense held both Bainbridge teams to exactly 32 points while the offenses were busy racking up points as the Rebels and Rebelettes took both ends of a Region 1-AA high school basketball doubleheader here Saturday night.

Coach Stanley Simpson's Berrien Rebels trounced the Bearcats, 49-32, while his Rebelettes trimmed the Bearkittens, 63-32.

Donna Jernigan spearheaded the Rebelette scoring by totaling 31 points for the night. George Sorrell was the only Rebel in double figures with 25, while James Love paced the Bearcats with 11.

The victory left the Rebelettes unbeaten after three starts and holding a 1-0 region record. The Rebels are now 2-1 overall and 1-0 in region standings.

GIRLS				
Berrien	14	32	45	63
Bainbridge	6	13	24	32

BERRIEN (63) – Jernigan 31, Bailey 14, McMillan 8, Langford 7, Brown 3, Swain, Rudesal, Carter, Barber, Carey. Team totals: field goals 25, free throws 13 of 16, fouls 15.

BAINBRIDGE (32) – Williams 22, Davis 5, Griffin 3, Lang 2, Spooner, Stewart, Morris, Brown. Team totals: field goals 12, free throws 8 of 17, fouls 14.

BOYS				
Berrien	8	23	31	49
Bainbridge	2	13	23	32

BERRIEN (49) – Sorrell 25, Wright 8, Tucker 8, B. Taylor 5, Guess 3, Harrell, W. Taylor. Team totals: field goals 17, free throws 15 of 27, fouls 6.

BAINBRIDGE (32) – James Love 11, Nelson 8, Spears 6, Boyd 4, Thigpen 2, Boyette 1, Johnson. Team totals: field goals 14, free throws 4 of 5, fouls 13.

The Tifton Gazette, page 4, December 10, 1969

Berrien Posts Two Victories Over Lanier

Special to Gazette

NASHVILLE – Berrien County took a pair of basketball contests Tuesday night from Lanier County.

The girls remained unbeaten with an easy 59-27 victory. The boys had more difficulty, but they were 48-44 victors.

Grace Bailey spearheaded the Berrien girls with 27 points, but she had double digit support from Marla Brown and Donna Jernigan who contributed 14 and 13, respectively. The Berrien squad is now 4-0 for the campaign.

In the skirmish, David Harnage tallied 15 and George Sorrell 12 to lead the victors. Patton, Lee and Felts chipped in 15, 13, and 10, respectively, for the losers. Berrien now boasts 3-1 credentials.

The Berrien teams play again next Tuesday night against Cook County at Adel.

The Valdosta Daily Times, page 17, December 10, 1969

Lanier Co. Loses Pair to Berrien

Special to the Times

LAKELAND – Lanier County's Bulldogs' five game winning streak came to an end here Tuesday night as Berrien's Rebels and Rebelettes took both ends of a high school basketball doubleheader.

Coach Billy Pafford's Bulldogs were undefeated until coach Stanley Simpson's Rebels handed them a 48-44 defeat. In the girls game Berrien's undefeated sextet downed coach Angie DeVivo's Bulldogettes, 59-27.

The victories left Simpson's girls with a 4-0 record while the Rebels are now 3-1. The losses left the Bulldogs 5-1 and the Bulldogettes, 4-2.

Lanier's quintet was slowed by the absence of Drew Dickson, a 6-5 senior who suffered a leg injury in a game last week.

Harris Patten led the scoring for the Bulldogs with 15 points. David Harnage paced the Rebs with 15 points.

In the girls game Mary Grace Bailey led the Rebelettes with 27 points, while Chris Boyette paced the Bulldogettes with 10.

BOYS				
Lanier	7	22	36	44
Berrien	9	20	38	48

LANIER (44) – Lee 13, Patten 15, Felts 10, Robinson 5, Brockington 1, Benefield. Team totals: field goals 16, free throws 12 of 18, fouls 15.

BERRIEN (48) – Taylor 2, Conway, Guess 9, Carey, B. Taylor 2, Harnage 15, Tucker 2, Howell, Wright 8, Sorrells 10. Team totals: field goals 19, free throws 10 of 21, fouls 14.

GIRLS				
Lanier	3	11	19	27
Berrien	18	33	49	59

LANIER (27) – Boyette 10, Moore 9, Keene 8, Ivey, Sirmans, Pierce, J. Pierce, Calhoun, Johnson. Team totals: field goals 11, free throws 5 of 12, fouls 13.

BERRIEN (59) – Bailey 27, Brown 14, Jernigan 13, Langford 2, Williams 2, Bennett 1, Carey, Barber, Carter, Swain, Parr, McMillan. Team totals: field goals 24, free throws 11 of 19, fouls 12.

The Berrien Press, page 8, December 11, 1969
Photo caption:
UP AND OVER – Berrien High School Rebel's leading scorer with 22 points, Roger Guess, crossed under the basket and shot, hard pressed by a Lowndes County Viking. Backing him up are George Sorrell (20) hiding David Harnage (40) and Bobby Taylor (nearest the camera). The Rebels continued their winning ways against Bainbridge Saturday night and Lanier County Tuesday night, taking their neighbors to the south 48-44.

The Berrien Press, page 11, December 11, 1969

Basketball Teams Start Season With Wins
By Tim Moore

The Berrien High Rebels and Rebelettes have kicked off their 1969-70 basketball season in fine style as they played three varsity games this past week and came away with only one defeat in six games. The Rebelettes put down three opponents without too much trouble and the Rebels, after dropping the season opener to Tift, came on real strong over the weekend to push their record to two and one.

A strong defensive and some fine shooting by Donna Jernigan and Marla Brown led the way in the Tifton game, won by the Rebelettes 40-16. Lenna Carey, Peggy Barber, and Andrea Carter completely put the lock on the Tift forwards as they held Tift to only 16 points. The boys game was a big upset as the Tift boys came on strong at the finish to defeat the local club 46-45 in a thriller. Foul trouble and lack of defensive reaction led to the Rebels' defeat.

On Friday evening the home season was launched with the Lowndes High Vikings and Vikettes. The Rebelettes again looked strong as they defeated the Lo-Hi girls, 51-30, behind another strong defensive game by Carey, Barber and Carter, Jernigan and Brown with 29 and 13 points, leading the offense.

Roger Guess pumped in 22 points to lead the Rebs past the Vikings 58-40. George Sorrell and Charles Wright controlled the boards for Berrien.

The Bainbridge Bearcats and Kittens came to town on Saturday and took the long trip home with two additional losses attached to their records as Berrien rolled over the 1-AA opponents, 63-32, in the girls' game and 49-32 in the boy's game. The Berrien girls were led by Donna Jernigan and Debra Swain and George Sorrell with 25 points and 24 rebounds paved the way for the Rebels.

Coach Stanley Simpson stated he was proud of both teams during their first week of action, but added that both teams had a lot of improving to do before he would call them a good ball club. Simpson took full blame for the boys loss to Tift saying that "Coach Orwell did a better job of preparing the Tift boys than I had done for the Rebels." The teams will see action again on Tuesday Dec. 16 when they travel to Adel to face Cook High.

The Berrien Press, page 14, December 11, 1969
Photo captions:
HOME OPENER – The Berrien High Rebelettes opened the home court season with a 51-30 win over the Lowndes County Vikings. Marla Brown in white shoots for another score as Jo Ann Langford comes in for a backup.

TRYING – David Harnage (40) goes up high in trying to defend the goal from a Viking from Lowndes County.

TRYING – David Harnage (40) was caught by The Berrien Press camera in an almost identical action in defending the goal from a Viking from Lowndes County.

The Tifton Gazette, page 5, December 17, 1969
Berrien Hoopsters Defeat Cook Twice
Special to Gazette

ADEL – Basketball meetings of two Tiftarea schools found invading Berrien County dominating her Tuesday night over Cook County.

Coach Stanley (Ramrod) Simpson's unbeaten girls blasted Cook, 63-33. His powerful boys triumphed, 59-47.

Marla Brown, Donna Jernigan and Grace Bailey score 26, 18 and 17 points, respectively, in the Rebelettes' well-balanced attack. The victory was No. 5.

Cheryl Griffin tallied 16 and Lyn Futch 15 for Cook. The losers are winless after seven tries.

The Berrien boys who, only once in five tries – that coming to Tift County – were spearheaded by George Sorrell's 22 points. Charles Wright chipped in 14.

Cook, which slumped to 2-5 for the campaign, had a 15 point performance from Robert Ray.

Berrien hosts Tiftarea foe Worth County in Friday night play at Nashville. Cook visits Norman Park the same night.

Girls' Game

Berrien (63)		Cook (33)
Brown 26		Futch 15
Jernigan 18		C. Griffin 16
Bailey 17		Nipper 2
Carey		Chapman
Barber		Shiflette
Carter		Ward

Berrien subs – Williams (2), Rudeseal, Swain, Bennett, McMillan, Langford. Cook subs – M. Griffin, McEven, Davis, Giddens.

Score by Quarters

Berrien	18	15	20	10 --	63
Cook	6	13	5	9 --	33

Boys' Game

Berrien (59)		Cook (47)
Guess 2		Ray 15
B. Taylor 9		Moore 6
Tucker 7		Tucker 10
Wright 14		Jenurette 10
Sorrell 22		Shackelford 6

Berrien subs – Harnage (3), W. Taylor (2), Harrell, Slaughter, Conway. Cook subs – Purvis, Sanders.

Score by Quarters

Berrien	11	14	13	21 --	59
Cook	10	11	11	15 --	47

The Valdosta Daily Times, page 32, December 17, 1969

Berrien Is Victor Over Cook

Special to the Times

ADEL – The powerful Berrien Rebels and Rebelettes did it again – and this time they did it to Cook as they took both ends of a high school basketball twin-bill here Tuesday night.

It was the fourth time in five starts that coach Stanley Simpson's Berrien teams took both ends of doubleheaders as the Rebels defeated Cook's Hornets, 59-47 and the Rebelettes trimmed the Wasps, 63-33.

The victories brought the Rebelettes to a perfect 5-0 record, while the Rebels are 4-1. Coach Hansel Faulkner's Hornets now own a 2-5 record while the Wasps of coach Lamar Chapman have yet to win after seven starts.

Marla Brown, Donna Jernigan and Grace Bailey shared the Berrien scoring with 26, 18 and 17 points respectively. Cheryl Griffin and Lyn Futch paced the Wasps with 16 and 15 points.

George Sorrell tallied 22 points to pace the Rebels while Robert Ray led the Hornets with 15 points.

(Box Scores Omitted)

The Moultrie Observer, page 14, Thursday, December 18, 1969

Berrien Cagers Top Cook Twice

NASHVILLE, Ga. – The Berrien County Rebels and Rebelettes tripped up the Cook County basketballers here last night for a twin-bill victory in Region 1-A.

In the opener the Nashville sextet bombed the Cook sextet 63-33 behind the sharp shooting of Marla Brown, Gray Bailey and Donnie Jernifer with 26, 19 and 16 points respectively.

Lyn Futch and Mary Griffin paced the Cook hoopsters offensive with 15 and 16 points respectively.

In the nightcap it was the powerful Berrien Rebels all the way as they notched the victory over the Hornets, 59-47.

George Sorrell was the big gun for the winners with 22 points and Charles Wright took runner-up honors with 14 markers.

Three Hornets placed in double figures but that was still not enough to pull the Cook team through with the victory. Robert Ray led the scoring with 17 points followed by Bobby Tucker and Don Jenerette with 10 each.

The Cook cagers next game will be Friday night when they invade Norman Park to battle the Trojans and Trojanettes in a non-region contest.

[Compiler's note: The article was typed as it appeared in the newspaper, including misspellings of names.]

The Berrien Press, front page, December 18, 1969

Berrien Rebels Defeat Cook High Tuesday

By Tim Moore

The Berrien High Rebels and Rebelettes traveled to Adel on Tuesday night and came home with two more wins over the Cook High Hornets and Wasps. The Berrien B team boys and girls also continued their winning ways as they rolled past the Cook teams also.

In the varsity girl's game, it was simply too much Berrien scoring, Marla Brown, Grace Bailey, and Donna Jernigan poured 63 points into the bucket with Brown's 26 leading the way. The Cook Wasps could only muster 33 points against Berrien's defense of Lenna Carey, Peggy Barber, Andrea Carter along with reserve guards Debra Swain, Brenda Rudeseal and Sandy McMillan.

The Berrien boys got a stern test from the Cook High boys before they pulled away in the closing seconds for a 59-47 victory. George Sorrell, Charles Wright, Bobby Taylor and Richard Tucker spotlighted the fourth victory of the season for the Rebels.

The Rebelettes now stand with a record of 5-0 and the Rebels are 4-1. The Berrien B teams made the evening complete in Adel as the girls dropped Cook 35-14 and the B boys winning 46-32.

The local teams close pre-Xmas action on Friday evening as they host the Worth High teams here in the local gym. The teams from Sylvester are much improved over last year and the basketball teams of Berrien expect plenty of action on Friday.

The Berrien B boys get the action underway at 5:30, when they face the Worth B boys, and the Berrien Freshman teams continue weekend action against Worth on Saturday morning when they duel Worth at 11 a.m.

The Tifton Gazette, page 3, December 20, 1969
Berrien Hoopsters Outclass Worth
Special to Gazette

NASHVILLE – Powerful Berrien County swept a varsity basketball doubleheader here Friday night from Tiftarea foe Worth County. The boys triumphed, 70-32, and the girls won 56-15.

In the boys' contest, Berrien ran its record to 5-1 behind the 23-point firing of George Sorrell, while Wayne Taylor came off the bench to score 11. Nobody for Worth hit in double figures.

The unbeaten Berrien girls, who registered their sixth victory, got double digit scoring from Donna Jernigan, Marla Brown and Grace Bailey who tallied 21, 19 and 12 points, respectively. The guard corps of Lenna Carey, Peggy Barber and Andrea Carter was also superb. Worth was paced by James' 13 points.

Coach Stanley Simpson's Berrien squads now prepare for the Lowndes Christmas Tournament, which begins Dec. 26.

Girls' Game

Worth (15)	Berrien (56)
Hall 1	Brown 19
D. James 13	Jernigan 21
Pendley 1	Bailey 12
Eldridge	Carey
Parr	Barber
Smith	Carter

Worth subs – Booth, Sullivan, Bridges, Stone, Bonnan, G. James. Berrien subs – Langford (2), Williams (2), McMillan, Bennett, Rudeseal, Swain.

Field goals: Worth, 6; Berrien, 23; Free throws: Worth, 3-9; Berrien 10-19; Personal fouls: Worth, 14; Berrien 10.

Boys' Game

Worth (32)	Berrien (70)
Bridges 9	Guess 2
Napier 5	B. Taylor 2
W. Monk 1	Tucker 10
Sams 4	Wright 9
D. Willis 1	Sorrell 23

Worth subs – Barney (2), Ellerbee (4), B. Monk (6). Berrien subs – Harnage (4), W. Taylor (11), Harrell (6), Slaughter (2), Conway (1), Carey, Bobo.

Field goals: Worth, 12; Berrien, 26. Free throws: Worth, 8-14; Berrien, 18-27; Personal fouls: Worth, 20; Berrien, 11.

The Valdosta Daily Times, page 10, December 20, 1969
Berrien Zips Past Worth Co.
Special to the Times

NASHVILLE, Ga. – Berrien's Rebels and Rebelettes turned on their scoring power while the defense turned off Worth's as they posted wide-margin wins in both ends of a high school basketball doubleheader here Friday night.

The Rebels of Coach Stanley Simpson hit for 70 points while holding the Rams to only 32. Simpson's Rebelettes held the Worth sextet to only 15 points while chalking up 56 for themselves.

The victory was the fifth in a row for the Rebels, who are now 5-1, while the Rebelettes are still undefeated after six games.

Donna Jernigan, Marla Brown and Grace Bailey paced the Rebelette scoring with 21, 19 and 12 points respectively. Donna James was high scorer for Worth with 13.

In the boys game, George Sorrell led the way for Berrien hitting for 23 points, while Ken Bridges totaled nine to pace the Rams.

(Box Scores Omitted)

The Valdosta Daily Times, page 11, December 20, 1969
Holiday Tourney Field Completed
By Times Staff Writer

The field is complete and the pairings have been drawn for the 18th annual Christmas Invitational high school basketball tournament to be held in the Lowndes High gym during the holidays.

A total of 14 teams, seven boys and seven girls, will take part in the event which calls for four nights of hoop action over a five-day period this coming weekend.

A total of six first round games, three each night, are on tap for this coming Friday and Saturday. There will be no tourney action Sunday. The semi-finals are set for Monday with the finals on tap for Tuesday.

Berrien's Rebels and Rebelettes have captured both titles for the past two years. Last year they defeated Lowndes 56-50 in the boys final and, 59-44, in the girls title game.

In 1967 Berrien won both trophies by downing Valdosta's Wildcats, 50-41, in the boys showdown and defeating Lowndes, 51-41, in the girls finals.

The tournament began in 1952 at Hahira High, but was moved to the Lowndes site in 1967 when Hahira and Lowndes County Highs consolidated into Lowndes High.

Composing the list of boys squads are top-seeded Georgia Christian (Dasher), Tift County (Tifton), Lowndes, Berrien (Nashville), Cook (Adel), Echols County (Statenville) and Valdosta.

Entered in the girls competition are top-seeded Berrien, Clinch County (Homerville), Tift, Echols, Cook, Valdosta and Lowndes.

The pairings for the first round call for Tift to meet Lowndes, Berrien vs. Cook and Echols vs. Valdosta, while Georgia Christian gets a bye.

The girls schedule calls for first round games of Clinch vs. Tift, Echols vs. Cook, and Valdosta vs. Lowndes, while Berrien has a bye.

The tourney schedule is as follows:

Friday – Clinch vs. Tift (girls), 6:30 p.m.; Echols vs. Valdosta (boys), 7:45 p.m.; and Valdosta vs. Lowndes (girls) 9 p.m.

Saturday – Berrien vs. Cook (boys), 6:30 p.m.; Echols vs. Cook (girls), 7:45 p.m.; and Tift vs. Lowndes (boys), 9 p.m.

Monday – Berrien vs. Clinch-Tift winner (girls), 5:30 p.m.; Berrien-Cook winner vs. Echols-Valdosta winner (boys), 6:45 p.m.; Echols-Cook winner vs. Valdosta-Lowndes winner (girls), 8 p.m.; Georgia Christian vs. Tift-Lowndes winner (boys), 9:15 p.m.

Tuesday – girls finals, 7:30 p.m.; boys finals, 8:45 p.m.

The Tifton Gazette, page 5, December 22, 1969

Four Different Events

6 Tiftarea Teams Go In Holiday Tourneys

By Doug Hawley
Gazette Sports Editor

Six of Tiftarea's seven basketball-playing schools are competing in Christmas tournaments.

Three will battle for honors in the Lowndes Christmas Tournament scheduled Friday, Saturday, next Monday and Tuesday at Valdosta. The schools, which are being represented by both boys' and girls' teams, include Tift County, Berrien County and Cook County.

Actually, one Tiftarea school, Turner County, has already kicked off play in the Wilcox Christmas Tournament. The girls were eliminated Friday by Cochran, while the boys were defeated by Wilcox, 56-54.

Atkinson County's squads compete tonight in the opening of the two-night Coffee County Christmas Tournament at Douglas.

Meanwhile, the Worth County boys prepare for the Albany Christmas Tournament slated Friday, Saturday and next Monday.

Only Fitzgerald High, which finished its football season nine days ago, will not be competing in a tournament. The school has no girls' squad.

In the Lowndes' festivities, Berrien's squads will be defending championships for both divisions. Coach Stanley Simpson's two teams are aiming for a third consecutive tourney sweep.

The unbeaten Berrien Girls (6-0) are top-seeded, along with the undefeated Georgia Christian boys (8-0).

There are seven teams entered in each division. These schools with both boys and girls squads include Tift, Berrien, Cook, Lowndes, Valdosta and Echols County.

Georgia Christian has only a boys' representative. Clinch County sends just a girls team.

The 18th annual tournament was originally held at Hahira. This marks the third year on the Lowndes' premises.

Tift's girls go in the tourney's opening game Friday against Clinch at 6:30 p.m. The local boys face Lowndes in Saturday play slated for 9 p.m.

Lowndes' Tournament

Friday, Dec. 26 – 6:30 p.m. (girls), Tift Co. vs. Clinch Co.; 7:45 p.m. (boys), Echols Co. vs. Valdosta; 9 p.m. (girls), Valdosta vs. Echols Co.

Saturday, Dec. 27 – 6:30 p.m. (boys) Berrien Co. vs Cook Co., 7:45 p.m. (girls), Echols Co. vs. Cook Co.; 9 p.m. (boys), Tift Co. vs. Lowndes Co.

Monday, Dec. 29 – 5:30 p.m. (girls) Berrien Co. vs. Clinch-Tift winner; 6:45 p.m. (boys), Berrien-Cook winner vs. Echols-Valdosta winner; 8 p.m. (girls), Echols-Cook winner vs. Valdosta-Lowndes winner; 9:15 p.m. (boys), Georgia Christian vs. Tift-Lowndes winner.

Tuesday, Dec. 30 – 7:30 p.m. (girls), finals; 9 p.m. (boys), finals.

Atkinson's boys and girls will be going in a four school tournament tonight at Douglas. The other representatives are Nichols, Coffee County and Broxton.

Both Atkinson teams face Nichols tonight. The girls batter at 3 p.m., and the boys compete at 5:30 p.m.

Then, the Coffee County and Broxton girls go in a 7:30 p.m. duel. Those schools' two boys' squads then have a 9 p.m. collision.

Four games are slated Tuesday, including:

3 p.m. (girls), tonight's two losers; 5:30 p.m. (boys), tonight's two losers; 7:30 p.m. (girls), tonight's two winners; 9 p.m. (boys), tonight's two winners.

In the Albany Christmas Tournament, Worth will be part of an eight-team boys' field. The others are host Albany, Westover, Dougherty County, Marion County, Plains, Moultrie and Pelham.

Worth faces an unenviable task Friday night at 9 o'clock against defending champion Albany. The other pairings have not been released.

The Tifton Gazette, page 4, December 24, 1969
<u>Tift, Cook Play Too</u>

Berrien Teams Seeking Third Tourney Title

VALDOSTA – Berrien County's two top-notch basketball teams will be going after their third consecutive tourney sweep here beginning Friday when roundball play opens in the Lowndes Christmas Tournament.

Ironically, this marks the third year also that the event – held in Hahira for 15 years – will be staged on the Lowndes premises.

The Berrien girls, coached by Stanley Simpson and undefeated in six outings, are top-seeded among the female teams. The boys, also coached by Simpson, are not seeded as high, but are given a good chance to take home all the marbles.

Altogether, seven teams are competing in both the boys' and girls' divisions, including Tiftarea representatives Tift County High and Cook County High – in addition to Berrien.

The Friday schedule calls for the following games:

Friday, Dec. 26 – 6:30 p.m. (girls), Tift Co. vs Clinch Co.; 7:45 p.m. (boys), Echols Co. vs. Valdosta; 9 p.m. (girls), Valdosta vs. Echols Co.

Meantime, Worth County High's basketball Rams will be going against Albany's defending champs at 9 p.m. Friday in the annual Albany Christmas Tournament. A field of eight boys' teams is competing in that event.

The Valdosta Daily Times, page 14, December 24, 1969

Holiday Tourney Has Fast Field

By Sammy Glassman
Times Sports Editor

After the high school basketball fans in this area get through celebrating Christmas on Thursday, they can turn their attention to what is annually one of the top hoop attractions in this section.

I'm talking about the Christmas Invitational Tournament. The 18th edition of this popular and historic basketball event is set to begin Friday night at the Lowndes High gym.

The tourney was launched back in 1952 at Hahira High. After that school was consolidated with Lowndes County High in 1966 and the combination became Lowndes High, the event was moved to the new school in 1967.

This year the tourney slate calls for four nights of action over a five-day period. Friday and Saturday will be devoted to the playing of six first round games. There will be no cage action Sunday. The semi-finals are on tap Monday and the finals are slated for Tuesday night.

One strong appeal of the tournament is that it brings teams from schools of all sizes together. This time the entries range in class from "C" to "AAA."

And as you hoop fans already known the quintets and sextets from the smaller schools quite often trip up the cagers from the larger schools.

One of the top favorites in the boys division this time is Georgia Christian (Dasher). Coach Jon Hazelip's Generals, who campaign in Region 1-C, will bring a perfect 9-0 record into the tourney.

Previous Winners

As recently as 1966 Manor, a Class B school, ruled as the tourney's girls champion. And the year before that, 1965, Atkinson County (Pearson), another "B" delegate, won the boys title.

A full list of previous winners, by divisions, goes like this:

Boys – 1952, Valdosta; 1953, Valdosta; 1954, Lanier County; 1955, Irwin County; 1956, Hahira; 1957, Hahira; 1958, Echols County; 1959, Hahira; 1960, Valdosta; 1961, Valdosta; 1962, Coffee County; 1963, Valdosta; 1964, Valdosta; 1965, Atkinson County; 1966, Lowndes; 1967, Berrien and 1968, Berrien.

Girls – 1952, Tifton; 1953, Atkinson County; 1954, Valdosta; 1955, Valdosta; 1956, Valdosta; 1957, Atkinson County; 1958, Berrien; 1959, Valdosta; 1960, Valdosta; 1961, Valdosta; 1962, Valdosta; 1963, Hahira; 1964, Valdosta; 1965, Lowndes; 1966, Manor; 1967, Berrien and 1968, Berrien.

Can Berrien Repeat?

If you'll put the two lists together, you'll see that coach Stanley Simpson's Berrien Rebels and Rebelettes have made a clean sweep of title honors two years in a row.

The only other school to do that in the history of the tourney was Valdosta when it put double title wins back-to-back in 1960 and 1961.

If Berrien can make a third consecutive sweep it will be a tourney first. Since the Rebs are 5-1 and the Rebelettes are 5-0, both certainly must be rated as strong contenders.

Besides GCS and Berrien in the boys bracket, coach Joe Wilson's VHS Wildcats (4-0) and coach Charles Cooper's Lowndes Vikings (5-3) must be ranked high.

In the girls section, coach Steve Kebler's Lowndes Vikettes (6-2) must be considered when you talk about possible winners.

But basketball is unpredictable, especially in a tournament, and the field is so well balanced that the outcome is going to be in doubt until the final game is finished.

The Valdosta Daily Times, page 14, December 24, 1969

Holiday Tourney to Begin Friday
By Times Staff Writer

Play in the 18th edition of the Christmas Invitational high school basketball tournament is to begin her Friday night with strong competition expected in both the boys and girls divisions.

The tourney, to be staged at the Lowndes High gym, will have four nights of cage action over a five-day period. Friday and Saturday will be devoted to first round games. The semi-finals are set Monday and the finals are on tap for Tuesday.

In the field are 14 teams, seven boys and seven girls, representing schools in this area ranging from Class AAA to Class C size.

The entries and their won-loss records follow:

Boys – Georgia Christian (Dasher), 9-0; Valdosta, 4-0; Berrien (Nashville, Ga.), 5-1; Lowndes, 5-3; Echols County (Statenville), 4-7; Cook (Adel), 3-5; and Tift County (Tifton), 2-4.

Girls – Berrien, 6-0; Lowndes, 6-2; Tift, 2-4; Echols, 2-5; Clinch County (Homerville), 2-6; Valdosta, 1-3; and Cook, 0-8.

Coach Jon Hazelip's small, but talented Generals from Dasher with their 9-0 record are top seeded in the boys bracket. Coach Joe Wilson's Valdosta Wildcats, also unbeaten at 4-0; coach Stanley Simpson's defense-minded Berrien Rebs (5-1) and coach Charles Cooper's home-standing Lowndes Vikings (5-3) are other quintets which rate high on the pre-tourney form chart.

In the girls bracket Berrien's coached by Simpson, are top-seeded with their perfect 6-0 record. Coach Steve Kebler's Lowndes Vikettes (6-2) also have a high place on the form chart.

Berrien has made a sweep of title honors for two years in a row, winning both the boys and girls championships in 1967 and again in 1968. Valdosta also put double wins back-to-back in 1960 and 1961, but no school has won both crowns three years in a row. If Berrien can repeat, it will be a tourney first.

The schedule follows:

Friday – Clinch vs. Tift (girls), 6:30 p.m.; Valdosta vs. Echols (boys), 7:45 p.m.; Lowndes vs. Valdosta (girls), 9 p.m.

Saturday – Berrien vs. Cook (boys), 6:30 p.m.; Echols vs. Cook (girls), 7:45 p.m.; Lowndes vs. Tift (boys), 9 p.m.

Monday – Berrien vs. Clinch-Tift winner (girls), 5:30 p.m.; Echols-Valdosta winner vs. Berrien-

Cook winner (boys), 6:45 p.m.; Valdosta-Lowndes winner vs. Echols-Cook winner (girls), 8 p.m.; Georgia Christian vs. Tift-Lowndes winner (boys), 9:15 p.m.

Tuesday – girls finals 7:30 p.m.; boys finals 8:45 p.m.

The Berrien Press, page 10, December 25, 1969

Berrien Zips Past Worth Co.

Berrien's Rebels and Rebelettes turned on their scoring power while the defense turned off Worth's as they posted wide-margin wins in both ends of a high school basketball doubleheader here Friday night.

The Rebels of Coach Stanley Simpson hit for 70 points while holding the Rams to only 32. Simpson's Rebelettes held the Worth sextet to only 15 points while chalking up 56 for themselves.

The victory was the fifth in a row for the Rebels, who are now 5-1, while the Rebelettes are still undefeated after six games.

Donna Jernigan, Marla Brown and Grace Bailey paced the Rebelette scoring with 21, 19 and 12 points respectively. Donna James was high scorer for Worth with 13.

In the boys game, George Sorrell led the way for Berrien hitting for 23 points, while Ken Bridges totaled nine to pace the Rams.

The Tifton Gazette, page 3, December 30, 1969

Third Straight Sweep Tonight?

Berrien Teams Eye Repeats at Valdosta

Special to Gazette

VALDOSTA – Coach Stanley (Ramrod) Simpson's Berrien County High basketball teams will be seeking their third consecutive sweep of the Lowndes Christmas Tournament here tonight.

Berrien's girls advanced to the finals with a Monday night victory over Tift County, 57-36. The boys took a semi-final triumph at the expense of Valdosta, 53-43.

Opposing Berrien's two championship-minded squads tonight will be host Lowndes. The boys knocked top-seed Georgia Christian from the unbeaten ranks in overtime, 72-68, and the girls decisioned Echols County, 63-48.

The girls' squads pair off for the title tonight at 7:30 o'clock. The boys' championship match is scheduled for 9 o'clock.

Tremendous scoring balance was exhibited by Berrien in its victory over Tift as Grace Bailey, Donna Jernigan and Marla Brown scored 24, 18 and 15 points, respectively. Juanita Dickens tallied 21 for the Angels.

Tift trailed by only six points at halftime, 20-26. However, the Rebelettes had a 19-11 third quarter advantage and romped home free.

In the Berrien boys' victory, Roger Guess led the way with 14 points, while Bobby Taylor contributed 12 and Richard Tucker 11. Don Golden was the only Valdosta player in double digits by way of 19.

The Rebels trailed early in the game, but they led at the first quarter turn, 13-10. Berrien held 28-23 and 41-32 advantages at the next two junctures.

Donnie Wisenbaker of Georgia Christian emerged the night's shooting sensation with 46 points in his team's first loss. The better-balanced Lowndes attack showed Curtiss Jones, Henry Otis Register, Jerome Register and Martin Hendrix bucketing 21, 19, 14 and 10, respectively.

Kay Price potted 39 points for the Lowndes girls. Donna Deloach reciprocated with 26 on the Echols' ledger.

Girls' Game

Tift (36)					Berrien (57)
Dickens 21					Brown 15
B. Evans 9					Jernigan 18
Cole 2					Bailey 24
Whittington					Carey
Crowley					Barber
K. Evans					Carter

Tift subs – Conner (4), Taylor, Hawkins. Berrien subs – Langford, Rudeseal, Swain.

Score by Quarters

Tift	10	10	11	5 --	36
Berrien	13	13	19	12 --	57

Field goals: Tift, 15; Berrien, 23. Free throws: Tift, 6-8; Berrien, 11-20; Personal fouls: Tift, 15; Berrien, 6.

Boys' Game

Berrien (53)					Valdosta (43)
Guess 14					Golden 19
B. Taylor 12					Rome 8
Tucker 11					Taylor 6
Wright 8					White 2
Sorrell 8					Webb 8

Berrien subs – None. Valdosta subs – Jones, Baker.

Score by Quarters

Berrien	13	15	13	12 --	53
Valdosta	10	13	9	11 --	43

The Valdosta Daily Times, page 8, December 30, 1969

Lowndes, Berrien In Finals

By Julian Miller
Times Staff Writer

It will be Lowndes going against Berrien in the finals of the 18th annual Christmas Invitational high school basketball tournament here tonight.

In action at the Lowndes High gym, the girls title game is set for 7:30 p.m. and the boys finals are scheduled for 8:45 p.m.

Monday's semi-finals round action in the boys division saw coach Charles Cooper's Lowndes Vikings trim coach Jon Hazelip's Georgia Christian (Dasher) Generals, 72-68, in overtime and coach Stanley Simpson's Berrien (Nashville, Ga.) Rebs beat coach Joe Wilson's Valdosta Wildcats, 53-43. GCS had won nine straight and 'Dosta had clicked off five straight wins before both bowed last night.

In the girls bracket, coach Steve Kebler's Lowndes Vikettes defeated Echols County (Statenville), 63-48, and Berrien's Rebelettes, also coached by Simpson, sailed past the Tift County (Tifton) Angels, 57-36.

Berrien's Rebs will enter the boys final with a 7-1 record and the Nashville quintet is riding the crest of a seven-game victory streak. The Vikes own a 7-3 mark.

The Rebelettes from Nashville are unbeaten at 7-0 and the Vikettes they are to face have an 8-2 chart.

Berrien has made a clean sweep of title honors in the tournament for the past two years and will be going for a third double triumph tonight.

Both Lowndes teams reached the finals in 1968, bowing 59-44 in the girls championship and falling, 56-50, in the boys title game last year.

The Lowndes girls were also runners-up in 1967 and claimed the title in 1965. Lowndes' boys won their division championship in 1965.

Recap of Monday's games shows:

BERRIEN 57 – TIFT 36

At first it seemed as if Tift's guards were going to be able to stay with the Berrien's defense trio as the first stanza became a defensive exhibit with Berrien taking a 13-10 lead.

But mid-way the second quarter, the Tift girls began to slow down while the Rebelettes guard trio of Lenna Carey, Peggy Barber and Andrea Carter held the Angels. In the second half, the three Berrien forwards Marla Brown, Donna Jernigan and Grace Bailey opened up and Tift's hopes sank.

Bailey, who sparkled in the last stanza, hit for 24 points followed by Jernigan, and 18, and Brown, 15. High scorer for the Angels was Jaunita Dickens with 21 points.

Coach Sandra Withrow's Angels leave the tourney with a 3-5 record.

BERRIEN 53 – VALDOSTA 43

The Wildcats took a 4-2 lead in the opening minutes, but that was as far as the Rebels let them get. With 4:05 remaining in the first quarter Berrien was ahead 8-6 on a field goal by Richard Tucker and although the lead lagged between 4 and 12 points the 'Cats never caught up.

Berrien kept the back boards clean and kept the fouls down to 11, compared to Valdosta's 14.

A balanced Rebel attack of Roger Guess, 14; Bobby Taylor, 12; Richard Tucker, 11; Charles Wright, 8; and George Sorrell, 8, won Berrien.

On the Valdosta side there was Don Golden with 15; Roger Rome, 12; Benji Webb, 8; Warrick Taylor, 6; and William White, 2.

[Compiler's note: The report of other games in the tournament was omitted here.]

(Box Scores Omitted)

Photo caption:
Berrien's George Sorrell (21) gets one finger on the basketball. – Times Staff Photo

The Tifton Gazette, page 3, December 31, 1969
Berrien's Third Straight Sweep

Simpson's Teams Garner Lowndes' Honors Again

Special to Gazette

VALDOSTA – If the annual Lowndes Christmas Tournament changes its name to the Berrien County Christmas Tournament, it would be understandable.

For the third consecutive year, Coach Stanley (Ramrod) Simpson's Berrien squads have swept to titles for both divisions. Host Lowndes was the victim Tuesday night.

The Berrien girls decisioned Lowndes, 44-37. The boys not to be outdone followed with a 48-37 victory over the tourney host.

In both contests, the Berrien squads leaped off to sizeable early leads. The girls were ahead, 9-0, and the boys, 8-0, before the Lowndes squads knew what hit them.

Berrien's girls received a 26-point effort from Donna Jernigan. Marla Brown contributed 14.

Lowndes, which did pull twice within two points during the first half, was sparked by Kay Price's 16-point production.

In the boys' title clash, Charles Wright bucketed 14 points and George Sorrell 11 to pace the winners. Nobody for Lowndes hit double figures.

Berrien held a 15-6 first quarter advantage and a comfortable 29-12 halftime lead.

Girls' Game

Berrien (44)	Lowndes (37)
Brown 14	Price 16
Jernigan 26	Shaw 6
Bailey 4	Passmore 9
Carey	Vann
Barber	Wheeler
Carter	Lumley

Berrien subs – Langford, McMillan, Rudeseal.
Lowndes subs – Lineberger (6), Mitchell.

Score by quarters:

Berrien	13	11	9	11 --	44
Lowndes	5	14	4	14 --	37

Field goals: Berrien, 16; Lowndes, 14;
Free throws: Berrien, 12-21; Lowndes, 9-17.
Personal fouls: Berrien, 16; Lowndes, 14.

Boys' Game

Berrien (48)	Lowndes (37)
Guess 9	Jones 6
Taylor 9	J. Register 9
Tucker 5	Hendrix 7
Wright 14	H. Register 4
Sorrell 11	Haines

Berrien subs – Conway. Lowndes subs – Thomas (2), Saengerhausen (5), Deloach.

Score by quarters:

Berrien	15	14	11	8 --	48
Lowndes	6	6	14	11 --	37

Field goals: Berrien, 18; Lowndes, 16; Free throws: Berrien, 12-22; Lowndes, 5-9; Personal fouls: Berrien, 8; Lowndes, 14.

Photo caption:

UNBEATEN BERRIEN CHAMPIONS – Members of the unbeaten Berrien County basketball team, who captured the girls' championship in the Lowndes Christmas Tournament for the third consecutive year, include (front row, from left) Sandra McMillan, Donna Bennett, Pat Williams, Andrea Carter, Debra Swain and Donna Jernigan; (top row) Gloria Mathis, Peggy Barber, Marla Brown, Grace Bailey, Lenna Carey, Jo Ann Langford, Brenda Rudeseal and Coach Stanley (Ramrod) Simpson. (Staff Photo).

The Valdosta Daily Times, page 8, December 31, 1969

Berrien Sweeps Tourney Honors

By Sammy Glassman
Times Sports Editor

Berrien's Rebels and Rebelettes from Nashville, Ga., made a clean sweep of title honors as the 18th annual Christmas Invitational high school basketball tournament came to a close here Tuesday night.

It was Berrien against host Lowndes in the finals, and the cagers from Nashville won in the boys game, 48-37, and triumphed in the girls contest, 44-37.

This marks the third consecutive year that the Berrien teams, both coached by Stanley Simpson, have gone home with all the tourney crowns, and that's never been done before in the event which dates back to 1952.

While coach Charles Cooper's Lowndes Vikings and coach Steve Kebler's Vikettes battled hard all the way, both fell behind early and then couldn't catch up.

Last night's triumph was the eight in as many starts this season for the Rebelettes. The Rebs are now 8-1 and have an eight-game victory streak going. The losses left the Vikes with a 7-4 mark and the Vikettes with an 8-2 chart.

In the boys game the Berrien fivesome of Charles Wright, George Sorrell, Roger Guess, Bobby Taylor and Richard Tucker combined their talents to offer a balanced attack and a super tough defense. Wright, with 14 points, and Sorrell, with 11, were the scoring leaders.

Berrien's defense was so effective Lowndes didn't have anyone who scored in double figures. The Vike leader was Jerome Register, 9; Martin Hendrix, 7; and Curtis Jones, 6.

Berrien jumped off to a quick 8-0 lead. The Rebs went on to stretch their advantage to 17 points at the half. Lowndes began to chip away at Berrien's lead, but had whittled it down to only 11 points at the finish.

The girls game featured some sparkling guard play at both ends of the court. The defensive leaders for Berrien were Lena Carey, Peggy Barber and Brenda Rudeseal. Those for Lowndes were Kristine Wheeler, Debbie Lumley and Earlie Mitchell.

On offense, Donna Jernigan racked up 26 points and Marla Brown scored 14 to lead the way for Berrien. Kay Price, with 16 points, and Peggy Passemore, with 9, led the way for the Vikettes.

The sextet from Nashville moved to the front 9-0 early in the opening stanza. From there on the Vikettes had the task of trying to catch up.

Lowndes got within two points twice in the second period, fell behind by 10 in the third stanza and then pulled up within six twice in the closing period, but could never quite make up all the lost ground.

(Box Scores Omitted)

Photo captions:
Rebs' Roger Guess (22) Reaches Out to Guard Vikes' Curtis Jones – Times Staff Photo

January 1970

The Tifton Gazette, page 4, January 1, 1970
Photo caption:
BERRIEN'S TOURNAMENT CHAMPIONS – Members of the Berrien County High basketball team who claimed the boys' division championship of the Lowndes Christmas Tournament earlier this week for the third consecutive year include (front row, from left) Wayne Taylor, Roger Guess, Bobby Conway, Jerry Slaughter, David Bobo and Bobby Taylor; (back row) George Sorrell, Richard Tucker, Karl Harrell, David Harnage, Charles Wright and Coach Stanley (Ramrod) Simpson. (Absent from picture was Kim Carey). (Staff Photo).

The Berrien Press, front page, January 1, 1970

Calendar Girl For January
The new 1970 vehicle license plates are due to go on sale Friday at the office of Lorene Dorminey, tax commissioner of Berrien County. And a reminder for tag buyers is Sandra McMillan, holding the tag of a neighbor, Bobby Rowan, state senator of Eighth District, and another tag close ('70) to the year. Daughter of Mr. and Mrs. Maurice McMillan of Enigma, Sandra is a senior at Berrien High School, forward on the BHS Rebelette basketball team, member of B Club, Beta Club, Student Council and President of Senior Tri-Hi-Y.

The Valdosta Daily Times, page 13, January 1, 1970
Double Challenge Fine With Coach
By Sammy Glassman
Times Sports Editor

W. Stanley (Ramrod) Simpson rested his elongated frame against a wall at one end of the Lowndes High gym, flashed a friendly smile and said with a serious tone in his voice, "Our kids worked hard and we were lucky."

The 18th annual Christmas Invitational high school basketball tournament had just come to a close on Tuesday night and Simpson's Berrien Rebels and Rebelettes from Nashville, Ga., had just swept the championship honors in the event for the third year in a row. That's something no other school has done since the tourney was launched back in 1952.

Simpson came out with that remark about his players working hard and being lucky in answer to a question about what was Berrien's secret of success in the Yule event.

Perhaps, as some contend, it takes at least a touch of luck to win in any athletic contest. But when you view the overall record of the Berrien cage teams since Simpson arrived on the scene nine years ago, well, you know his coaching skill has been the major factor.

It was once a rather common practice for high schools in these parts to have one coach for both the boys and girls teams.

Now Simpson, who is 32 years old, is one of just a few prep hoops mentors who are still pulling double duty.

Worries A Lot

By his own admission Simpson worries a lot and he doesn't try to discount the fact that coaching two teams puts extra wear and tear on his nerves, but he also sees it as a challenge and he's quite happy with his situation.

After those tourney triumphs Simpson's Rebels are 8-1 and his Rebelettes are 8-0. His boys lost their season opener and haven't been licked since.

But winning teams are something he has been turning out at Berrien for nine years. The overall mark for his boys is 150-66 and for his girls the total is 166-46.

Put the two together and you come up with the amazing record of 316-112.

Down through the years Simpson's quintets and sextets have been noted for their defensive ability and their smooth well-coordinated attacks.

Both the Rebels and Rebelettes of 1969-70 are cut from that same pattern.

Title Contenders

The Rebs' starters include Roger Guess (6-0, jr), Bobby Taylor (6-0, jr). Richard Tucker (6-2, sr), Charles Wright (6-5, jr.) and George Sorrell (6-5, jr).

Among the front-liners for the Rebelettes are forwards Marla Brown (5-9, sr.), Donna Jernigan (5-4, jr.), and Grace Bailey (5-10, sr.) and guards Lena Carey (5-10, sr.), Peggy Barber (5-8, sr.), Andrea Carter (5-6, sr.) and Brenda Rudeseal (5-8, jr.).

Simpson is one of those do-it-then-brag coaches, so you won't catch him climbing out on any limbs right now. But both the Rebs and Rebelettes must be rated as title contenders in both divisions of Region 1-AA.

It just may be both will be making state tourney appearances this year. That certainly would put the pressure on Simpson and keep him busy. But he's been that route before and the friendly man from Nashville would enjoy facing that kind of double challenge again.

The Thomasville Times-Enterprise, page 6, January 3, 1970

Rebels Edge Syrupmakers

NASHVILLE – Cairo's Syrupmakers suffered their second loss of the season last night as Berrien County gained a 30-29 victory.

Both teams played a slow game and Berrien led only 10-7 at halftime. The Syrupmakers had an 11-10 margin in the third quarter but the Rebels led 20-18.

Cairo pulled within one point with 58 seconds remaining in the game and played for one shot. The Syrupmakers shot and missed and tied the ball.

Joel Rackley grabbed the tip but failed to get a shot off before the final buzzer sounded.

The Syrupmakers held a 12-11 edge in field goals, but the Rebels were eight for 15 at the free throw line while Cairo was five for seven.

"We played good enough to win," said Cairo Coach Tommy Taylor. "But, we missed too many shots under the goal."

Tom Taylor was the only player to score in double figures with 13 points.

The Syrupmaids dropped a 55-38 game to the Rebelettes. Marla Brown scored 29 points to lead all scorers.

The Rebelettes jumped off to a 13-8 lead in the first quarter and held a 25-14 margin at halftime. Berrien then outscored Cairo 30-14 in the second half for the victory.

Coach Jeff McCord's Cairo B team upped their record 6-0 with a 53-39 victory. Melvin Ray scored 18 points, Craig Taylor 12 and Terry Prince 11 to pace Cairo.

In the Cairo ninth grade game the Rebels were 35-34 victors. Melvin Ray paced the Syrupmakers with 20 points and Andrew Davis had eight.

*****

CAIRO GIRLS (12 – 4 – 28) – Rineer 2-2-6; Ponder 2-1-5; Thrower 3-0-6; Wight 0-0-0; Womble 3-0-6; Avery 1-0-2; Massey 1-1-3; Guards: Dukes, Furgerson, Whitfield.

BERRIEN COUNTY (21 – 13 – 55) – Brown 12-5-29; Jernigan 1-2-4; Bailey 2-3-7; Langford 4-0-8; McCillian 1-2-3; Williams 0-0-0; Bennett 1-2-4; Guards: Carey, Barber, Radenseal.

| Cairo | 8 | 6 | 5 | 9 – 28 |
| Berrien | 13 | 12 | 13 | 17 – 55 |

CAIRO BOYS (12 – 5 – 29) – Burt 1-0-2; Rackley 4-0-8; Montgomery 0-0-0; Ready 0-2-2; Kravig 2-0-4; Taylor 5-3-13.

BERRIEN COUNTY (11 – 8 – 30) – Guest 1-1-3; Taylor 1-2-4; Tucker 4-0-8; Wright 3-3-9; Sorrell 2-2-6.

| Cairo | 4 | 3 | 11 | 11 – 29 |
| Berrien | 6 | 6 | 10 | 10 – 32 |

The Tifton Gazette, page 3, January 3, 1970

Berrien Sweeps Cairo

Special to Gazette

NASHVILLE – Berrien County's boys captured a scintillating one-point decision over perennial power Cairo here Friday night, 30-29.

By virtue of the victory, Berrien gained a sweep for the evening. In the opener, the unbeaten local girls stormed to a convincing 55-28 triumph.

In the boys' skirmish, Berrien and ball-control Cairo were knotted at the first quarter, 4-4. The Rebels held 10-7 and 20-18 advantages following the next two junctures and never trailed down the stretch.

Tommy Taylor of Cairo emerged the contest's double-digit scorer with 13 points. Berrien's Charles Wright tallied nine.

Berrien extended its record to 10-1, the lone loss coming in the season opener to Tift County. Cairo fell to 9-2.

The girls' battle found Marla Brown outscoring the Cairo team with a 29-point effort. Nobody for the visitors registered in double figures.

Berrien extended its perfect mark to 10-0. Cairo now has 8-3 credentials.

The Berrien squads go on the road tonight to face Lowndes at Valdosta.

(Box Scores Omitted)

The Valdosta Daily Times, page 8, January 3, 1970
Berrien's Cagers Turn Back Cairo
Special to the Times

NASHVILLE, Ga. – Cairo's Syrupmakers gave Berrien's Rebels the closest game since they started their nine-game winning streak, but a last-minute gamble didn't payoff and Berrien took both ends of a high school basketball doubleheader here Friday night.

When the dust had settled the Rebels had taken a 30-29 victory over the Cairo five and the Rebelettes of coach Stanley Simpson trounced the Syrupmaids, 55-28. The Berrien girls are now 9-0

With nearly two minutes remaining, a free throw put the Rebs ahead 30-29. Cairo froze the ball for nearly a minute and a half then put all its hopes on a field goal with three seconds remaining. The shot missed and Berrien won.

Cairo's Rick Taylor was high scorer with 13 points while Charles Wright paced the Berrien quintet with 9 points. The victory boosted the Rebels to a 9-1 record. The Syrupmakers are now 9-2.

In the girls game, Berrien took a quick lead in the first stanza and easily held on to it to stage their 55-28 victory.

Marla Brown dominated the scoring for Berrien with 29 points to her credit while Mary Rineer, Kay Thrower and Sandra Rumble teamed-up to lead Cairo with six points each.

Berrien is scheduled to see action again tonight when it travels to Valdosta to meet Lowndes Vikings and Vikettes. That twin-bill is scheduled to begin at 7 p.m. in the Lowndes gym.

(Box Scores Omitted)

The Tifton Gazette, page 3, January 5, 1970
Berrien Teams Wax Lowndes

VALDOSTA – Berrien's girls played it close during the first half, but came on strong in the second to score their 10th straight victory of the year over Lowndes' girls here Saturday night.

Meantime, the Berrien boys had to rally behind the scoring punch of William Taylor to down Lowndes' boys in the second game. It was the Rebels' 10th victory against one loss (to Tift County). [Compiler's note: Incorrect identification. Wayne, not William.]

Marla Brown's 14 points paced the Berrien girls in their victory. Berrien led only 13-9 at half, but opened up in the second half to gain the 37-29 victory.

Berrien's boys trailed 25-16 at halftime, but came on strong in the second half. They pulled to within four points by the end of the third period and scored 18 more in the fourth to wrap up the 45-39 victory. Taylor's 12 points were high for Berrien.

(Box Scores Omitted)

The Valdosta Daily Times, page 12, January 5, 1970

Berrien Cagers Defeat Lowndes

By Julian Miller
Times Staff Writer

Lowndes' Vikings almost did it Saturday night, but the Rebels showed them "almost" wasn't enough as Berrien took both ends of a high school basketball doubleheader here Saturday night.

The Vikings of coach Charles Cooper jumped off to a quick lead and built it up as far as 15 points before the Rebs of coach Stanley Simpson started a rally which didn't end until they had a 47-39 victory. Simpson's Rebelettes had earlier defeated coach Steve Kebler's Vikettes, 37-29.

It was the third time this season the Berrien teams from Nashville, Ga. have defeated Lowndes' cagers.

In the girls' game the lead changed hands four times in the first quarter before the Rebelettes broke a 7-7 tie with two quick field goals by Marla Brown.

Berrien moved five points ahead, but that was as far as Lowndes would allow before the Vikettes finally caught the visitors at the end of the third stanza. But at the start of the final period Donna Jernigan and Grace Bailey sank a field goal and two free throws each to set the Rebelettes up for the victory.

Kay Price was high scorer for the Vikettes with 19 points.

Brown paced the Rebelettes with 14 points, while Donna Jernigan chipped in with 13.

In the boys game, Lowndes had a surprise for the Rebels as it jumped off to a quick lead at the start of the game and expanded it to a 15 point margin in the third stanza. But in that same period, the Rebels started a rally which turned into a 10-point lead for Berrien.

With 2:49 remaining in the third stanza, the Rebels' Charles Wright and Bobby Taylor took turns at sinking three field goals each before Lowndes could get the ball down court. Berrien continued this type action in the final quarter to register its victory.

Wayne Taylor, a Berrien substitute, led the scoring for the Rebels by hitting six field goals in as many attempts for 12 points. Following was Richard Tucker, with 10 points. For Lowndes, Jerome Register took the lead with 16 points, while Barry Saengerhausen got in 10.

The victories moved the Rebels to a 10-1 record, with a 10-game win streak. The Rebelettes are undefeated at 10-0. The Vikings are now 8-5, while the Vikettes are 9-4.

Berrien's "B" teams defeated the Lowndes boys, 31-26, and the LHS girls, 25-23.

GIRLS				
Lowndes	7	9	24	29
Berrien	11	13	24	37

LOWNDES (29) – Price 19, Shaw 7, Lineberger 3, Passmore, Mitchell, Vann, Wheeler, D. Lumley. Team totals: field goals 10, free throws 9 of 11, fouls 15.

BERRIEN (37) – Brown 14, Jernigan 13, Bailey 8, Langford 2, Carey, Barber, Rudeseal. Team totals: field goals 13, free throws 11 of 21, fouls 9.

BOYS				
Lowndes	13	25	31	39
Berrien	7	16	27	47

LOWNDES (39) – J. Register 16, Saengerhausen 10, H. Register 6, Hendrix 5, Jones 2, Haines. Team totals: field goals 16, free throws 7 of 10, fouls 11.

BERRIEN (47) – W. Taylor 12, Tucker 10, Wright 8, B. Taylor 7, Sorrell 5, Guess 3, Conway 2. Team totals: field goals 19, free throws 7 of 14, fouls 7.

The Valdosta Daily Times, page 11, January 6, 1970

Berrien to Host Valdosta Cagers

By Times Staff Writer

Valdosta's Wildcats will have revenge on their minds when they take on the one team that has defeated them, Berrien's Rebels, as the two schools meet in a high school basketball doubleheader tonight in Nashville, Ga.

Coach Joe Wilson's Wildcats will put a 6-1 record on the line. The Rebels are 10-1 and have a 10-game winning streak going. Coach Bill Davis' VHS Kittens will be looking for their third win in seven starts when they take on Berrien's undefeated (10-0) Rebelettes at 7 p.m.

The Rebels, coached by Stanley Simpson, defeated the 'Cats, 53-43, in the semi-finals of the Lowndes Christmas Tournament last week. Berrien's only defeat came at the hands of Tift County's Blue Devils in the season opener in Tifton.

That VHS-Berrien duel heads a list of five doubleheaders and one single game involving an are cage team tonight.

Other slated action calls for Cook (Adel) to play at Central (Thomasville), Echols County (Statenville) at Atkinson County (Pearson), Brooks County (Quitman) at Thomasville and Clinch County (Homerville) at Charlton County (Folkston). Hamilton County (Jasper, Fla.) is scheduled to take on Madison, Fla., in a boys game at Madison.

Coach Ray Rollyson's Hamilton County Rebels will be trying to put their record above the .500 mark when they travel to Madison. The Rebs are now 2-2.

Clinch County's Panthers of coach Austin DeLoach will be trying to expand on a 5-3 record when they take on Charlton County's Indians in Folkston.

The Tifton Gazette, page 5, January 7, 1970

Berrien Boys Make Big Comeback

Special to Gazette

NASHVILLE – Berrien County's boys overcame an eight-point lead in the fourth quarter to defeat visiting Valdosta here Tuesday night, 56-52.

In the opener, the Berrien girls remained unbeaten with a convincing 42-20 victory over Valdosta.

The boys' contest found Berrien being outscored from the field, 24-16, but the Rebels had the superiority at the free throw line, 24-4. The victory was the Rebels' 11th straight, running the overall mark to 11-1.

Bobby Taylor, Roger Guess and George Sorrell paced the Rebels attack with 16, 15 and 11 points, respectively. Don Golden tallied 20 and Warrick Taylor 14 for the Wildcats.

In the girls' skirmish, Berrien – which recorded its 11th win – got a 21 point performance from Marla Brown. Valdosta's Joy Johnson tallied 13.

The Valdosta boys now stand 6-2 for the campaign. The girls are 3-5.

Berrien's squads have action Friday night against Crisp County at Cordele.

Girls' Game

Valdosta (20)	Berrien (42)
M. Stephenson 4	Brown 21
Johnson 13	Jernigan 9
Robertson 3	Bailey 4
B. Stephenson	Carey
Brantley	Barber
Graham	Rudeseal

Valdosta subs – Flanders, Lumpkin. Berrien subs – McMillan (6), Langford (2), Swain.

Score by quarters:

Valdosta	3	8	4	5 – 20
Berrien	8	10	7	17 – 42

Field goals: Valdosta, 9; Berrien, 15. Free throws: Valdosta, 2-9; Berrien, 12-16. Personal fouls: Valdosta, 11; Berrien, 10.

Boys' Game

Valdosta (52)		Berrien (56)	
Taylor	14	Guess	15
Jones	4	B. Taylor	16
Webb	6	Tucker	9
Golden	20	Sorrell	11
Rome	6	Wright	4

Valdosta subs – Barker (2), White. Berrien subs – W. Taylor (1).

Score by quarters:

Valdosta	12	10	20	10–52
Berrien	10	12	12	22–56

Field goals: Valdosta, 24; Berrien, 16. Free throws: Valdosta, 4-10; Berrien, 24-32. Personal fouls: Valdosta, 20; Berrien, 9.

The Valdosta Daily Times, page 11, January 7, 1970

Berrien Cagers Defeat Valdosta

Special to the Times

NASHVILLE, Ga. – Berrien's Rebels did some sharp-shooting from the foul line as they posted a 56-52 high school basketball victory over Valdosta here Tuesday night.

Berrien made it a sweep as the Rebelettes turned back VHS' Kittens, 42-20, in the girls game.

Coach Stanley Simpson's Berrien boys are now 11-1 after winning 11 in a row. His girls are unbeaten after 11 starts. Coach Joe Wilson's 'Cats are 6-2 and coach Bill Davis' Kittens have a 2-5 mark.

In the boys game the count was deadlocked at the half and VHS had a 12-point edge after the third period. But the Rebs tallied 22 points in the final stanza to rally and win. For the night Berrien hit 24 of 32 from the charity line.

Roger Guess, 15, and Bobby Taylor, 16, were attack leaders for the Rebels. Don Golden, with 20 points, and Warrick Taylor, with 14, were leaders for the 'Cats.

Marla Brown got 21 points to pace the Rebelettes. Top scorer for the Kittens was Joy Johnson with 13 markers to her credit.

(Box Scores Omitted)

The Berrien Press, front page, January 8, 1970

Coach Stanley Simpson Steers Teams to Crowns

W. Stanley (Ramrod) Simpson rested his elongated frame against a wall at one end of the Lowndes High gym, flashed a friendly smile and said with a serious tone in his voice, "Our kids worked hard and we are lucky."

The 18th annual Christmas Invitational high school basketball tournament had just come to a close on Tuesday night and Simpson's Berrien Rebels and Rebelettes from Nashville, Ga., had just swept the championship honors in the event for the third year in a row.

That's something no other school has done since the tourney was launched back in 1952.

Simpson came out with that remark about his players working hard and being luck in answer to a question about what was Berrien's secret of success in the Yule event.

Perhaps, as some contend, it takes at least a touch of luck to win in any athletic contest.

But when you view the overall record of the Berrien cage teams since Simpson arrived on the scene nine years ago, well, you know his coaching skill has been the major factor.

It was once a rather common practice for high schools in these parts to have one coach for both the boys and girls teams.

Now Simpson, who is 32 years old, is one of just a few prep hoop mentors who are still pulling double duty.

WORRIES A LOT

By his own admission Simpson worries a lot and he doesn't try to discount the fact that coaching two teams puts extra wear and tear on his nerves, but he also sees it as a challenge and he's quite happy with his situation.

After those tourney triumphs Simpson's Rebels are 8-1 and his Rebelettes are 8-0. His boys lost their season opener and haven't been licked since.

But winning teams are something he has been turning out at Berrien for nine years. The overall mark for his boys is 150-66 and for his girls the total is 166-46.

Put the two together and you come up with the amazing record of 316-112.

Down through the years Simpson's quintets and sextets have been noted for their defensive ability and their smooth well co-ordinated attacks.

Both the Rebels and Rebelettes of 1969-70 are cut from that same pattern.

TITLE CONTENDERS

The Rebs' starters include Roger Guess (6-0, jr), Bobby Taylor (6-0, jr). Richard Tucker (6-2, sr), Charles Wright (6-5, jr.) and George Sorrell (6-5, jr).

Among the front-liners for the Rebelettes are forwards Marla Brown (5-9, sr.), Donna Jernigan (5-4, jr.), and Grace Bailey (5-10, sr.) and guards Lena Carey (5-10, sr.), Peggy Barber (5-8, sr.), Andrea Carter (5-6, sr.) and Brenda Rudeseal (5-8, jr.).

Simpson is one of those do-it-then-brag coaches, so you won't catch him climbing out on any limbs right now. But both the Rebs and Rebelettes must be rated as title contenders in both divisions of Region 1-AA.

It just may be both will be making state tourney appearances this year. That certainly would put the pressure on Simpson and keep him busy.

But he's been that route before and the friendly man from Nashville would enjoy facing that kind of double challenge again. – Sammy Glassman in Valdosta Times.

The Berrien Press, page 2, January 8, 1970
For Record Third Time

Berrien Basketball Teams Wins Lowndes Tournament

By TIM MOORE

The Berrien Basketball teams brought a record Tuesday, Dec. 30 when they won the Lowndes County Christmas Tournament for the third straight year.

The Berrien County Rebels started their drive for the first place trophy Monday, Dec. 27, when they put the Cook County Hornets down, 64-36.

Scoring for the Rebels was led by George Sorrell with 22 points followed by Roger Guess and Wayne Taylor with 9 points each; Charles Wright and David Bobo both had 7 points, Karl Harrell had five, Bobby Conway had 3 and Jerry Slaughter had 2.

Bobby Tucker led the Hornets, scoring 18 points.

This game put the Berrien County boys in the semi-finals with Valdosta.

The Berrien girls played their first game of the tournament Monday night in the semi-finals against the Tift County Angels. The Rebelettes downed the Angels, 57-36.

Scoring for the Rebelettes was led by Grace Bailey with 24 points. Donna Jernigan had 18 points and Marla Brown had 15. Berrien's defense was led by Lenna Carey. Peggy Barber and Andrea Carter with Brenda Rudeseal and Debra Swain serving as defensive substitutes.

High scorer for the Angels was Juanita Dickens with 21 points.

Monday night also brought the Berrien County boys another win as they downed the Valdosta Wildcats, 53-43.

Roger Guess scored highest for the Rebels with 14 points, Bobby Taylor with 12, and Richard Tucker with 11. Also scoring for the Rebels was Charles Wright and George Sorrell with 8 points each. George Sorrell also pulled down 15 rebounds.

High scorer for Valdosta was Donnie Golden with 19 points.

The Rebels took a quick close lead in this game and held it to the end. These wins put both Berrien teams up against the Lowndes County teams in the finals which were played Tuesday night, December 30.

In the finals the girls got past their contest by the score of 44-37. Leading Berrien's offense was Donna Jernigan with 26 points, followed by Marla Brown with 14 points, and Grace Bailey with 4 points. Offensive subs for Berrien were Jo Ann Langford and Sandy McMillan. Heading the Rebelette's defense were Lenna Carey, Peggy Barber and Andrea Carter with Brenda Rudeseal substituting.

Scoring highest for Lowndes was Kay Price with 16 points and Passmore with 10 points.

The Rebels took their game by the score 48-37. High scorer for the Rebels was Charles Wright with 14 points. George Sorrell made 11 points and jerked 18 rebounds off the boards. Roger Guess and Bobby Taylor both had 9 points and Richard Tucker had 5.

The only player for Lowndes who was close to double figures was Jerome Register with 9 points.

The Berrien Press, page 3, January 8, 1970

Berrien High Basketball Teams Chalk Up Victories
By TIM MOORE

The Berrien County basketball teams took both games from the Cairo Syrupmakers and Syrupmaids Friday night, Jan. 2 in Nashville.

The Berrien girls had their game pretty well in the clear for the greater part of the game as they beat the Syrupmaids, 55-28. Leading the scoring for the Rebelettes was Marla Brown with 29 points, followed by Jo Ann Langford with 8 points, Grace Bailey with 7 points, Donna Jernigan and Donna Bennett with 4 points each; Sandy McMillan with 3 points. The starting guards for Berrien were Lenna Carey, Peggy Barber, and Brenda Rudeseal.

High scorers for Cairo were Rineer, Thrower, and Womble each having 6 points. Starting guards for Cairo were Dukes, Demorest and Clark.

The boys game consisted mainly of a tough defensive battle for both teams. The Rebels could muster only 30 points against Cairo's tough defense, but that was enough to beat Cairo's 29 points against Berrien's equal defense.

High scorer for the Rebels was Charles Wright with 9 points. Richard Tucker followed with 8 points. George Sorrell with 6 points, Bobby Taylor with 4 points and Roger Guess with 3 points.

Leading the Syrupmakers offense was Tommy Taylor with 13 points.

These 2 wins brought the Rebelettes record to 9-0 and the Rebels record to 9-1.

The Berrien County Rebels and Rebelettes beat the Lowndes County basketball team again Saturday night, Jan. 3, in Valdosta for the third straight time this season.

The Lowndes girls trailed the Rebelettes slightly during the first and second quarters. The Rebelettes led 11-7 at the end of the first juncture, and at half time they were leading 13-9. By the end of the third period the Vikings had come up to tie the Rebelettes, 24-24. The Rebelettes finally broke the tie in the fourth period and came on to win the game, 37-29.

Scoring for the Berrien team was Marla Brown with 14 points, Donna Jernigan with 11 points, Grace Bailey with 10 points and Jo Ann Langford with 2 points. Playing on the defense for the Rebelettes were Lenna Carey, Peggy Barber and Brenda Rudeseal.

High scorer for Lowndes was Kay Price with 19 points.

The boys game was really an exciting one, especially for the Berrien fans. The Vikings took an early lead which had the Rebels trailing, 13-7, at the start of the second quarter, and at half time they were still leading, 25-16. The third quarter started with the Vikings grabbing a 15-point lead on the Rebels before they could score again. Finally, the Berrien boys started closing the gap, and at the end of the third period Berrien was close behind the Vikings 31-27. In the fourth quarter Berrien pulled ahead and held their lead for 45-39 victory that displayed Berrien's valuable "stickability."

Richard Tucker scored 10 points for Berrien, followed by Charles Wright with 8 points, Bobby Taylor with 7, George Sorrell with 5 and Roger Guess with 3. Substitutes for Berrien were Wayne Taylor (who was also high scorer of the night with 12 points), David Harnage, and Bobby Conway.

Photo caption:
CLOSE – In the tight defensive game with Cairo, the Berrien Rebels try for another score as George Sorrell goes up for the basket, backed by Richard Tucker, George Sorrell and Bobby Tucker.

The Tifton Gazette, page 3, January 8, 1970

Berrien's 'Ramrod' Is 'Defensive'

By Johnny Futch
Special to Gazette

NASHVILLE – If Ramrod Simpson stays on the "defensive" a lot when he talks about his Berrien High School Rebel basketball team, it's understandable. The Rebs stay on the defensive a lot themselves.

Matter of fact, defense is a Simpson, Berrien County trademark largely responsible for the 11-1 season record the Rebels are carrying into the second half of their season. They dropped their opener 45-46 to Tift County on the road but they have been unstoppable ever since.

The 11-game win skein has been built on a stingy defense that has yielded an average of 39.7 points per game countered by an unspectacular but deliberately effective offense that has been picking opponents apart at the rate of 52.0 points an outing.

That defense is built around 6-0 Roger Guess, 6-0 Bobby Taylor and 6-2 Richard Tucker outside and Charles Wright and George Sorrell, both 6-5, underneath. Co-captain Tucker is the only senior starter – the rest are juniors.

Sorrell, a second started and the other co-captain, is the "big" man for the team in more ways than one. Hitting at a 14.3 point pace, he has been hauling down an average of 16.1 rebounds per game.

Wright, playing his first year of organized basketball, has picked off 9.4 rebounds a game while averaging 8.9 points. Taylor's 6.5, Tuckers' 6.4 and Guess' 7.9 averages round out the balanced Berrien attack.

The Rebels got their biggest test of the season last weekend when they locked up with Cairo, a mirror image ringer for Berrien in both defensive ability and offensive deliberateness. With both teams allowing shots only from third row, balcony, or farther out, the halftime score was 10-7. The Rebs finally won it in a hairline receding finish, 30-29, to preserve a home court win string stretching back more than three years.

The Tifton Gazette, page 3, January 10, 1970

Berrien Warms Up for Tift Tilts by Sweeping Homestanding Crisp

Special to Gazette

CORDELE – Berrien County's basketball teams, which host Tift County tonight at Nashville, used balanced scoring attacks and sound defenses to turn back homestanding Crisp County High here Friday night.

The Berrien girls, in running their record to 12-0 for the season, turned back Crisp, 42-26. Donna Jernigan with 17 points and Marla Brown with 14 provided the scoring punch. Cason had 17 for Crisp.

The balanced Berrien attack was even more evident in the boys' game as the Rebels ran their season chart to 12-1 by downing Crisp, 55-43.

Four Rebels hit in double figures – Roger Guess with 14, Bobby Taylor with 13, Richard Tucker with 11, and George Sorrell with 10. Jerry David had 18 points and Mike Phillips 16 for Crisp.

The Cordele girls are now 5-5 on the season, while the boys are 5-4.

Berrien meets Tift County at home tonight. The girls have beaten the Angels twice already this season, while the Rebel boys' lone loss has come at the hand of the Tift boys.

GIRLS'				BOYS'			
Berrien (42)	**Crisp (26)**			**Berrien (55)**	**Crisp (43)**		
Jernigan 17	Cason 17			Guess 14	David 18		
Brown 14	Griffin 9			Sorrell 10	Phillips 16		
Bailey 2	Whitaken			Taylor 13	Ray 3		
Carey	Lochett			Tucker 11	Standard 4		
Barber	Bramlett			Wright 4	Childrees 2		
Rudeseal	David						

GIRLS': Berrien subs – McMillan (9), Williams, Bennett, Swain and Harrell. Crisp subs: Dean and Bullington.

Berrien	7	24	35	42
Crisp	8	16	21	26

BOYS': Berrien subs – Taylor, W. Harnage 3. Crisp subs – Rogers.

Berrien	12	22	36	55
Crisp	5	16	25	43

The Valdosta Daily Times, page 8, January 10, 1970

Berrien Is Victor Over Crisp

Special to the Times

CORDELE – Crisp County's Rebelettes made the fatal mistake of leading Berrien's Rebelettes by one point in the first quarter and were buried in a sea of field goals and free throws as Berrien took both ends of a Region 1-AA high school basketball doubleheader here Friday.

Coach Stanley Simpson's Berrien girls handed Crisp's Rebelettes a 42-26 loss after trailing 8-7 in the first stanza while Berrien's quintet took up where the girls left off and trounced Crisp, 55-43.

The victories left Simpson's Rebels at 12-1 overall with a 12-game winning streak, while his girls are still undefeated at 12-0. With the losses, Crisp's girls are 5-5 and the quintet is 5-4.

Donna Jernigan and Marla Brown scored 17 and 14 points respectively to lead Berrien while Janie Eson hit for 17 to pace the Crisp girls.

In the boys game, Roger Guess scored 14 points to lead Berrien, followed by Bobby Taylor 13, Richard Tucker 11 and George Sorrell, 10. Gary David and Mike Phillips scored 18 and 16 points respectively for Crisp.

Berrien is scheduled to see action again tonight when it plays host to Tift County's Blue Devils and Angels.

(Box Scores Omitted)

The Tifton Gazette, page 3, January 12, 1970

Angels Give Scare to Unbeaten Berrien in 32-27 Defeat; Blue Devils Shellacked by Revenge-Minded Rebels, 50-31

By Staff Writer

NASHVILLE – Tift County High's girls provided unbeaten Berrien County a scare here Saturday night before losing, 32-27. In the nightcap, the homestanding Rebels – who obviously had revenge on their minds – dumped the Blue Devils, 50-31.

A four-game preliminary marathon card found Tift winning only one contest. The boys' B-team decisioned Berrien, 45-35. In other preliminary play, the Berrien boys' Freshman team eked out a 54-53 win. The Nashville Freshman and B-team girls gained 29-26 and 47-26 victories, respectively.

"I think it was the best team effort so far," Angels' coach Mrs. Sandra Withrow said of her team's performance. She was particularly happy with the guards' play, citing as their "best game by far."

Coach Stanley Simpson's Berrien girls, who chalked up their 13th triumph, trailed the Angels into the fourth quarter, 18-17. The lead changed hands several times in the fourth stanza before the Rebelettes stashed away for good.

Donna Jernigan sparked the winning girls with 14 points. Marla Brown pitched in 12.

The Angels' guard corps of Sherri Whittington, Gerry Crowley, Kathy Evans and Glenna Taylor provided the defensive spark. Juanita Dickens led the attack with 15 for the Angels who now stand 3-7.

In the varsity boys' game, Berrien took its 13th consecutive victory, running the season mark to 13-1. The lone loss came in the season opener to Tift, 46-45.

Simpson's Rebels charged to a 13-8 first quarter lead and held a 25-14 halftime advantage. Berrien increased the margin to 34-19 down the stretch.

George Sorrell was the chief point-maker for the Rebels with 19 points. Bobby Taylor pumped in 14.

Edd Dorminey emerged the only Blue Devil in double figures, by virtue of a 13-point effort. Coach Arthur Otwell's quintet is now 2-7 for the campaign.

In the Tift boys' B-team victory, Brad R__den registered 12 points. Robert Hodge sacked 18 points and snagged 20 rebounds for the Baby Blue Devils' Freshman squad.

Debbie Bruce tallied 10 points for the Tift girls' Freshman squad, and Karen Jones bucketed 16 in the B-team contest. Donna Bennett and Cathy Watson tallied 16 and 19, respectively, for Berrien.

Tift's squads host Valdosta in Tuesday night play at the local gym. The varsity girls go at 7 o'clock, with the boy's varsities slated for 8:30 o'clock.

A pair of Freshman contests are scheduled today at the local gym against Valdosta. The girls are slated for 4:30 p.m. and the boys 5:30 p.m.

Girls' Game

Tift	Fg	Ft	Pf	Pts	Berrien	Fg	Ft	Pf	Pts
* Dickens	7	1-1	0	15	* Brown	5	2-4	0	12
* B. Evans	3	0-1	0	6	* Jernigan	5	4-5	2	14
* Cole	3	0-0	1	6	* McMillan	0	2-4	0	2
* Whittington	0	0-0	2	0	* Carey	0	0-0	0	0
* Crowley	0	0-0	4	0	* Barber	0	0-0	1	0
* K. Evans	0	0-0	3	0	* Swain	0	0-0	0	0
Connor	0	0-0	0	0	Bailey	2	0-2	0	4
Taylor	0	0-0	2	0	Rudeseal	0	0-0	1	0
Totals	13	1-2	12	27	Totals	12	8-15	4	32

Score by quarters:

Tift	4	12	2	9 – 27
Berrien	7	3	7	15 – 32

Boys' Game

Tift	Fg	Ft	Pf	Pts	Berrien	Fg	Ft	Pf	Pts
* Dorminey	3	7-12	02	13	* Guess	3	1-2	3	7
* Winkler	1	0-0	4	2	* B. Taylor	5	4-6	2	14
* Parkman	1	0-0	1	2	* Sorrell	9	1-2	4	19
* Henderson	3	0-1	2	6	* Wright	2	0-0	1	4
* Mims	1	2-3	2	4	* Tucker	1	2-3	1	4
Thompson	0	0-0	1	0	W. Taylor	1	0-0	0	2
Luke	0	0-0	0	0	Conway	0	0-0	0	0
Chestnutt	0	0-0	0	0	Harnage	0	0-0	2	0
Reinhardt	0	0-0	0	0	Carey	0	0-1	1	0
King	1	2-2	1	4	Harrell	0	0-1	1	0
Totals	10	11-18	13	31	Bobo	0	0-0	0	0
					Slaughter	0	0-1	1	0
					Totals	21	8-16	16	50

Score by quarters:

Tift	8	6	5	12 – 31
Berrien	13	12	9	16 – 50

* - Denotes starters.

The Valdosta Daily Times, page 13, January 12, 1970
Tift Co. Is Beaten By Berrien
Special to the Times

NASHVILLE, Ga. – Berrien High's Rebels avenged their only loss of the season by thumping Tift County's Blue Devils, 50-31, as the Nashville, Ga., teams took both ends of a high school basketball doubleheader here Saturday night.

In the girls game, coach Stanley Simpson's Rebelettes outscored the Blue Angels, 32-27, for their third win over the Tifton girls. The Rebels avenged a 46-45 loss handed them by the Devils in the season opener.

The victory left the Rebels with a 13-1 record and a 13-game win streak. The Rebelettes are still undefeated after 13 starts.

For Tift County the losses left the boys with a 2-7 record while the girls are 7-3.

Donna Jernigan and Marla Brown led the scoring for the Rebelettes with 14 and 12 points respectively.

In the boys game George Sorrell hit for 19 points for Berrien.

(Box Scores Omitted)

The Berrien Press, front page, January 15, 1970
BHS Basketball Teams Continue Victory Streaks
BERRIEN vs. VALDOSTA
The Berrien County Rebels and Rebelettes continued their winning streak Tuesday night, Jan. 6, as they defeated the Valdosta Wildcats and Kittens.

In the girls' game the Rebelettes took the lead from the start, and were leading the Kittens 8-3 at the end of the first quarter. They kept the Kittens trailing 18-11 and 25-15 at the ends of the next two junctures. Berrien held their lead when the buzzer sounded the decision was in Berrien's favor, 42-20.

The Rebelettes scoring was led by Marla Brown with 21 points. Donna Jernigan tallied 9, Grace Bailey 4, Jo Ann Langford 2, and Pat Williams 6. The Rebelettes' defense was led by Lenna Carey, Peggy Barber, and Brenda Rudeseal. Debra Swain was defensive sub.

Joy Johnson led Valdosta's offensive play with 13 points. Serving as guards for the Kittens were Stephenson, Brantley, and Graham.

The boys' game was really a nerve-wracking one for the Rebel fans as the Rebels had to come from behind again to take their game.

The Wildcats had the Rebels down 12-10 at the end of the first period of play, and at halftime they were tied up 22-22. At the end of the third quarter the Rebels were trailing again, 42-34. Although it seemed almost impossible, they finally took the lead with 3 minutes left in the game and held it for a 56-52 victory. Free-throws was one of the main things that saved the Rebels as they were hitting 75% on them – 24 out of 32 attempted.

Scoring for the Rebels were Bobby Taylor with 16 points, Roger Guess 15, George Sorrell 11, Richard Tucker 9, Charles Wright 4, and Wayne Taylor 1.

High scorer for the Wildcats was Don Golden with 20 points.
BERRIEN vs. CRISP
The Berrien County Rebels and Rebelettes picked up a couple of wins from their tough Region 1-AA foe Crisp Co. Friday night, Jan. 9, in Cordele.

The Rebelettes got off to sort of a slow start in their game, and the end of the first quarter found them lagging behind, 8-7. They began to warm up in the second quarter though, and when the buzzer sounded for the halftime, they had pulled ahead 24-16. They had widened the margin in their favor, 35-21, by the end of the third quarter and held this lead throughout the rest of the game for a final decision of 42-26.

Berrien's scorers were Donna Jernigan 17, Marla Brown 14, Sandy McMillan 9, Grace Bailey 2. The defensive side of Berrien's teams was played by Lenna Carey, Peggy Barber, Brenda Rudeseal, Debra Swain, and Debbie Harrell.

High scorer for Crisp was Eason with 17 points.

Berrien's boys had their game in the bag the whole game as they were leading the Crisp Co. Rebels 12-5, 22-16, 36-25, and 55-43 at the ends of the four quarters.

High scorers for Berrien were Roger Guess 14, Bobby Taylor 13, Richard Tucker 11, and George Sorrell 10. Sorrell also jerked 21 rebounds off the boards. Charles Wright and David Harnage also scored for Berrien with 4 and 3 points respectively.

High scorers for Crisp were Jerry David 18 and Mike Phillips 16.

BERRIEN vs. TIFT

The Berrien County Rebels and Rebelettes chalked up 2 more wins to their records Saturday night, Jan. 10, in Nashville.

The Rebelettes had a tough time taking the Tift Co. Angels. Although the Rebelettes grabbed an early lead which had the Angels trailing 7-4 at the end of the first quarter, the Angels stepped up their pace and was leading 16-10 by the end of the second. By the end of the third quarter the Rebelettes had come back to within one point of the Angels, 18-17; and in the final round came on strong to defeat the Angels 32-27.

Donna Jernigan boosted the Rebelettes scoring with 14 points. Marla Brown followed with 12 points, Grace Bailey with 4, and Sandy McMillan with 2. Berrien defense was played by Lenna Carey, Peggy Barber, Brenda Rudeseal, and Debra Swain.

Tift's high scorer was Juanita Dickens with 15 points.

This win brought the Rebelettes' record to 13-0.

The Rebels had their game a little easier. They took a quick lead and kept the Devils the underdogs for the rest of the game. At the ends of the 4 quarters the Devils were behind 13-8, 25-14, 34-19, and 50-31.

The Rebels scoring was led by George Sorrell and Bobby Taylor, both registering in the double figures with 19 and 13 points respectively. Sorrell also pulled 19 rebounds off the boards. Following in the scoring for the Rebels were Roger Guess with 7, Charles Wright and Richard Tucker with 4 each, Wayne Taylor 2, and Karl Harrell 1. Slaughter, Carey, Harnage, and Bobo also substituted during the last few minutes of play.

Tift's high point man was Ed Dorminey with 11 points.

This win brought the Rebels' record to 13-1. This one defeat for the Rebels came earlier in the season when the Tift Co. Blue Devils beat them in their opener 46-45.

Photo caption:
REBELS – The 1970 edition of Berrien High School Rebel basketball team, left to right, include: Front, Jerry Slaughter, Roger Guess, Kim Carey, Bobby Conway; second row, Wayne Taylor, David Harnage, Karl Harrell, David Bobo, Bobby Taylor; back row, coach Stanley Simpson, assistant coach Wayne Harris; managers Tim Moore, Lamar Jones and Tim Tygart; co-captains Richard Tucker and George Sorrell; Charles Wright.

The Berrien Press, page 6, January 15, 1970

Photo caption:
CRITICAL – The climax of the Berrien-Cairo defensive game was the final two minutes with Cairo putting on the freeze, missing a field goal with only three seconds to go. The scoreboard showed two seconds to go with Berrien still leading 30-29, as the ball was tossed up for a jump.

The Tifton Gazette, page 2, January 15, 1970

Berrien Now 3rd in State

ATLANTA – Berrien County is rated No. 3 for Class AA boys basketball in Georgia.

In the latest Atlanta Journal weekly ratings, Berrien trails only Carver of Atlanta and Newton County. Beach of Savannah, Bacon County, Harris County and Springfield Central are leaders of AAA, AA, B, and C, respectively.

The rankings include:

AAA – 1. Beach, 2. Ballard Hudson, 3. Savannah, 4. Douglass, 5. Carver (Columbus), 6. Mark Smith, 7. Forest Park, 8. Dalton, 9. Decatur, 10. Druid Hills.

AA – 1. Carver (Atlanta), 2. Newton Co., 3. Berrien Co., 4. Waycross, 5. Lakeshore, 6. Pepperell, 7. East Atlanta, 8. Central (Newnan), 9. North Springs, 10. Sandy Springs.

A – 1. Bacon Co., 2. Early Co., 3. Stone Mountain, 4. Central (Carrollton), 5. Cairo, 6. Americus, 7. Monroe Area, 8. Murray Co., 9. South Gwinnett, 10. Effingham Co.

B – 1. Harris Co., 2. East Laurens, 3. Vienna, 4. Roswell, 5. Stockbridge, 6. Johnson Co., 7. Hogansville, 8. Charlton Co., 9. Clinch Co., 10. Claxton.

C – 1. Springfield Central, 2. Arlington, 3. Savannah Country Day, 4. Crawford Co., 5. Taylor Co., 6. Dawson Co., 7. Pike Co., 8. St. Pius X, 9. Georgia Christian, 10. Adairsville.

The Thomasville Times-Enterprise, page 6, January 16, 1970
Central Hosts Pelham Teams; 'Dogs Travel
[Excerpts:]

Central High's Yellow Jackets and Jackettes host the Pelham High Hornets and Hornettes tonight in the Central gym while Thomasville High's Bulldogettes and Bulldogs travel to Nashville to play the Berrien County Rebels and Rebelettes.

…

Thomasville's Bulldogs must face the sixth-ranked Rebels of Berrien. Berrien has a 12-0 record.

The Thomasville Times-Enterprise, page 6, January 17, 1970
Bulldogettes Beat, 49-47 By Berrien

NASHVILLE – Thomasville High's Bulldogettes could not overcome a strong first half effort by the Berrien County Rebelettes and dropped their third game of the season, 49-47, here last night.

The Rebels rolled to a 55-28 victory over the Bulldogs in other action.

Berrien's girls trailed 16-14 at the end of the first quarter but outscored the Bulldogettes, 16-5, in the second quarter to take a 30-21 halftime lead.

In the first half the Berrien girls hit 13 of 18 shots from the field for a torrid 72 per cent. The Rebelettes finished the game with a 58 per cent average after connecting on 18 of 31 shots.

In the third quarter both teams score 11 points, but Thomasville began a comeback effort in the final period.

The Bulldogettes outscored the Rebelettes, 15-8, but the rally fell short as the game ended.

The Bulldogettes were 16 for 44 from the field for 36.5 per cent.

Anne Rumble dropped in 24 points to pace the Bulldogs while Joy Alligood added 13 and Susan Wine nine.

Marla Brown and Donna Jernigan each hit 21 points for the winners.

The Bulldogettes are now 9-3 and the Rebelettes 14-0.

The Bulldogs trailed 32-18 at halftime and Berrien added to the margin in the second half by outscoring Thomasville 22-10.

George Sorrell and Roger Guess paced Rebels with 24 and 15 points, respectively. The Rebels are now 13-1.

Lloyd Austin led the Bulldogs with 12 points and pulled down 20 rebounds. "Austin played his best game of the season," said coach Jerry Studdard. "He did a real fine job."

It's the first time this season Austin has scored in double figures.

Kenneth Gatlin added 10 points to the attack. Gatlin, a sophomore, has started only the last two games and has scored in double digits in both games.

The Bulldogs are now 5-7. The Bulldogettes and Bulldogs take a break for semester tests before playing Cairo at home on Thursday, Crisp County in Cordele on Friday and Early County at home on Saturday.

THOMASVILLE BOYS (11-16-28) – Thornton 1-1-3; Mathes 1-0-2; Austin 4-4-12; Keadle 0-0-0; Gatlin 5-0-10; Brinson 0-1-1.

BERRIEN COUNTY (24-7-55) – Guess 7-1-15; L. Taylor 1-1-3; Tucker 2-0-4; Wright 2-0-4; Sorrell 10-4-24; Harnage 1-0-2; W. Taylor 0-1-1; Bobo 1-0-2.

THOMASVILLE	10	8	7	3 – 28
BERRIEN	14	19	11	11 – 55

*****

THOMASVILLE GIRLS (16-15-47) – Rumble 8-8-24; Wine 4-1-9; Alligood 4-5-13; Laing 0-1-1; Dekle 0-0-0; Guards: Davis, Jones, Fletcher, Hall, Sollami.

BERRIEN COUNTY (18-13-49) – Brown 7-7-21; Jernigan 9-3-21; Bailey 2-3-7; Guards: Carey, Barber, Rudeseal, Carter.

THOMASVILLE	16	5	11	15 – 47
BERRIEN	14	16	11	8 – 49

The Tifton Gazette, page 5, January 17, 1970

Berrien Defeats T'ville

Special to Gazette

NASHVILLE – Berrien County's unbeaten girls had their closest call of the season in a 49-47 victory here Friday night over Region 1-AA foe Thomasville.

The Berrien boys gained a varsity sweep for the night with a convincing 55-28 victory at the expense of Thomasville.

In the girls' contest, Berrien chalked up its 14th victory behind the 21 point firings of Marla Brown and Donna Jernigan. Thomasville's Ann Rumble scored 24.

George Sorrell tallied 24 points and Roger Guess 15 for the winning boys who captured their 14th straight contest and extended the season mark to 14-1. Bill Austin had 12 for the losers.

(Box Scores Omitted)
Girls' Game

The Valdosta Daily Times, page 8, January 17, 1970

Berrien Trips Up Loop Foe

Special to the Times

NASHVILLE, Ga. – Berrien's Rebels and Rebelettes increased their winning streaks to 14 as they took both ends of a Region 1-AA high school basketball twin-bill from Thomasville here Friday night.

Coach Stanley Simpson's Rebels mowed down the Thomasville Bulldogs, 55-28 while Simpson's Rebelettes hit the Bulldogettes for a 49-47 victory.

The wins give the Rebs a 14-1 overall record and a 14-game win streak while the Rebelettes are still undefeated at 14-0. Both teams carry 3-0 records in region affairs.

Marla Brown and Donna Jernigan teamed up to tally 21 points each for the Rebelettes while Grace Bailey added the other seven points. Ann Rumble lead the Bulldogettes with 24 with Joyce Allegood adding 13 more.

George Sorrell was high point-maker for the Rebels with 24 followed by Roger Guess with 15. James Austin led the Bulldogs with 12 points.

Berrien is scheduled to see action again tonight when it travels to Cairo for another double-header.

(Box Scores Omitted)

The Thomasville Times-Enterprise, page 8, January 19, 1970
Syrupmakers, 'Maids Defeated by Berrien

CAIRO – Cairo's Syrupmaids failed to end Berrien County Rebelettes' winning streak but they did make the visitors earn their 14th victory.

The Syrupmaids led 41-36 going into the final quarter and failed to score in the final minutes as the Rebelettes rolled to a narrow 48-47 margin.

Berrien's Rebels used a strong third quarter to defeat the Syrupmakers, 40-25.

The Rebelettes, now 14-0, outscored the Syrupmaids 12-6 in the final quarter. The Berrien girls held a 15-11 first period margin before the Syrupmaids outscored the Rebelettes 18-9 in the second quarter.

"The girls are really improving," said Syrupmaid coach Billy Daniels. "They are playing the type ball we're capable of playing."

Berrien had defeated the Cairo girls by 27 points in an earlier meeting of the two teams this season. The Syrupmaids are now 8-7.

Rita Ponder scored 31 points to lead the Syrupmaids' losing effort while Sally Wight added 11.

Marla Brown hit 26 points to pace the winners while Donna Jernigan chipped in 15.

The Rebels, sixth-ranked in Class AA, rolled to a 19-14 halftime lead. Berrien outscored the Syrupmakers by 10 in the third quarter, 15-5, to put the game out of reach.

Cairo, now 12-3, was sixth-ranked in Class A. The Rebels are now 13-1.

Steve Montgomery was the top scorer for Cairo with nine. Joe Rackey and Tom Taylor each added six.

The Cairo B team registered its ninth win against no losses with a 54-22 win over Berrien. Terry Prince and Craig Taylor paced the way with 16 points each.

Melvin Ray, Mitchell Glenn and Paul Alred all scored eight points in the Cairo ninth grade team's 42-28 loss to Berrien. Mike Jones led Berrien with 21.

(Box Scores Omitted)

The Tifton Gazette, page 3, January 19, 1970
Berrien, Cook Gain Cage Sweeps
By Staff Writer

Berrien County and Cook County gained basketball sweeps Saturday night on enemy courts to head the Tiftarea scene.

Coach Stanley Simpson's Berrien boys shocked homestanding Cairo by 15 points, 40-25. His girls remained unbeaten, but the margin was only one point, 48-47.

Cook's boys edged Echols County, 60-58. The girls triumphed 53-42.

In other Tiftarea play, homestanding Atkinson County dropped a pair to Bacon County. The girls lost 52-45, and the boys fell, 72-58.

Meanwhile, Fitzgerald lost a boys' varsity struggle to Wilcox by a scant one point, 51-50.

The Berrien boys, who rolled to their 15th consecutive victory (15-1), got tremendous defensive play as evidenced by no Cairo player in the double figure scoring column. Bobby Taylor and George Sorrell shared honors for the winners with 11 points apiece.

(Box Scores Omitted)

The Valdosta Daily Times, page 14, January 19, 1970

Berrien Extends Victory Streak

Special to the Times

CAIRO – Berrien's Rebels and Rebelettes pushed their winning streaks to 15 by defeating Cairo in a high school basketball doubleheader here Saturday night.

Coach Stanley Simpson's Rebels, dropped Cairo's Syrupmakers, 40-25, while Simpson's Rebelettes had to come from behind to beat the Syrupmaids, 48-47.

The victories give the Rebs a 15-1 record with a 15-game win streak, while the Nashville, Ga., girls are still undefeated at 15-0. The Syrupmakers are now 13-3 while the Cairo sextet is 12-4.

The Rebelettes, who trailed by five at the half, hit a streak in the third and fourth quarters when they outscored their opponents 16-1 to take the lead.

Marla Brown was the top scorer for Berrien, with 26 points, followed by Donna Jernigan, with 15. Rita Ponder led the way for the Syrupmaids with 31 points, while Sally Wight added 11.

In the boys duel, Bobby Taylor and George Sorrell scored 11 points each to pace the Rebels while Steve Montgomery's nine points were the highest for any Syrupmaker.

GIRLS				
Berrien	15	24	36	48
Cairo	11	29	41	47

BERRIEN (48) – Brown 26, Jernigan 15, Bailey 5, Langford 2, Carey, Barber, Rudeseal, Carter. Team totals: field goals 21, free throws 6 of 11, fouls 6.

CAIRO (47) – Ponder 31, Rineer 5, Wight 11, Dukes, DeMorris, Clark. Team totals: field goals 21, free throws 5 of 7, fouls 11.

BOYS				
Berrien	10	19	34	40
Cairo	9	14	19	25

BERRIEN (40) – Guess 6, B. Taylor 11, Tucker 3, Wright 9, Sorrell 11. Team totals: field goals 15, free throws 10 of 14, fouls 10.

CAIRO (25) – Burt 2, Rackley 6, Montgomery 9, Reynolds 2, Taylor 6. Team totals: field goals 10, free throws 5 of 9, fouls 10.

The Tifton Gazette, page 5, January 21, 1970

Berrien Rips Cook Twice

Special to Gazette

NASHVILLE – Berrien County's powerful basketball teams swept a doubleheader from Tiftarea foe Cook County here Tuesday night.

Coach Stanley Simpson's unbeaten girls captured their 16th game to the tune of 56-21. His boys took their 16th consecutive victory, 68-36, running the season mark to 16-1.

Donna Jernigan, Joann Langford, and Marla Brown spearheaded the well-balanced Berrien girls' attack with 20, 18 and 17 points, respectively. Lyn Futch bagged 16 for the loser.

In the boys' skirmish, George Sorrell sparked the winners with 22 points, while Charles Wright and Roger Guess bagged 12 each. Robert Ray tallied 13 for Cook.

Both Cook teams have identical 3-12 season records.

Berrien's next action comes Saturday on the road at Central of Thomasville. Cook entertains Norman Park in Friday night play at Adel.

Girls' Game

Cook (21)	Berrien (56)
Futch 16	Jernigan 20
Griffin 2	Langford 18
Nipper 3	Brown 17
Chapman	Carey
Ward	Barber
B. Shiflit	Carter

Cook subs– S. Shiflit. Berrien subs – McMillan (1).

Score by Quarters:

Cook	13	1	7	0 – 21
Berrien	19	15	13	7 – 56

Field goals: Cook, 9; Berrien, 26. Free throws: Cook, 3-7; Berrien, 4-5. Personal fouls: Cook, 6; Berrien, 8.

Boys' Game

Cook (36)	Berrien (68)
Ray 13	Sorrell 22
Tucker 3	Wright 12
Jenerette 1	Guess 12
Purvis 3	B. Taylor 6
Shackleford 5	Tucker 2

Cook subs – Moore (11). Berrien subs – Harnage (8), W. Taylor (2), Harrell (2), Conway (2).

Score by Quarters:

Cook	3	4	9	20	– 36
Berrien	20	12	16	20	– 68

Field goals: Cook, 12; Berrien, 33. Free throws: Cook, 12-18; Berrien, 2-3. Personal fouls: Cook, 4; Berrien, 12.

The Valdosta Daily Times, page 13, January 21, 1970

Berrien Cagers Sweep Twin-Bill
Special to the Times

NASHVILLE, Ga. – Berrien's Rebels and Rebelettes, still even in their winning streaks, added another victory to the list by taking both ends of a high school basketball doubleheader from Cook's Hornets and Wasps here Tuesday.

The Rebels bounced their way to a 68-36 victory over coach Hansel Faulkner's Hornets, while the Rebelettes threw the Wasps for a 56-21 loss.

Coach Stanley Simpson's Berrien squads pushed their winning streaks to 16 with the victories. The Rebs are 16-1 overall, while the girls are still undefeated at 16-0.

Coach Lamar Chapman's Wasps were within six points of the Rebelettes at the end of the first quarter, but that was as close as they got. By the half the Rebelettes were 30 points ahead and sailed on in for the win.

Simpson's Rebels took a 20-3 lead at the first quarter and kept the pace going almost that way for the rest of the game.

Donna Jernigan, Jo Ann Langford and Marla Brown led the Rebelettes with 20, 18 and 17 points respectively. Lyn Futch was the Wasp leader with 16.

In the boys game George Sorrell took the lead for Berrien with 22 points, with Roger Guess and Charles Wright notching 12 each. Robert Ray led the Hornet attack with 13.

(Box Scores Omitted)

The Berrien Press, front page, January 22, 1970

BHS Basketball Teams Continue Victory Streaks
By Tim Moore

BERRIEN vs. THOMASVILLE

Friday night, Jan. 16, brought the Berrien teams 2 more wins as they overthrew their 1-AA rivals, the Thomasville Bulldogs and Bulldogettes.

The Rebelettes didn't seem to be able to "get with it" in the beginning of their game, so Thomasville grabbed a quick lead which had Berrien lagging, 16-14, after the first quarter of play. The Rebelettes stepped up their pace in the next 2 periods though, and gained the lead over Thomasville 30-21 and 41-32 at the ends of these periods. During the final turn the Bulldogettes came back up to challenge the Rebelettes, but they held their ground for a 49-47 victory.

Marla Brown and Donna Jernigan paced the Rebelettes scoring with 21 points each. Grace Bailey scored 7. The team's defensive positions were filled by Lenna Carey, Peggy Barber, Brenda Rudeseal, and Andrea Carter.

Thomasville's high scorer was Ann Rumble with 24 points.

The Rebels took their game with a convincing final decision of 55-28. The Rebels charged the Bulldogs from the start and lead them 14-10, 33-18, 44-25, and 55-28 at the ends of the four stanzas of the game.

George Sorrell sparked the Rebels on with 24 points, followed by Roger Guess with 15, Richard Tucker and Charles Wright with 4 each, and Bobby Taylor with 3. David Bobo and David Harnage also had 2 each, and Wayne Taylor had 1. Also playing for the Rebels were Harrell, Slaughter and Conway.

High point man for Thomasville was Bill Austin with 12 points.

BERRIEN vs. CAIRO

The Berrien Co. Rebels and Rebelettes traveled to Cairo Sat. night, Jan. 17, and came back with 2 more wins to add to their records. This brought the girls record to 15-0 and the boys to 15-1.

The Rebelettes barely escaped defeat as they gave the Syrupmaids a heart-breaking 48-47 loss. Although the Rebelettes took the early lead of 15-11 at the end of the first quarter, Cairo girls took over the lead 29-24 and 41-36 at the ends of the next 2 quarters.

At one point in the fourth quarter the Rebelettes had fallen behind 11 points. They finally got down to business though, and pulled back up front to lead the Syrupmaids through the remaining part of the game.

Marla Brown sparked the Rebelettes on with 26 points. Donna Jernigan pumped in 15, Grace Bailey 5, and Jo Ann Langford 2. Playing Berrien's defense was Lenna Carey, Peggy Barber, Brenda Rudeseal, and Andrea Carter.

Ponder lead the Syrupmaids scoring with 31 points.

The Rebels came on strong in their game to give the Syrupmakers one of the worst defeats they have ever received on their home court. The Rebels led Cairo all the way through with the scores 10-9, 19-14, 34-19, and a final decision of 40-25.

George Sorrell and Bobby Taylor paced the Rebels scoring with 11 points each. Sorrell also cleaned 14 rebounds off the boards. Other scorers for Berrien were Charles Wright 9, Roger Guess 6, and Richard Tucker 3.

Cairo's high scorer was Montgomery with 9 points.

Photo Caption:

HIGH POINT – George Sorrell (20) goes up for another toss into the Berrien basket to lead the scoring against the Thomasville Bulldogs with 24 points.

The Tifton Gazette, page 3, January 24, 1970
Berrien Cited Again
ATLANTA – A powerful Berrien County boys' basketball team, which boasts a 16-1 record – the only defeat coming in the opening game to Tift County – has gained another No. 2 state ranking for Class AA.

Coach Stanley Simpson's Berrien squad has gained the rating in this week's Atlanta Constitution poll. Earlier, the Rebels were named to the same position for the Atlanta Journal's list.

Carver of Atlanta boasts the No. 1 spot for Class AA. Other leaders include Carver of Columbus, AAA; Early County, A; East Laurens, B; Stratford Academy, C.

The Constitution's rankings include:

AAA – 1. Carver (Columbus), 2. Ballard Hudson, 3. Douglass, 4. Beach, 5. Forest Park, 6. Savannah, 7. Decatur, 8. Albany, 9. Druid Hills, 10. Valdosta.

AA – Carver (Atlanta), 2. Berrien Co., 3. Newton Co., 4. Pepperell, 5. East Atlanta, 6. Lakeshore, 7. Central (Newnan), 8. Wills, 9. Baldwin, 10. Waycross.

A – 1. Early Co., 2. Central (Carrollton), 3. East Hall, 4. Stone Mountain, 5. Vienna, 6. Bacon Co., 7. Cairo, 8. Murray Co., 9. Americus, 10. Monroe Area.

B – 1. East Laurens, 2. Roswell, 3. Harris Co., 4. Springfield Central, 5. Hogansville, 6. Johnson Co., 7. Blackshear, 8. Waynesboro, 9. Jackson, 10. Stockbridge.

C – 1. Stratford Academy, 2. Arlington, 3. Crawford Co., 4. Georgia Industrial, 5. Dawson Co.

The Thomasville Times-Enterprise, page 8, January 26, 1970
Berrien Teams Cop Victories Over Central
Berrien County's Rebels and Rebelettes rolled to a pair of victories over the Central High Jackets and Jackettes in the Central gym Saturday night.

The Rebels were 48-19 victors over the Jackets and the Rebelettes defeated the Jackettes, 55-23.

"The boys played a good defensive game," said Central coach Wesley Blair. "We stopped their two big boys. Most of their points were scored under the basket after pulling down rebounds."

The Rebels took a 15-4 first quarter lead and held a 25-11 command at halftime.

The Jackets scored three points in the opening minutes of the third quarter to pull within 12 points but Berrien held the Jackets scoreless the remainder of the period and added two points to their lead.

The Rebels rolled up a 17-5 third quarter margin.

"We just couldn't score," added Blair.

Johnson Thompson led the Jackets with six points, Martin Milton added five and Vann Murphy four.

The Rebelettes jumped off to a 28-10 halftime lead and outscored the Jackettes 17-6 in the third quarter and 10-7 in the fourth period to cap the win.

Nancy Speaker paced the losers with 18 points.

Central teams host Cairo teams Tuesday night in the Central gym.

(Box Scores Omitted)

The Tifton Gazette, page 3, January 26, 1970
Berrien Sweeps Central
Special to Gazette

THOMASVILLE – Those awesome Berrien County basketball teams continue to roll like "Ole Man River," their latest victories coming here Saturday night at the expense of Thomasville's Central High.

Coach Stanley Simpson's unbeaten girls charged to their 17th victory in a 55-23 waltz. Not to be outdone, his boys, now 17-1 for the season, gained an easy 48-19 conquest.

During the girls' skirmish, Marla Brown, Grace Bailey and Donna Jernigan scored 16, 15 and 12 points, respectively, in balance at its best. Central's Nancy Speaker captured game honors with 18 points, but she received minimum defensive support.

George Sorrell was the big gun for the Berrien boys with 26 points to outscore the Central team himself by seven points. The 6-5 jumping jack also snared 15 rebounds.

The Central girls and boys have 8-8 and 4-12 campaign marks, respectively.

Girls' Game

Berrien (55)	Central (23)
Brown 16	Speaker 18
Jernigan 12	Hallman 4
Langford 3	Baker 1
Carey	Dollar
Barber	Palmer
Carter	Beckham

Berrien subs – Bailey (15), McMillan (8), Bennett (1), Rudeseal, Swain, Harrell. Central subs – Fletcher, Spence, Cone, Reeves.

Berrien	10	18	17	10 – 55
Central	5	5	6	7 – 23

Field goals: Berrien, 21; Central, 8. Free throws: Berrien, 13-25; Central, 7-11. Personal fouls: Berrien, 10; Central, 18.

Boys' Game

Berrien (48)	Central (19)
Guess 4	Thompson 6
B. Taylor 6	Martin 5
Tucker	Murphy 4
Wright 5	Davis 2
Sorrell 26	Highsmith 2

Berrien subs – Conway (2), Slaughter (2), W. Taylor (2), Harnage (1). Central subs – None.

Score by quarters:

Berrien	15	11	5	17 – 48
Central	4	7	3	5 – 19

Field goals: Berrien, 19; Central, 6. Free throws: Berrien, 10-13; Central, 7-10. Personal fouls: Berrien, 9; Central, 9.

The Valdosta Daily Times, page 13, January 26, 1970

Berrien Cagers Extend Streaks

Special to the Times

THOMASVILLE – Berrien's Rebels and Rebelettes continued their streaks by licking Central's Yellow Jackets and sextet in a high school double-header here Saturday night.

The Rebels outdistanced the Yellow Jackets, 48-19, while the Rebelettes posted a 55-23 victory over the Central girls.

The victories pushed the win streaks of both Stanley Simpson's Berrien teams to 17 games. The Rebels are now 17-1 while the Berrien girls are still undefeated at 17-0.

George Sorrell was the leading scorer for the Rebels with 26 points and was the only boy in double figures. John Thompson led the Jackets with six points.

In the girls game, Marla Brown and Grace Bailey notched 15 points each to lead the Rebelettes, with Donna Jernigan and Sandy McMillan adding 12 and 8 points respectively. Nancy Speaker score 18 points for the Lady Jackets.

(Box Scores Omitted)

The Valdosta Daily Times, page 13, January 27, 1970

Berrien, Lanier In Feature Duel

By Times Staff Writer

Berrien is to host Lanier County in the feature attraction on tonight's schedule for area high school basketball teams.

In other area action tonight, Waycross is to be at Clinch County (Homerville), Cook (Adel) at Brooks County (Quitman) and Madison, Fla., at Hamilton County (Jasper, Fla.)

When Berrien's Rebels and Rebelettes host Lanier County's Bulldogs and Bulldogettes to night at Nashville, Ga., all four teams will put impressive records on the line.

Berrien's Rebels are 17-1 and the girls from Nashville have a 17-0 mark. The Bulldogs from Lakeland, Ga., are 13-1 and the Lanier sextet has an 8-5 mark.

When they met earlier in the season Berrien posted a pair of victories, winning in the boys game, 48-44, and triumphing in the girls contest, 59-27.

Both Berrien teams have 17-game victory streaks going. The Lanier boys have won eight straight since their four-point loss to the Rebels.

Hamilton County's Rebels from Jasper, who have a 9-2 overall record, will also put a seven-game winning streak on the line tonight when they host Madison.

The Tifton Gazette, page 5, January 28, 1970

Berrien Wins Pair

Special to Gazette

NASHVILLE – Berrien County's state-ranked basketball teams knocked off Class C foe Lanier here Tuesday night, the girls winning 54-46 and the boys capturing a 71-55 contest.

Marla Brown netted 28 big points for Stanley Simpson's Berrien girls, while Donna Jernigan added 12 and Grace Bailey chipped in 10 more tallies. Linda Moore and Chris Boyett each had 22 for Lanier.

In the nightcap, Berrien jumped out to a 38-27 halftime lead behind the balanced scoring punch of George Sorrell, Roger Guess, Bobby Taylor and Richard Tucker.

Sorrell finished the night with 24 points while Guess had 14, Taylor 12 and Tucker 10. Lanier's George Lee was the game's high scorer, however, with 33 points.

The Berrien boys stand 18-1 on the season, their only loss coming at the hands of Tift County. Lanier's boys are now 12-2, losing only to Berrien (twice). Lanier's girls are 8-5, while the Berrien girls are undefeated in 18 games.

*****

GIRLS				
Berrien	17	31	42	54
Lanier	8	20	30	46

BERRIEN (54) – Brown 28, Jernigan 12, Bailey 10, Langford 4, Carey, Barber, Carter. Team totals: field goals 17, free throws 20 of 25, fouls 19.

LANIER (46) – Moore 22, Boyette 22, Brogdon 2, Ivey, Sirmans, Calhoun, Keene. Team totals: field goals 13, free throws 20 of 27, fouls 19.

BOYS				
Berrien	19	38	49	71
Lanier	15	27	40	55

BERRIEN (71) – Guess 14, Taylor 12, Tucker 10, Wright 5, Sorrell 24, Conway 6, W. Taylor. Team totals: field goals 28, free throws 15 of 16, fouls 12.

LANIER (55) – Dickson 2, Lee 33, Patten 9, Felts 8, Robinson 3, Brockington. Team totals: field goals 19, free throws 17 of 19, fouls 13.

The Valdosta Daily Times, page 17, January 28, 1970

Berrien Trims Lanier County

Special to the Times

NASHVILLE – Berrien's Rebels, the only team to put a loss on Lanier County Bulldogs' otherwise perfect record, did it again Tuesday night to the tune of a 71-55 decision as Berrien took both ends of the high school basketball doubleheader here.

The Rebels of coach Stanley Simpson pushed their winning streak to 18 with the victory while Simpson's Rebelettes were busy defeating the Bulldogettes, 54-46.

The victories left the Rebels with an 18-1 overall record, while the Rebelettes are still undefeated with an 18-0 mark. The losses left coach Billy Pafford's Bulldogs with a 13-2 record, while coach Angie DeVivo's Bulldogettes are 8-7.

Marla Brown got in 28 points to lead the scoring for the Rebelettes with Donna Jernigan and Grace Bailey adding 12 and 10 points respectively. Linda Moore and Chris Boyette chalked up 22 points each to lead the Bulldogettes.

In the boys game, George Sorrell scored 24 points to lead the Rebels with Roger Guess, Bobby Taylor and Richard Tucker adding 14, 12 and 10 points respectively.

George Lee led the Bulldogs with 33 points.

(Box Scores Omitted)

The Berrien Press, front page, January 29, 1970

BHS Basketball Teams Continue Victory Streaks

By Tim Moore

The homestanding Rebels and Rebelettes swept two victories from the visiting Cook Co. Hornets and Wasps Tuesday night, Jan. 20.

The Rebelettes sewed up their game with a comfortable 56-21 victory over the Wasps. For the first time in three games, the Rebelettes held a good margin between them and their opponents throughout the game. They led the Wasps through the game with the scores 19-13, 34-14, 47-21, and 56-21.

Scoring for the Rebelettes were Donna Jernigan with 20, Jo Ann Langford with 18, Marla Brown with 17, and Sandy McMillan 1. Berrien's tough defense was played by Lenna Carey, Peggy Barber, Andrea Carter, Debra Swain, Brenda Rudeseal, and Debbie Harrell. Other subs for Berrien were Grace Bailey and Donna Bennett.

For Cook, Lynn Futch tallied 16 of their 21 points.

In the boys' game the Rebels came on strong to defeat the Hornets by a convincing 69-36 final decision. They had their game in the clear all the way through as they led the Hornets 20-3, 32-7, and 48-16 at the ends of the first three junctures.

George Sorrell paced the Rebels scoring with 22 points. Then came Roger Guess and Charles Wright who pumped in 12 apiece. David Harnage had 8, Bobby Taylor 6, and Richard Tucker, Wayne Taylor, Karl Harrell, and Bobby Conway all had 2 apiece.

Ray and Moore led Cook's scoring with 13 and 11 points respectively.

BERRIEN vs. THOMASVILLE CENTRAL

Saturday, Jan. 24, the Rebels traveled to Thomasville and took both rounds of a double-header from the Central Yellow Jackets.

In the girls' game the Jackettes gave the Rebelettes a little fight in the first quarter, but then fell behind and the Rebelettes took a 55-23 victory to bring their record to 17-0. Scores by quarters for Berrien were as follows: 20, 28, 45, 55. For Central: 5, 10, 16, 23.

Marla Brown sparked the Rebelettes' scoring with 16 points. Grace Bailey had 15, Donna

Jernigan 12, Sandy McMillan 8, Jo Ann Langford 3, and Donna Bennett 1. Berrien's guards were Lenna Carey, Peggy Barber, Andrea Carter, Brenda Rudeseal, Debra Swain and Debbie Harrell.

Nancy Speaker led Central's offense with 18 points.

The boys' game was about the same tune. The Rebels put a tough defense on the Jackets who could count only 19 points for the entire ball game. The Rebels got them down 15-4 at the end of the first quarter, and held them 26-11, 31-14, and 48-19 at the ends of the remaining quarters.

Scoring for the Rebels were George Sorrell 26, Bobby Taylor 6, Charles Wright 5, Roger Guess 4, Wayne Taylor, Jerry Slaughter, and Bobby Conway 2 apiece. Also playing for the Rebels were Richard Tucker, Karl Harrell, and David Bobo.

High scorer for Central was John Tompson with 6 points.

This win brought the Rebels' record to 17-1.

Photo caption (page 8):
SCORING – George Sorrell goes high for another shot for the Berrien Rebels in the 69-36 victory over Cook High School Hornets. Coming in on the left is Bobby Taylor while Charles Wright (42) comes in to back up the shot. The Rebels are ranked No. 2 in Class AA for the state. They play Crisp County here Friday night.

The Tifton Gazette, page 3, January 29, 1970

Berrien Holds Number 2 Spot In AA; Carver, Beach, Early, Lanier Leaders

ATLANTA – Tiftarea power Berrien County has kept its hold on the No. 2 spot in the State AA rankings for boys' basketball.

Carver of Atlanta remains the No. 1 Class AA team in the Atlanta Journal ratings. Beach of Savannah, Early County, East Laurens and Lanier County are the pace-setters for AAA, A, B and C, respectively.

The rankings include:

AA – 1. Carver (Atlanta), 2. Berrien Co., 3. Newton Co., 4. East Atlanta, 5. Hart Co., 6. Waycross, 7. Baldwin, 8. Central (Newnan), 9. Pepperell, 10. North Springs.

AAA – 1. Beach, 2. Ballard-Hudson, 3. Carver (Columbus), 4. Douglas, 5. Savannah, 6. Forest Park, 7. Decatur, 8. Mark Smith, 9. Albany, 10. Dalton.

A – 1. Early Co., 2. Central (Carrollton), 3. Bacon Co., 4. Monroe Area, 5. Murray Co., 6. Stone Mountain, 7. Americus, 8. Cairo, 9. Effingham Co., 10. East Hall.

B – 1. East Laurens, 2. Springfield Central, 3. Harris Co., 4. Roswell, 5. Hogansville, 6. Vienna, 7. Stockbridge, 8. Waynesboro, 9. Charlton Co., 10. Johnson Co.

C – 1. Lanier Co., 2. Pike Co., 3. Arlington, 4. Savannah Country Day, 5. Stratford, 6. Crawford Co., 7. Taylor Co., 8. St. Pius X, 9. Dawson Co., 10. Georgia Christian.

The Tifton Gazette, page 2, January 31, 1970

Berrien Sweeps Crisp

Special to Gazette

NASHVILLE – Those powerful Berrien County basketball teams rolled past invading Crisp County here Friday night. The girls triumphed, 48-27, and the boys won, 62-58, in the Region 1-AA meetings.

Coach Stanley Simpson's unbeaten girls, who captured their 19th contest, had balanced scoring at its utmost as forwards Marla Brown and Donna Jernigan scored 15 points each and Grace Baily 14. Candy Eason tallied 12 for the Crisp team which slumped to 7-9 for the campaign.

In the nightcap, Simpson's victorious boys – who extended their winning streak to 19 games and season mark to 19-1 – were sparked by the 26 point effort of George Sorrell. Charles Wright tallied 12, while Richard Tucker and Bobby Taylor bucketed 10 each.

Crisp, which now stands 7-9, got a 24 point performance from Jerry David. Jerry Norton contributed 16.

Berrien's squads take to the road tonight for battle against league opponent Bainbridge.

(Box Scores Omitted)

The Valdosta Daily Times, page 10, January 31, 1970

Berrien Extends Victory Streaks

By Times Staff Writer

NASHVILLE, Ga. – Berrien's Rebels and Rebelettes kept their winning streaks going strong by taking both ends of a Region 1-AA high school basketball twin-bill from Crisp County's Rebels and Rebelettes for the second time this season.

The Berrien Quintet put down the visiting Rebels 62-58 while the home-standing Rebelettes chalked up a 48-27 victory over the Cordele girls. Earlier in the season the Berrien boys took a 55-43 win while the girls won a 42-26 decision over the Crisp teams at Cordele.

The victories leave Coach Stanley Simpson's Rebels with a 19-1 record and a 19-game win streak, while his Rebelettes are still undefeated after 19 starts. Both teams are 4-0 in region games.

Marla Brown and Donna Jernigan notched 15 points each to pace the Berrien girls, while George Sorrell led the Nashville boys with 26 points.

The Berrien cagers are slated to play at Bainbridge tonight.

GIRLS				
Berrien	13	24	33	48
Crisp	8	11	16	27

BERRIEN (48) – Brown 15, Jernigan 15, Bailey 14, Langford 2, McMillan 2, Harrell, Swain, Rudeseal, Carter, Barber, Carey. Team totals: field goals 20, free throws 8 of 15, fouls 9.

CRISP (27) – Eason 12, Whitane 5, Dean 5, Smith 4, Griffin 1, Raines, Bullington, Winfree, David, Lockett. Team totals: field goals 10, free throws 7 of 9, fouls 11.

BOYS				
Berrien	15	35	51	62
Crisp	16	30	46	58

BERRIEN (62) – Sorrell 26, Wright 12, B. Taylor 10, Tucker 10, Guess 4, Conway, Harnage. Team totals: field goals 24, free throws 14 of 25, fouls 12.

CRISP (58) – David 24, Norton 16, Phillips 6, Standard 8, Childree 4, Ray. Team totals: field goals 23, free throws 12 of 18, fouls 17.

February 1970

The Berrien Press, front page, January 29, 1970

Calendar Girl For February

Berrien High Rebelettes have gone the season without a defeat but with some close scores on the basketball court. On the strong defense of the Rebelettes is Peggy Barber, The Berrien Press Calendar Girl for February. Kidded by the coach as "double nothing," she is a senior, member of the B Club and interested in a career as a teacher in elementary education. She is the daughter of Mr. and Mrs. Eston Barber of Nashville.

The Tifton Gazette, page 3, February 2, 1970

Berrien Squads Roll Like Ole Flint River

Special to Gazette

BAINBRIDGE – The Flint River runs through this South Georgia City and it just keeps rolling along, as folks here well know.

Bainbridge boosters, however, learned Saturday night that something else in South Georgia also just keeps rolling along – the Berrien basketball teams. That hard lesson was made plain as Stanley Simpson's squads swept their 20th doubleheader of the year by scores of 42-26 (girls) and 60-40 (boys).

The Berrien girls are 20-0 for the season, while the boys are 20-1.

In the girls' game, Marla Brown once again paced the fairer Rebels as she netted 17 points. Donna Jernigan added 14. Jackie Williamson of Bainbridge was high scorer in the contest with 22 points, but the home team's other two forwards could combine for only four points.

In the nightcap, George Sorrell burned the nets for 31 big points and Wayne Taylor came off the bench to add 13 more as the Rebels turned a close (28-22) halftime margin into a route. Ivey Thigpen and Gene Nelson each had 10 points for Bainbridge.

The Berrien squads see action again Friday night, meeting Thomasville in the Rose City.

(Box Scores Omitted)

The Valdosta Daily Times, page 21, February 2, 1970

Berrien Trips Up Loop Foe

Special to the Times

BAINBRIDGE – Berrien's Rebels and Rebelettes proved once again they were the top teams in Region 1-AA as they took both ends of a league high school basketball doubleheader from Bainbridge's Bearcats and Kittens here Saturday night.

The Rebels hit the 'Cats for a 60-40 victory while the Rebelettes won by a 42-46 score over the Kittens.

The victories left coach Stanley Simpson's Rebels and Rebelettes with 20-game winning streaks and 5-0 region records. The boys are now 20-1, while the girls are still undefeated at 20-0.

Marla Brown, Frances Jernigan and Grace Bailey paced the Rebelettes with 17, 14, and 11 points respectively. Jackie Williamson was the Kitten leader with 22.

In the boys game, Berrien's George Sorrell was the high scorer with 31 points.

GIRLS				
Berrien	10	17	30	42
Bainbridge	10	15	22	26

BERRIEN (42) – Brown 17, Jernigan 14, Bailey 11, Carey, Barber, Carter, Rudeseal. Team totals: field goals 14, free throws 14 of 24, fouls 7.

BAINBRIDGE (26) – Williamson 22, Long 2, Griffin 2, Tyson, Stewart, Morris, Brown. Team totals: field goals 11, free throws 4 of 9, fouls 16.

BOYS				
Berrien	15	28	44	60
Bainbridge	13	22	32	40

BERRIEN (60) – Sorrell 31, W. Taylor 13, Wright 9, B. Taylor 7, Guess, Tucker. Team totals: field goals 25, free throws 10 of 13, fouls 7.

BAINBRIDGE (40) – Thigpen 10, Gene Nelson 10, Robinson 8, Boyd 8, Boyette 4, Love. Team totals: field goals 17, free throws 6 of 9, fouls 10.

The Tifton Gazette, Doug's Digest, page 4, February 3, 1970

Personable Simpson of Berrien Puts 'Mustard' on His Rebels' 'Hot Dogs'

Following an opening-game boys loss to Tift County High, Berrien County Coach Stanley Simpson remarked, "We'll have a better ball club when I get through putting some mustard on my hot dogs."

Simpson was making reference to several players who appeared to be playing more for the spectators than the team.

As evidenced by his first paragraph quote, Simpson is quite a personable person. In fact, he's the type colleges like to have – a coach who can make the alumni forget how bad the team is.

However, Simpson should not be considered simply as personable. He is one tremendous basketball coach.

To say that Simpson put some "mustard" on his "hot dogs" would be putting it mildly. Since that fateful Dec. 46-45 loss to Tift, his Rebels have rolled unbeaten past 20 opponents.

Win In Self-Defense

Almost any coach would have to be considered a success with a 20-1 basketball record. Yet, the Berrien boys must win in self-defense.

After all, the Berrien girls are rolling along with an even slightly better record. They've compiled a perfect 20-0 mark.

Simpson also guides the girls, a two-way coaching proposition seldom seen in Georgia High School Association basketball – particularly for a larger school (Class AA). Can you imagine having a 40-1 cage coaching record in one year? Why, that's better than the red hot New York Knicks could do!

To show you how meticulous Simpson is, he says of his girls, "We thought here lately we could perform a little better than we have (20-0 record?) ... We've played in streaks ... look good for a few minutes and then look bad ... Experience has carried us ... five seniors in the starting lineup."

Regarding the boys' success, he stresses, "This team goes more on physical strength than any other I've had ... rely on brute strength to get the ball off the boards and on defense ... We've come a long way. We learned to play as a team more ... desire and effort ... the hustle has made the difference."

Those boys supplying the primary "brute strength" are center George Sorrell and forward Charles Wright, a pair of 6-5 juniors. The other starters include forward Richard Tucker (6-2), together with guards Roger Guess (6-0) and Bobby Taylor (6-0).

Of that starting quintet, only Tucker is a senior. Consequently, the Berrien foes can "look forward" to seeing the near-identical group next year.

Supplying depth include guards Wayne Taylor (5-10), Bobby Conway (6-0), Jerry Slaughter (5-11) and David Bobo (5-10); forwards David Harnage (6-1), Kim Carey (6-0) and Karl Harrell (6-3, jr.)

The veteran girls' group has a forward corps amazingly well-balanced in scoring, with Marla Brown, Donna Jernigan and Grace Bailey sharing almost equal honors for the year. The obstinate guard group includes Lenna Carey, Peggy Barber and Andrea Carter.

Forward bench strength comes from Jo Ann Langford, Donna Bennett, Sandy McMillan and Pat Williams. The backup defenders include Brenda Rudeseal and Debra Swain.

Records Not Accidental

For those who have kept up with Berrien basketball over the years, they realize these big winners this year are not by accident.

Heading into his ninth season at Berrien, the combined chart read 300 wins and 107 losses. Add a 40-1 mark to that, and you have 340-108, a tremendous 759 percentage.

Some opponents swear with good reason that Berrien does not know how to lose at home – either the boys or the girls. A check of the record would indicate some legitimate crying.

The boys' team has captured 50 consecutive home games. The last loss came in December of 1965 to Madison County, a North Georgia visitor.

On the girls' ledger, the home streak stands at 28. Northside of Warner Robins emerged the last outfit to win at Nashville, and that sextet emerged the State AA champion of two years ago.

Capacity crowds at Berrien County's home games have occurred for so long that Simpson cannot remember the last time every seat was not filled. It's been something like four years.

True, you will usually find winners being supported at home. The big test comes on the road.

Here, Berrien is in a class by itself for this section of the country. You will not find it uncommon to have more of their boosters attending games at foreign courts than the envious home teams.

All-Around Winner

Johnny Futch, who recently returned from Vietnam after serving a tour of duty with the U.S. Army, put out a booklet on Berrien's basketball teams which he headlined, "The Simpson Years."

In the first paragraph of the booklet, Futch starts out, "When Ramrod Simpson came to Berrien High School fresh out of Georgia Southern, basketball was awash in the doldrums of averageness."

…

Obviously, the tall slender native from Buford has changed things in a remarkable two-fold coaching career.

If Stanley (Ramrod) Simpson ever seriously ponders leaving Berrien County (he's reportedly had numerous offers), the folks of that community will likely get off their pocketbooks or whatever they have to do. He's a real winner – not only as a coach but as a person as well.

The Thomasville Times-Enterprise, page 10, February 4, 1970

Cairo 8th-Ranked In Prep Cage Poll

ATLANTA, Ga., (AP) – Savannah's Beach High continues in first place in the Atlanta Journal's weekly high school basketball poll.

Beach has been in top spot all season, and is has shown no sign of faltering.

Ballard-Hudson, Carver of Columbus and Forest Park are in the top four and all are given a good chance to wind up in the state AAA tourney.

Forest Park is unbeaten in 18 starts, while the others have been beaten once.

The rankings by classes:

AAA: Beach, Ballard-Hudson, Carver-Columbus, Forest Park, Savannah Douglas, Decatur, Mark Smith, Albany, Dalton.

AA: Carver-Atlanta, Berrien, East Atlanta, Newton County, Baldwin, Waycross, Hart County, Central-Newnan, North Springs, Pepperell.

A: Early County, East Hall, Central Carrollton, Bacon County, Monroe Area, Murray County, Stone Mountain, Cairo, Americus, Effingham County.

B: Springfield-Central, Harris County, Hogansville, East Laurens, Blackshear, Roswell, Vienna, Stockbridge, Johnson County, Waynesboro.

C: Pike County, Savannah Country Day, Taylor County, Lanier County, Stratford, Arlington, Crawford County, St. Pius X, Dawson County, Georgia Christian.

The Berrien Press, front page, February 5, 1970

"Big Package" Juniors Make Rebel Good News

Good things come in big packages – especially if the "packages" stand 6-5, haul down rebounds, put them back in and are for a high school basketball coach.

Take Ramrod Simpson, for example. The Berrien High coach's "packages", traveling under the aliases of George Sorrell and Charles Wright have been terrorizing south Georgia basketball circles all season. The junior twosome are the foundation Simpson has fashioned his Rebels around, a formula that has produced a 20-1 record going into the season homestretch.

Sorrell, who started last season as a soph. has been living up to pre-campaign expectations averaging 16-plus points and rebounds a game, but Wright has been the real surprise.

Wright, a transfer student from upstate New York, moved to Berrien County last year and is playing his first season of organized basketball. By the second game he had established himself as a starter.

The Sorrell-Wright duo fits well into the defensive-minded Rebel organization. Both delight in blocking shots as a reminder to opponents to stay away from the basket.

After Cairo held the ball for over a minute for a last-second first-half shot, Sorrell gleefully spiked the ball half the length of the court to the Cairo bench. Berrien won 40-25.

Wright, during the finals of the Lowndes-Hahira Invitational Tournament, blocked six straight shots the first six times Lowndes tried to penetrate the middle.

The Rebel defense, with Wright and Sorrell keeping people away under the basket, and Richard Tucker, Bobby Taylor, Roger Guess and to sub Wayne Taylor harassing opponents outside, has been yielding only 38.6 points per game.

Sorrell is hitting at a 17-point pace and picking off 15.6 rebounds an outing. He accounted for a career high 31 points in a 60-40 win over Bainbridge Saturday night. He collected 24 rebounds in an earlier meeting with Bainbridge.

Wright, playing in the shadow of Sorrell, is averaging 8.1 points and 8.7 rebounds.

The Rebels, who haven't lost since they got caught with their press notices down against Tift County 45-46 in the season opener, have two tough games left before tournament time.

Region foe Thomasville at Thomasville Friday and Valdosta at Valdosta the following Tuesday wrap up the regular season schedule.

DEFENSIVE - Lenna Carey, Andrea Carter and Peggy Barber had the Crisp girls taking long shots because of their close defensive play. The Rebelettes won 48-27.

Photo caption:
BIG PACKAGE – George Sorrell goes higher to get one past Lanier's tall Dixon, aiding the Rebels' cause with 24 points in the 71-55 defeat of the Bulldogs from Lakeland. On the backup on the right is Charles Wright, with Bobby Taylor in mid-court and Richard Tucker on the left.

[Compiler's note: This same article without the pictures appeared in the February 5, 1970 edition of The Tifton Gazette under the headline "Good Things Come in Big Packages, Berrien Coach Simpson Discovering".]

The Berrien Press, front page, February 5, 1970
BHS Basketball Teams Continue Victory Streaks
By Tim Moore

Unstoppable George Sorrell dropped 31 points as Berrien County's Rebels dumped region foe Bainbridge, 60-40 Saturday night. This win completed a three-game sweep for the week as they spilled Class C's top rank team, Lanier County, 71-55, on Tuesday night, and slipped by tough Crisp Co., 62-58 on Friday night.

Coach Stanley Simpson's Rebelettes pushed their perfect record to 20-0 with wins of 54-46 over Lanier, 48-27 over Crisp, and 42-26 over Bainbridge.

George Sorrell pumped in 24 point Tuesday night as the Rebels took the Lanier Bulldogs. He also snatched 20 rebounds off the boards. The Rebels had a 11 point lead of 38-27 at half time, and the Bulldogs never came closer than 9 point to them during the remainder of the game. Sorrell was followed in scoring by Roger Guess who bucketed 14 points, Bobby Taylor 12, and Richard Tucker 10.

In the girls' game the Rebelettes held a safe margin the entire game with Marla Brown leading the way as she tallied 28 points. Donna Jernigan, Grace Bailey, and Jo Ann Langford added 12, 10, and 4 points respectively.

In the game with Crisp Friday night both teams were fighting hard for the leading position, and at the end of the first quarter the Berrien Rebels were behind 16-15. In the second quarter they took a 5-point lead though, and held it throughout the rest of the game. Again, George Sorrell paved the way for Berrien's scoring with 26 points aided by Charles Wright's 12 points and 14 rebounds, Richard Tucker's 10 points, and Bobby Taylor's 10.

The girls' game with Crisp wasn't as close, as the Berrien team held a good margin all the way. Marla Brown and Donna Jernigan dropped in 15 points apiece to pace Berrien's offense. Also contributing to Berrien's scoring were Grace Bailey 14, Jo Ann Langford 2, and Donna Bennett 2.

Saturday night as the Berrien teams finished their 3 sweeps of the week, the Bearkittens gave the Rebelettes a fight to start with, but fell farther and farther behind as the game continued. Marla Brown sparked the Rebelettes scoring with 17 points, followed by Donna Jernigan with 14, and Grace Bailey with 11. Lenna Carey, Peggy Barber, Andrea Carter, and Brenda Rudeseal mainly handled Berrien's defensive side of game.

The boys' game went about the same, and it seemed as if George Sorrell couldn't miss the basket as he pumped in 31 of Berrien's 60 points. Wayne Taylor came off the bench to spark the Rebels with 13 points.

Photo captions (page 6): **CLOSE** – Richard Tucker cuts loose with another shot at the basket in the close 62-58 win over Crisp County. Closing in on the left was Charles Wright (42), George Sorrell (20) on the right and Taylor just behind him.

The Thomasville Times-Enterprise, Sports Line, by George Lassiter, Sports Editor
page 6, February 5, 1970

Sub-Region Preview

Thomasville High's Bulldogettes have never won a region or sub-region title in basketball and the outlook is a rough one this season.

Basketball fans will get a preview of the subregion tournament Friday night when the Rebelettes of Berrien County invade the Thomasville gym.

Thomasville, Berrien County, Crisp County and Bainbridge are all in Sub-Region 1-AA. When tournament time rolls around Feb. 19-20-21 the Bulldogettes and Rebelettes will be the top two seeded teams.

The way it looks now Thomasville will battle Crisp in the first round and Berrien meets Bainbridge. The winners of the games – to be played at the THS gym – will automatically advance to the Region 1-AA tournament.

Berrien and Appling County were the victors in Region 1-AA last season and represented the league at the state meet. The Rebelettes won their first game but dropped the second game to Wheeler – 40-35 – in the second round. Wheeler won the state crown with a 33-31 victory over Hart County.

The Berrien girls bring an impressive 20-0 record to Thomasville – including a 49-47 victory over the Bulldogettes earlier this season.

The Bulldogettes are 14-5 but three of the losses are by only nine points. The THS girls have been defeated by Class A Early County twice – 40-39 and 60-51 – Bainbridge – 51-44 – and Crisp County – 38-32.

Berrien Has Great Forwards

In the 40-39 loss to Early the Bulldogettes played most of the game without leading scorer Anne Rumble. Rumble injured her leg in the early minutes of the first quarter and managed to score only four points. She is averaging 18.3 a game.

The loss to Crisp was 'just one of those nights' when everything goes wrong.

And the two point defeat by Berrien – well. The Rebelettes had a tremendous night from the field, hitting on 78 per cent of their shots in the first half and finishing the game well over the 50 per cent mark.

"Berrien keeps the ball until they get the open shot," said Bulldogettes coach Guy Sullivan. "They usually shoot above 50 per cent."

"Berrien has great outside shooters, but their offense is centered around clearing out the middle and driving for a good shot," added Sullivan.

And the Berrien guards are not bad either – "They are probably the best in South Georgia," said Sullivan.

I think Coach Sullivan was overlooking the depth he has at guard when that statement was made.

The Thomasville guards – all six of them – have done a tremendous job this season.

They have improved on the number of turnovers (losing the ball) each game and the handling of the ball has been a key part of every win.

Depth at Guard Pays Off

Betty Sue King is the only girl of the six that starts in every game. "Betty Sue has really contributed to the cut down of turnovers this season," said Sullivan, "And developed into a top flight guard."

King missed the last game with Berrien County with a hurt neck which she suffered in a wreck.

The Bulldogettes depth at guard helps when a starter gets in foul trouble. Sullivan does not hesitate to play any of the six at anytime.

Although he prefers to start King, Janet Jones and Joyce Fletcher when the Bulldogettes are facing quick forwards. But, Yvonne Hall, Kathy Sollami and Melissa Davis are waiting on the bench to help out.

Davis is a strong rebounder and has the height to stop a good forward from shooting from the outside.

Fletcher is probably the quickest guard on the team. "She played well before Christmas and seems to be regaining early season form," said Sullivan.

"Sollami has strength and quickness and unlimited ability," Sullivan continued, "and experience is the only thing Kathy needs to become an outstanding guard." Sollami is a sophomore.

Jones is versatile. Sullivan thinks she is easy coached. Jones had her best game in THS's 72-45 romp when she held Bainbridge's Jackie Williamson to only 25 points.

Good Control Game Needed

Williamson had scored 43 against the Bulldogettes the first time the two teams met and was averaging 32 going into the game.

Hall is one of the most experienced on the team. She is a co-captain and playing for the third year.

Hall, Sollami and Fletcher combined to keep Cairo's Sally Wight from scoring a field goal Tuesday night in the Bulldogettes narrow 49-46 victory over the Syrupmaids.

"We have to control the ball to beat Berrien," noted Sullivan.

He continued, "We have three girls that can score on any guards. But, we can't force anything on the Berrien girls. We will have to keep the turnovers down and not miss any scoring chances."

"It's just a case of who has the best guards and shooters."

Sullivan says there is no special defense to stop the Berrien forwards.

So, it will be a man-to-man defense – excuse me – girl-to-girl to see who's best.

The Tifton Gazette, page 2, February 5, 1970

Berrien Boys Hold Second in AA Ratings

ATLANTA – Tiftarea representative Berrien County continues to hold the No. 2 ranking for State AA basketball.

Carver of Atlanta, the defending State AA champion, remains as the No. 1 team in the Atlanta Journal's weekly rankings. Beach of Savannah, Early County, Springfield Central and Pike County are the pace setters for AAA, A, B and C, respectively.

The ratings include:

AA – 1. Carver (Atlanta), 2. Berrien Co., 3. East Atlanta, 4. Newton Co., 5. Baldwin, 6. Waycross, 7. Hart Co., 8. Central (Newman), 9. North Springs, 10. Pepperell.

AAA – 1. Beach, 2. Ballard-Hudson, 3. Carver (Columbus), 4. Forest Park, 5. Savannah, 6. Douglass, 7. Decatur, 8. Mark Smith, 9. Albany, 10. Dalton.

A – 1. Early Co., 2. East Hall, 3. Central (Carrollton), 4. Bacon Co., 5. Monroe Area, 6. Murray Co., 7. Stone Mountain, 8. Cairo, 9. Americus, 10. Effingham Co.

B – 1. Springfield Central, 2. Harris Co., 3. Hogansville, 4. East Laurens, 5. Blackshear, 6. Roswell, 7. Vienna, 8. Stockbridge, 9. Johnson Co., 10. Waynesboro.

C – 1. Pike Co., 2. Savannah Country Day, 3. Taylor Co., 4. Lanier Co., 5. Stratford, 6. Arlington, 7. Crawford Co., 8. St. Pius X, 9. Dawson Co., 10. Ga. Christian.

The Thomasville Times-Enterprise, page 6, February 7, 1970

Rebels Roll, 45-27 Over Thomasville

By George Lassiter
T-E Sports Editor

"It's the best defense we have faced this year," said Berrien County coach Stanley Simpson.

And the Thomasville High Bulldogs held the Rebels to only 45 points last night but the 'Dogs could not find the range and managed only 27.

The Bulldogettes had their problems also – and scoring was the major problem as the Rebelettes rolled to a 50-38 victory.

The Bulldogs trailed only 10-8 to the sixth-ranked Rebels at the end of the first quarter and by seven points, 19-12 at halftime.

But, the third quarter was the big difference as the Rebels rolled up a 12-4 margin.

Berrien's two giants – George Sorrell and Charles Wright – were held below their scoring average. Sorrell scored 15 points, seven in the last quarter after the Bulldogs' Lloyd Austin fouled out.

Most of the Berrien points came from under the basket on short jumpers. Wright had 14 points and Bobby Taylor nine.

The Bulldogs trailed by 10 points most of the third and final quarter until Austin and Angelo Mathes went to the bench with five fouls.

Then the Rebels netted eight straight points for the final winning margin.

Ronnie Thornton led the Bulldogs with 10 points.

The Bulldogs shot 40 times from the field and hit on 12 attempts for a 30.5 percentage mark.

Thornton shot 21 of the shots and connected on only five for a frigid 23.8 per cent. Mathes added six points and Bubba Wadley four.

The Berrien boys are now 21-1. The Bulldogs are 5-15.

In the girls' game, the Thomasville guards stayed in foul trouble most of the game and the Berrien forwards took advantage.

Berrien beat the THS girls by only one goal – 16-15 – but held an 18-8 edge at the free throw line.

The Bulldogettes were charged with 18 fouls in the game to only eight for the Rebelettes. Berrien was charged with only two in the first half.

The Bulldogettes trailed 12-10 at the end of the first quarter and 25-17 at halftime.

In the third quarter Thomasville fell behind, 33-22, with four minutes remaining in the period.

Susan Wine hit a goal and Anne Rumble a free throw and goal to pull the Bulldogettes within six, 33-27.

But, two quick goals in the final 45 seconds of the quarter boosted the Rebelette lead back to nine points, 36-27. The Berrien girls then held this throughout the remainder of the final quarter.

Donna Jernigan paced the Rebelettes with 25 points while Marla Brown added 25. Berrien has an undefeated 21-0 mark.

Rumble led the Bulldogettes with 25 points. She scored 16 in the second half. Joy Alligood was below her 15 point average with only six points while Wine added six.

The Berrien girls shot 38 per cent from the field for the night – including a 50 per cent effort in the second half. The Bulldogettes had a percentage mark of 31.5 from the field.

Thomasville is open tonight and finish the regular season against Cook County Tuesday night in Adel.

(Box Scores Omitted)

The Tifton Gazette, page 5, February 7, 1970
Berrien Takes Thomasville Teams
Special to Gazette

NASHVILLE – Berrien County's undaunted basketball duo rolled on again Friday night, capturing a doubleheader from hapless Thomasville.

The Berrien girls ran over Thomasville, 50-38, in the first game, with the boys' completely outclassing the visitors, 45-27, in the nightcap. They now stand 21-0 and 21-1, respectively.

Donna Jernigan netted 25 points for the Rebelettes, while Marla Brown was tallying 22 more. Ann Rumble scored 25 for Thomasville.

In the boys' game, the powerful Berrien front line of George Sorrell and Charles Wright was more than Thomasville could handle as the duo dominated both scoring and rebounding.

Sorrell finished with 15 points, while Wright added 14. Ronnie Thornton, with 10 points, was the only Thomasville player to reach a double figure.

(Box Scores Omitted)

The Valdosta Daily Times, page 15, February 7, 1970
Berrien Triumphs Over Thomasville
Special to the Times

THOMASVILLE – Berrien Rebels and Rebelettes completed their Region 1-AA schedule for the 1969-70 season in their usual fashion, by taking both ends of a basketball doubleheader from Thomasville, here, Friday night.

The Rebels took a slight lead in the first quarter and never gave it up as they hit Thomasville's Bulldogs for a 45-27 victory. Meanwhile, the Rebelettes used the same type attack, defeating the Bulldogettes, 50-38.

Both of coach Stanley Simpson's Berrien teams were undefeated in region play with 6-0 records. And both now have 21-game winning streaks with the boys owning a 21-1 mark and the Rebelettes still undefeated at 21-0.

Donna Jernigan and Marla Brown scored 25 and 22 points respectively to lead the Rebelette attack. Grace Bailey accounted for the other three points. Ann Rumble led the attack for Thomasville with 25 points.

George Sorrell and Charles Wright paced the Rebels with 15 and 14 points respectively. Ronnie Thornton was the only Bulldog in double figures with 10 points.

GIRLS				
Berrien	12	25	36	50
Thomasville	10	17	27	38

BERRIEN (50) – Jernigan 25, Brown 22, Bailey 3, Langford, Carey, Barber, Carter. Team totals: field goals 16, free throws 18 of 26, fouls 8.

THOMASVILLE (38) – Rumble 25, Wine 7, Alligood 6, King, Davis, Jones, Fletcher. Team totals: field goals 15, free throws 8 of 10, fouls 18.

BOYS				
Berrien	10	19	31	45
Thomasville	8	12	16	27

BERRIEN (45) – Sorrell 15, Wright 14, B. Taylor 9, Tucker 6, Guess 1, W. Taylor, Conway. Team totals: field goals 17, free throws 11 of 22, fouls 4.

THOMASVILLE (27) – Thornton 10, Mathis 6, Austin 2, Keadle 2, Wadley 4, Drake 1, Gatlin 2. Team totals: field goals 12, free throws 3 of 5, fouls 14.

The Tifton Gazette, page 3, February 10, 1970

Berrien Girls Are Shooting to Finish Unbeaten Tonight
By Staff Writer

With Tift County High's basketball teams idle tonight, the Tiftarea spotlight focuses on Berrien County's girls.

One last foe remains tonight for Berrien County High's girls to complete an unbeaten regular season. Homestanding Valdosta represents the final hurdle against the Nashville girls who have chalked up 21 victories.

The school's boys boast a 21 game winning streak following an opening game loss to Tift County. Stanley Simpson has been the coach behind the Berrien teams' combined 42-1 record.

Two other Tiftarea schools also conclude regular season play tonight as Cook County hosts Thomasville, and Fitzgerald visits Vienna.

Turner County goes on the road tonight to combat Wilcox. Then, the Ashburn representative finishes at home Friday night against Doerun.

Tift's teams finish regular campaign activity Friday against Westover at Albany. Atkinson County does likewise that night by hosting Clinch County.

Worth County terminated play this past weekend.

Records of the Tiftarea schools include:

Tift (girls, 11-10; boys, 9-11), Atkinson (girls, 13-7; boys, 7-13), Turner (girls, 8-11; boys, 11-8), Worth (girls, 8-12; boys, 9-11), Cook, (girls, 5-12; boys 4-14), and Fitzgerald (boys only, 4-10).

The Valdosta Daily Times, page 11, February 10, 1970

'Dosta, Lowndes At Home Tonight
By Times Staff Writer

Valdosta's Wildcats and Kittens are scheduled to host Berrien's Rebels and Rebelettes, while Lowndes' Vikings play host to Live Oak, Fla., in high school basketball action here tonight.

Tonight's games will close the regular season for Valdosta, Lowndes and Berrien teams. They will, however, see more action in region tourneys slated next week.

Other area action tonight sees Blackshear at Clinch County (Homerville), Lanier County (Lakeland) at Echols County (Statenville) and Thomasville at Cook (Adel).

Coach Joe Wilson's 'Cats and coach Bill Davis' Kittens will try to put an end to 21-game winning streaks held by both of coach Stanley Simpson's Berrien squads.

The 'Cats will take a 16-4 record into battle while the Kittens have a 9-10 mark.

Simpson's Rebels are now 21-1 and have already defeated the Wildcats twice. They posted a 53-43 victory in a Christmas tournament and later defeated the 'Cats, 56-52, in Nashville, Ga. The Rebelettes are still undefeated after 21 starts and earlier registered a 42-20 win over the Kittens in Nashville.

Coach Charles Cooper's Vikings will close out their regular season when they meet Live Oak, Fla., tonight. Lowndes' boys will take a 16-4 overall record into battle against the Florida foes. They went 13-2 in Region 1-AAA. The Vikettes have already closed their regular season and won't play tonight since Live Oak does not field a girls team.

Action is to begin with the girls game at 7 p.m. at Valdosta's gym on the Valdosta Junior High School campus and with a boys' "B" team game at 7 p.m. at Lowndes High's gym.

The Tifton Gazette, page 4, February 11, 1970
Boys Finish 22-1

Berrien Girls Get Unbeaten Season

Special to Gazette

VALDOSTA – Berrien County's girls terminated a perfect season here Tuesday night, but it did not come without a battle down to the wire against Valdosta and an eventual 26-21 victory.

In the nightcap, the Berrien boys rolled to a 48-38 victory over the Region 1-AAA representative.

Coach Stanley (Ramrod) Simpson saw his two Berrien teams finish regular season play with a fantastic 44-1 combined record. The girls went 22-0 and the boys 22-1.

With 42 seconds left in the girls' game, Berrien trailed by one point, 20-21, which prompted Simpson to tell the Gazette, "I didn't think for a while it was meant to be … We didn't play well, but we won."

In the final seconds, Marla Brown – who emerged game high with 15 points – sacked two free throws and a field goal, while Donna Jernigan contributed a pair of gratis tosses.

Berrien's boys had minimum difficulty in posting their 22nd consecutive victory following an opening game loss as Roger Guess and George Sorrell scored 13 points each. Roger Romer bucketed 12 for the victims.

The Berrien squads will compete Feb. 19-21 in the Region 1-AA West Tournament at Thomasville.

Valdosta's boys saw their record decrease to 15-5. The girls fell to 9-11.

(Box Scores Omitted)

The Valdosta Daily Times, page 13, February 11, 1970

Berrien Cagers Defeat Valdosta

By Sammy Glassman
Times Sports Editor

Berrien's Rebels and Rebelettes continued their impressive victory streaks by sweeping a high school basketball doubleheader with Valdosta here Tuesday night.

Coach Stanley Simpson's Rebs lead all the way as they trimmed coach Joe Wilson's VHS Wildcats, 48-38. And Simpson's Rebelettes rallied in the closing moments of the game to nip coach Bill Davis' Valdosta Kittens, 26-21.

Both teams from Nashville, Ga., have now won 22 games in a row. The Rebelettes became the first team in Berrien's hoop history to go undefeated in regular season play. The Rebs, who bowed in their season opener, closed out their regular slate with a 22-1 mark.

The Wildcats are now 16-5 and the Kittens are 9-11. The VHS cagers have also ended regular season play.

Valdosta's and Berrien's teams will be playing in region and sub-region tourneys in the near future.

Last night's girls game saw some brilliant defensive play by the Kittens' and the Rebelettes' guard corps. It was primarily the work of VHS' Nita Brantley, Evelyn Graham and Debbie Stephenson and Berrien's Lena Carey, Peggy Barber and Andrea Carter which accounted for the low score.

Valdosta took an early lead and stayed out front by from one to four points until Marla Brown sank a pair of free throws with just 49 seconds showing on the clock to put Berrien ahead 22-21. In the time remaining the Rebelettes added four insurance points.

Brown finished as the game's leading scorer with 15 points. Donna Jernigan was next in line for Berrien with nine. The VHS scoring was divided among Joy Johnson, 8; Ann Sutton, 7, and Marsha Stephenson, 6.

In the boys game the Rebels jumped off to a quick four point lead then stayed out front to the finish. By the middle of the third stanza Berrien was 14 markers ahead and VHS couldn't get within eight points of the Rebs after that.

Roger Guess and George Sorrell, each with 13, led the BHS attack. Roger Rome, with 12 points, was the only Wildcat in double figures.

GIRLS				
Valdosta	9	15	16	21
Berrien	7	13	15	26

VALDOSTA (21) – Sutton 7, Johnson 8, M. Stephenson 6, D. Stephenson, Brantley, Graham. Team totals: field goals 6, free throws 9 of 12, fouls 15.

BERRIEN (26) – Brown 15, Bailey 2, Jernigan 9, Carey, Barber, Carter, Langford. Team totals: field goals 8, free throws 10 of 18, fouls 18.

BOYS				
Valdosta	11	18	24	38
Berrien	18	27	36	48

VALDOSTA (38) – Jones 6, Webb 2, Golden 8, Rome 12, White 4, Taylor, Baker 2, Mabry, Rowe 4, Johnson. Team totals: field goals 16, free throws 6 of 12, fouls 8.

BERRIEN (48) – Guess 13, Harnage, Tucker 7, Wright 6, Sorrell 13, Taylor 9. Team totals: field goals 19, free throws 10 of 16, fouls 9.

Photo caption:
'Cats' Don Golden Keeps the Basketball Away from George Sorrell – Times Staff Photo

The Berrien Press, page 8, February 12, 1970
Berrien Basketball Teams Trim Thomasville Friday
BERRIEN vs. THOMASVILLE
The Rebels and Rebelettes lengthened their string of victories to 21 straight Friday night at the expense of their 1-AA opponents, Thomasville.

Due to the balanced scoring of Marla Brown and Donna Jernigan, with 25 and 22 points respectively, the Rebelettes came through their game with an eight to twelve-point lead after the first quarter to take a 50-38 win from the Bulldogettes. Also scoring for the Rebelettes was Bailey with three points.

The boys game was a carbon copy as the Rebels came on after the first quarter to a 45-27 victory. Sorrell led Berrien's scoring again with 15 points, and also snagged 14 rebounds. Wright got 14 points, B. Taylor nine, and Tucker six.

The Rebels had one season game left before tournament time. That was played in Valdosta Tuesday night.

The Tifton Gazette, page 3, February 12, 1970
Berrien Ends Up Second
ATLANTA – Berrien County's boys, who finished regular season play with a 22-1 record, hold the No. 2 position in the State AA basketball ratings.

East Atlanta is still the leader for Class AA in the Atlanta Journal rankings. Other pacesetters include Beach, AAA; Early County, A; Springfield Central, B; Pike County, C.

The ratings for this week include:

AAA – 1. Beach, 2. Ballard-Hudson, 3. Carver (Columbus), 4. Forest Park, 5. Savannah, 6. Decatur, 7. Mark Smith, 8. Douglass, 9. Albany, 10. Dalton.

AA – 1. East Atlanta, 2. Berrien Co., 3. Newton Co., 4. Carver (Atlanta), 5. Baldwin, 6. Central (Newnan), 7. Waycross, 8. Pepperell, 9. Wills, 10. Hart Co.

A – 1. Early Co., 2. East Hall, 3. Central (Carrollton), 4. Monroe Area, 5. Stone Mountain, 6. Murray Co., 7. Bacon Co., 8. Americus, 9. Cairo, 10. Effingham Co.

B – 1. Springfield Central, 2. East Laurens, 3. Hogansville, 4. Blackshear, 5. Harris Co., 6. Roswell, 7. Stockbridge, 8. Johnson Co., 9. Waynesboro, 10. Vienna.

C – 1. Pike Co., 2. Taylor Co., 3. Savannah Country Day, 4. Crawford Co., 5. Stratford, 6. Arlington, 7. Lanier Co., 8. St. Pius X., 9. Georgia Christian, 10. Dawson Co.

The Valdosta Daily Times, page 17, February 12, 1970

Prep Cagers Eye Tourney Titles

By Sammy Glassman
Times Sports Editor

It's that time of the year when prep basketball coaches go into shock and the fans bounce around in a high state of excitement.

Tournament action, with sub-region and region titles up for grabs, is ready to begin.

In the area are quintets and sextets ranging in classification from "AAA" to "C" and it has been a good year for many teams in this section.

How many will emerge as champs or runners-up in their regions and move on into the state playoffs remains to be seen. But I'm going to be surprised if several in the area don't make the grade.

Let's run down the list by regions and at least try to do some guessing about how area delegates might do.

The 1-AAA boys event is slated here next week at the Lowndes High gym. Albany's Indians will be top-seeded and the title favorite, but Lowndes' Vikings and Valdosta's Wildcats figure to be contenders along with Monroe and fast-improving Tift County.

Coach Charles Cooper's Lowndes Vikings (17-6) closed regular season play with six straight wins and nine triumphs in their last 10 outings. Coach Joe Wilson's Valdosta Wildcats (16-5) lost in their regular season finale to non-region foe Berrien, but before that turned back three straight 1-AAA opponents.

The 1-AAA girls tourney is to be played week after next at Tifton and coach Steve Kebler's Lowndes Vikettes (17-5) are likely to be top-seeded. Coach Bill Davis' Valdosta Kittens are 9-11, but have come on strong near the finish of the season. Moultrie, Monroe, Albany and surging Tift are others with strong teams in the girls division.

Berrien Sparkles

As far as the Region 1-AA (West) tourney next week is concerned coach Stanley Simpson's Berrien Rebels and Rebelettes are right smack in the middle of the limelight. The Rebs bowed in their season opener and have since clicked off 22 straight wins. The Rebelettes went through a 22-game campaign without a loss. Berrien has its sights on a pair of titles.

Cook's Hornets and Wasps are the area delegates in the 1-A (East) meet opening tonight at Hazlehurst. The Hornets are 4-17 and the Wasps have a 7-12 mark. Bacon County (Alma) is a solid favorite in both the boys and girls bracket of this tourney.

Brooks County's Tigers (12-7) and Tigerettes (7-12) will be the area teams in the 1-B (East) tourney slated next week at Camilla. The Mitchell County girls and Turner County boys are top-seed in this meet, but don't count either of the Brooks teams out yet.

Clinch Hopeful

Clinch County's Panthers (12-7) and Pantherettes (7-13) will carry the area's colors into the 2-B (West) scramble at Douglas next week. The Panthers are top-seeded.

The Region 1-C boys tourney is slated Feb. 25-27 at Norman Park and Georgia Christian School's Generals (15-4) and Lanier County's Bulldogs (15-4) are a pair of area teams with title hopes.

The girls in this league will hold their tourney a week later at Doerun. The host Does, who are unbeaten, Whigham and Norman Park head the form chart. Lanier's Bulldogettes (10-9) rank as a "darkhorse."

Down in Florida the Hamilton County Rebels of Jasper, Fla., are going strong with a 14-3 mark. They're playing in the Suwanee Conference tourney that opens tonight at Gainesville, Fla. The Rebs rank just a notch back of top-seed P.K. Yonge on the form chart for this event.

All in all, it has been a very good season for high school basketball in this part of the country. And the tournaments this year promise to offer a lot more excitement for fans in the area.

The Tifton Gazette, page 2, February 16, 1970

Berrien Garners Firsts

Berrien County's powerful basketball teams will be top-seeded in the Region 1-AA West tournament slated for Thursday through Saturday at Thomasville.

Berrien's girls have a 7 p.m. date Thursday against Bainbridge. The boys from Nashville enter the competition Friday against Thomasville at 8:30 o'clock.

The Berrien girls have perfect 22-0 credentials for the year. The boys are 22-1.

Other girls' records include Thomasville, 14-7; Crisp County, 11-9; Bainbridge, 7-14.

In the boys' division, Bainbridge boasts the second best mark at 14-8. Following are Crisp County, 11-8; Thomasville, 6-15.

While the Region 1-AA West teams are battling at Thomasville, the Region 1-AA East representatives go the same nights at Baxley. The winners and runners-up from both the boys and girls compete Feb. 26-28 at Cordele in the Region 1-AA finals.

The Region 1-AA West Tournament schedule at Thomasville includes:

Thursday
7 p.m., (girls) Berrien Co. vs. Bainbridge; 8:30 p.m. (boys) Bainbridge vs. Crisp Co.
Friday
7 p.m. (girls) Thomasville vs. Crisp Co.; 8:30 p.m. (boys) Berrien vs. Thomasville.
Saturday
7 p.m., girls' championship; 8:30 p.m., boys' championship.

The Tifton Gazette, page 3, February 17, 1970

Berrien Takes No. 6

ATLANTA – Berrien County High's boys have finished No. 6 in one statewide basketball poll for Class AA.

Berrien got the No. 6 spot for regular season action by way of the Atlanta Constitution. Newton County boasts the top rung.

Other pace setters include Carver of Columbus, AAA; Early County, A; Roswell, B; Taylor County, C. The ratings include:

AA – 1. Newton Co., 2. Carver (Atlanta), 3. East Atlanta, 4. Lakeshore, 5, Central (Newman), 6. Berrien Co., 7. Baldwin, 8. Stephens Co., 9. Waycross, 10. Pepperell.

AAA – 1. Carver (Columbus), 2. Ballard-Hudson, 3. Beach, 4. Forest Park, 5. Savannah, 6. Douglass, 7. Decatur, 8. Mark Smith, 9. Dalton, 10. Druid Hills.

A – 1. Early Co., 2. Central (Carrollton), 3. East Hall, 4. Bacon Co., 5. Monroe Area, 6. Rockdale Co., 7. Murray Co., 8. Cairo, 9. Americus, 10. Statesboro.

B – 1. Roswell, 2. East Laurens, 3. Harris Co., 4. Central (Springfield), 5. Hogansville, 6. Union Co., 7. Vienna, 8. Blackshear, 9. Johnson Co., 10. Waynesboro.

C – 1. Taylor Co., 2. Crawford Co., 3. Pike Co., 4. St. Pius X, 5. Arlington.

The Thomasville Times-Enterprise, page 13, February 18, 1970
AT THOMASVILLE HIGH GYM

Sub-Region 1-AA Cage Tourney Begins Here Thursday

The West Sub-Region 1 AA basketball tournament opens play at the Thomasville High gym Thursday night with two games scheduled.

Girls and boys teams from Berrien County, Thomasville, Bainbridge and Crisp County compose the West sub-region.

The East sub-Region has boys teams from Dodge, Dublin, Dudley-Hughes, Waycross and Appling County competing and girls teams from all the schools except Dudley-Hughes. The East tournament will be staged at the Appling County gym in Baxley.

The undefeated Berrien County girls will take on the Bainbridge Bear Kittens at 7 p.m. Thursday to open the tournament play while the Bainbridge Bearcats and Crisp County Rebels play in the nightcap at 8:30.

Friday night both Thomasville teams get into action with the Bulldogettes taking on Crisp County's Rebelettes at 7 and the Bulldogs go against Berrien County boys at 8:30.

The Thomasville boys, who are the defending Region champions, have won only six games in 21 starts this season.

The Berrien boys have a 22-1 record and are top-seeded in the tournament. Tift County beat the Rebels in the opener this season but Berrien bounced back for 22 consecutive victories, including a 19-point win over Tift.

The Rebels have defeated the Bulldogs twice this year.

The Thomasville Bulldogettes have had their troubles since winning the Cairo Christmas tournament.

The Bulldogettes were 7-1 after the tournament and since have a 7-6 record, including a loss to the Crisp girls, 38-32. The THS girls also beat the Rebelettes, 38-32, in the fifth game of the season.

The Crisp girls have an 11-9 record. The Crisp girls have two losses to the Bainbridge and Berrien County teams.

The Berrien County Rebelettes are a solid favorite to win the sub-region for the third straight year.

The Berrien girls are 22-0 for the season with two victories over Thomasville, Bainbridge and Crisp teams.

The Bear Kittens are 7-14 for the season. Their biggest upset of the season was a 51-44 victory over the Bulldogettes early in the season.

The Bainbridge Bearcats, now 14-8, and the Crisp County Rebels (11-6) have played twice this season with the Bearcats winning both games. In the East tournament Dudley-Hughes is the top-seeded boys team while the Waycross has the top team in the girls' division.

Both Waycross teams are 17-3 for the season and should have no trouble advancing to the Region tournament next week at the Crisp County gym in Cordele.

The top two girls and boys teams from each sub-region will advance to the Region 1AA contest.

Thomasville High's boys and Berrien's girls are the defending Region champions.

Thomasville lost in the first round of the state tournament last season to Lakeshore of Atlanta, 58-57.

The Berrien girls beat College Park of Atlanta, 66-48 in the first round and lost to Wheeler County in the second night of play, 40-35.

The Valdosta Daily Times, page 23, February 18, 1970
Berrien Seeking Pair of Crowns
By Times Staff Writer

THOMASVILLE – With Berrien's Rebels and Rebelettes aiming for a double title sweep action in the Region 1-AA (West) high school basketball tournament is slated to begin here Thursday.

In the field for the three-day event along with the Berrien teams will be quintets and sextets from Thomasville, Bainbridge and Crisp County (Cordele).

The western sub-division winners and runners-up will join the teams from the eastern half of the region in the 1-AA playoffs slated for Feb. 26-28 at the Crisp County High gym in Cordele. At stake in the competition at Cordele will be state Class AA playoff berths.

For the tourney beginning here Thursday night, coach Stanley Simpson's high-riding Rebels and Rebelettes are top-seeded. Both have 22-game victory streaks going. The Rebs started their victory surge after losing their first game. The Rebelettes have gone all the way without a loss.

Records of other teams in the field are as follows: boys – Bainbridge, 14-8; Crisp, 11-8, and Thomasville 6-15. Girls – Thomasville, 14-7; Crisp, 11-9 and Bainbridge 7-14.

The pairings follow:

Thursday – Berrien vs. Bainbridge, girls, 7 p.m. Bainbridge vs. Crisp, boys, 8:30 p.m.

Friday – Thomasville vs. Crisp, girls, 7 p.m.; Berrien vs. Thomasville, boys, 8:30 p.m.

Saturday – girls championship game at 7 p.m.; boys championship game at 8:30 p.m.

The Berrien Press, front page, February 19, 1970
1-AA Basketball Tourney Action Begins Tonight
By Tim Moore

The Berrien High School Rebelettes open the action tonight in the 1-AA tournament in Thomasville, meeting Bainbridge at 7 p.m.

The Rebelettes put up an unblemished record in 22 games against the Bainbridge 7-14 score for the season.

Berrien Rebels play tomorrow night at 8:30 against the homestanding Thomasville boys with a 6-15 record. Berrien boys have dropped only one loss in 23 starts.

In boys' action tonight will be Bainbridge (14-8) and Crisp with an 11-8 season record.

The Thomasville girls start the action tomorrow night, putting their 14-7 record against Crisp with a 11-9 slate for the season.

Winners of the brackets in the girls meet at 7 p.m. Saturday and the boys' winners collide at 8:30 p.m. Saturday.

Tournament play continues next week with games Feb. 26, 27 and 28 at Cordele.

Twenty-six to twenty-one was the close note that the Rebelettes closed their regular season with, as they barely escaped defeat from the Valdosta Kittens.

After trailing the entire game, the Rebelettes finally slipped into the lead with only 42 seconds left on the clock. Marla Brown made two free throws making the score 21-20 Berrien's favor.

They held this small lead and added more to it in the few remaining seconds to keep their record spotless, bringing it to 22-0 for the season.

Marla Brown led the Rebelettes' scoring again with 15 points. Donna Jernigan had nine and Mary Grace Bailey had two. The guards were Carey, Barber, Carter and Rudeseal.

The Rebels led their game all the way taking an easy 48-38 victory from the Wildcats. Sorrell and Guess both netted 13 points for the Rebels followed by Bobby Taylor with nine, Tucker seven and Wright six.

The Rebels will take a 22-1 record into their tournament this week-end.

Photo captions:
FRESHMEN GIRLS – The Berrien High School freshmen girls' team, left to right, includes: Front, Catherine Carter, Donna Bennett, Cynthia Bailey, Cynthia Shearer; second row, Janice Boyd, Debbie Harrell, Heather Harrell, Carol Futch; back row, coach Dona Fields, Sherry McGill, Susan Rollins, and Peggy Jo Cook.
[Compiler's note: The photo reprinted here is not the published version but was taken at the same time.]

FRESHMEN BOYS – On the freshman boys' team of Berrien High School, left to right, are: Front, March Miller, Gary Ray, Gary Benjamin; second row, Pat Luke, Tony Slaughter, Kenneth Shaw, Bobby Moore; back row, coach Wayne Harris, Mitch Ray, Bobby Jones and manager Johnny Horne. Not shown are: Ned Wooten, Tommy Rice and Mickey Carter.
[Compiler's note: The photo reprinted here is not the published version but was taken at the same time.]

The Berrien Press, page 3, February 19, 1970
Photo caption:
B TEAM GIRLS – On the Berrien High School Girls B Team, left to right, are: Front, Kathy Flanders, Debbie Harrell, Debra Murphy; second row, Deborah Vickers, Donna Bennett, Freida Holland, Cathy Watson; back row, Judy McNabb, Sandie Parr, Carole McMillan, Carolyn Futch, manager Karen Griffin, Mrs. Dona Fields, coach.

The Thomasville Times-Enterprise, page 8, February 19, 1970
AT THS GYM
Sub-Region Tourney Opens Here Tonight
By George Lassiter
T-E Sports Writer

The West Sub-Region 1AA basketball tournament opens play in the Thomasville High gym tonight with two games scheduled.

The Berrien County Rebelettes battle the Bainbridge Bear Kittens at 7 p.m. and the Bainbridge Bearcats take on the Crisp County Rebels at 8:30.

The Thomasville teams go into action Friday night with the finals scheduled for Saturday night.

The THS Bulldogettes battle the Crisp County Rebelettes at 7 while the Bulldogs take on the Berrien County Rebels.

Both Berrien County teams are top-seeded in the tournament.

The Berrien girls are 22-0 including two victories over the Bainbridge girls. The Kittens are 7-14.

The Berrien girls depend on a tough defense and a balanced offense led by Marla Brown.

Jackie Williamson paced the Kittens scoring attack. Williamson, a senior, is averaging over 30 points a game. The Bainbridge have registered two victories over the Crisp boys but the Rebels are a threat to the Bearcats.

The Bearcats have a 14-8 record while Crisp is 11-8.

The Thomasville boys are the defending Region 1AA champions, but have to play Berrien County – and the Rebels own two victories over the Bulldogs this season.

Thomasville has a 6-15 record while the Rebels are 22-1. The only loss was to Tifton in the opener this year.

The Bulldogettes need a subregion victory to break a jinx.

The THS girls have never won a sub-region or region basketball game.

And the Crisp County guards have stopped the Bulldogette forwards scoring efforts in both games between the teams this season.

Thomasville defeated the Crisp girls 38-32 in the fifth game of the season and the Rebelettes topped the Bulldogettes by the same score two weeks ago.

In both games the THS forward had a poor shooting percentage.

In the victory over the Rebelettes, the THS forwards hit only three of 23 shots from the field for 13 percent in the first half and used a strong second half comeback to win, hitting on 10 of 22 attempts for 49 percent.

In the loss to Crisp, the Bulldogettes connected on seven of 15 shots from the field in the first half for a percentage mark of 47 per cent while Crisp was hitting on five of 22 for 40 per cent.

But, in the second half the Bulldogettes managed only three of 23 shots again for 13 percent. The THS guards limited the Rebelettes to only five shots and connected on three.

Anne Rumble continues to lead the Bulldogettes' scoring with a 22.5 average. Rumble – who missed school Wednesday with the flu – has hit 452 points in 20 games. She has also hit on 105 of 159 free throws for 66.6 percent.

Joy Alligood has an average of 15.7 a game with 331 points in 21 games. Alligood got off to a slow start this season but has led the Bulldogette scoring in recent games.

Alligood set a new school scoring record of 34 points and broke the record only a week later with a 38-point performance. She has hit on 77 of 111 free throws for a 69.3 percent.

Susan Wine has a 9.9 average and has connected on 37 of 61 free throws.

Kay Dekle leads the team in free throw percentage with a 71.4 percent mark. She has hit on 20 of 28 attempts. Dekle also has a six-point a game average.

The Tifton Gazette, page 11, February 19, 1970
Berrien, Atkinson Go in Tournaments
By Staff Writer

Two tournaments involving Tiftarea basketball teams commence activity tonight.

The Region 1-AA West Tournament, which encompasses Berrien County, begins tonight at Thomasville. Atkinson County's squads are competing in the Region 2-B West play slated for the South Georgia College gym at Douglas.

Berrien's girls face Bainbridge tonight at 7 o'clock. In the 8:30 o'clock finale, the boys teams of Bainbridge and Crisp County collide.

The Friday action calls for the Berrien boys to tangle with host Thomasville at 8:30 o'clock. The 7 o'clock matinee sends the Crisp girls against Thomasville.

Both Berrien teams are top-seeded. The girls have perfect 22-0 credentials, while the boys are 22-1.

At Douglas tonight, the Atkinson girls go in an 8:30 o'clock duel with Telfair County. The 7 o'clock game matches the Wilcox and Clinch County girls.

Atkinson's boys face Wilcox in 7 o'clock Friday action. The 8:30 o'clock tilt puts Clinch County against the Telfair boys.

The Berrien and Atkinson teams will be keeping close tabs on the Region 1-AA East and Region 2-B East Tournaments which begin tonight at Baxley and Jesup, respectively.

The Valdosta Daily Times, page 30, February 19, 1970
Berrien Favored in T'ville Meet
By Times Staff Writer

THOMASVILLE – With Berrien's Rebels and Rebelettes from Nashville, Ga., rated as the teams to beat, play in the Region 1-AA (West) basketball tourney is slated to begin here tonight.

Both of coach Stanley Simpson's Berrien teams will come into the tourney riding the crest of 22-game victory streaks. The Rebs bowed in their season opener, but haven't lost since. The Rebelettes are undefeated.

Records of other teams in the field are as follows: Boys – Bainbridge, 14-8, Crisp County (Cordele), 11-9, and Thomasville, 6-15. Girls – Thomasville, 14-7; Crisp, 11-9, and Bainbridge, 7-14.

The tourney will end Saturday with the winners and runners-up earning berths in the 1-AA playoffs slated for Feb. 26-28 at Cordele.

The schedule follows:

Tonight – Berrien vs. Bainbridge, girls, 7 p.m.; Bainbridge vs. Crisp, boys, 8:30 p.m.

Friday – Thomasville vs. Crisp, girls, 7 p.m.; Berrien vs. Thomasville, boys, 8:30 p.m.

Saturday – girls championship game at 7 p.m.; boys championship game at 8:30 p.m.

The Thomasville Times-Enterprise, page 8, February 20, 1970
BERRIEN GIRLS, BEARCATS ADVANCE TO FINALS

Bulldogettes, 'Dogs Open Sub-Region Bids Tonight

By George Lassiter
T-E Sports Editor

Thomasville High's Bulldogs and Bulldogettes begin West Sub-Region 1AA basketball tournament play tonight on their home court.

The Bulldogettes battle the Crisp County Rebelettes at 7 p.m. and the Bulldogs go against the top-seeded Berrien County Rebels at 8:30.

In last night's action the Berrien County girls advanced to the finals of the Sub-Region tournament with a 63-46 victory over the Bainbridge Bear Kittens.

The Bainbridge Bearcats also gained a berth in the finals of the Sub-Region with a 68-56 rout over Crisp County's Rebels.

The Bulldogs are 6-15 for the season while the Rebels are 22-1. Two of the Thomasville losses have been to Berrien.

The Bulldogettes and Crisp girls have met twice this season with bot winning a game 38-32.

The THS girls have a 14-7 record while the Rebelettes are 11-9.

Two years ago, Thomasville played the Crisp girls in the opening game of the sub-Region tournament and were upset by two points.

The Thomasville girls will be trying to break a sub-Region and Region jinx. The Bulldogettes have not won a game in either tournament.

In last night's action, Marla Brown, Donna Jernigan and Grace Bailey all hit high in double figures to pace the Berrien County Rebelettes victory.

Brown netted 28 points – 14 in each half – Jernigan added 20 and Bailey 15.

Jackie Williamson paced the Bear Kittens with 31 points – 22 in the first half. Pam Long added eight and Lessa Griffin seven for the Bainbridge girls.

Williamson scored all 15 of the Bainbridge points in the first quarter as the Kittens managed to take a 15-13 lead.

The Kittens led most of the first quarter until Bailey hit a short jump shot to tie the game at 13-13 with 14 seconds remaining.

In the second quarter the Kittens held the lead by two and four points before the Rebelettes – now 23-0 for the season – begin to roll.

With three minutes remaining until halftime Berrien went on a scoring spree that netted 11 straight points and boosted the Rebelettes into the lead for the first time in the game.

Brown and Bailey hit goals to tie the game at 26-26. Jernigan then scored four of her 10 points in the second quarter to up the lead to four points.

Brown then hit a free throw and a long set shot with 10 seconds left in the quarter to give the Rebelettes a 33-26 command. Long sank a goal as the buzzer sounded and Berrien led by only five at halftime.

Bainbridge cut the margin to four points, 46-42, as they outscored Berrien 14-13 in the third quarter, but the winners used the free throw line in the final period for a 17-4 scoring edge.

The Rebelettes hit on 12 of 14 free throws in the final quarter.

Williamson managed to score seven in the third quarter but was held to only a field goal by guard Lenna Carey in the fourth period.

In the boys' game, Bainbridge jumped off to a 5-0 lead but Crisp Rebels rallied back to tie the game at 7-7 before the Bearcats took a 13-7 command at the end of the first quarter.

With 6:57 remaining until halftime, Bainbridge led 15-11 but the Bearcats drilled in eight straight points in a two minute span to lead the Rebels, 23-11.

The Rebels could not close the margin and trailed by 10 points, 32-22, at halftime.

The Bearcats then outscored the Rebels 17-11 in the third quarter and led by a margin of 22 points, 56-34, with 7:10 remaining in the game.

The Rebels pulled back within 10 points, 64-54, with 50 seconds remaining, but the charge was too late to catch Bainbridge.

Rodger Robinson and Ivey Thigpen led the Bainbridge scoring attack with 18 and 16 points, respectively. Paul Boyd and Jerry Boyett each added 10, James Love dropped in eight – all in the fourth quarter – and Eugene Nelson added six.

Jerry David was the only Crisp player in double figures. David scored 28 – 15 in the first half and 13 in the final quarter.

The Bearcats are now 15-3 and the Rebels finished the season 11-9.

*****

BERRIEN COUNTY (21-21-63) – Brown 8-12-28; Jernigan 7-6-20; Bailey 6-3-15; Guards: Carey, Barber, Carter, Rudeseal, Swain.

BAINBRIDGE (15-16-46) – Williamson 10-11-31; Long 4-0-8; Griffin 1-5-7; Guards: Stewart, Morris, Brown, Tyson.

Berrien field goals, 21; free throws, 21-28; personal fouls, 17. Bainbridge field goals, 15; free throws, 16-20; personal fouls, 17.

BERRIEN	13 20 13 17 – 63
BAINBRIDGE	15 13 14 4 – 46

The Tifton Gazette, page 2, February 20, 1970

Berrien Girls Win Easily

THOMASVILLE – Berrien County's girls, who went unbeaten during regular season play (22-0), gained an opening night 63-46 victory in the Region 1-AA West Tournament over Bainbridge here Thursday night.

In other first round play the Bainbridge boys took the measure of Crisp County, 68-56.

Tonight's action calls for the Berrien boys (22-1) to tackle host Thomasville at 8:30 o'clock. A 7 o'clock girls' contest puts Thomasville against Crisp.

Berrien's girls showed tremendous offensive balance against Bainbridge as Marla Brown, Donna Jernigan and Grace Bailey scored 26, 22 and 15 points, respectively. Jackie Williamson for Bainbridge emerged game high with 31.

The Berrien sextet trailed at the first quarter turn, 13-15. However, the unbeaten team turned a 33-28 halftime advantage and won going away.

In the boys' skirmish, Roger Robinson scored 18 points for Bainbridge. Crisp's Jerry David tallied 28.

(Box Scores Omitted)

The Valdosta Daily Times, page 20, February 20, 1970

Berrien's Girls Beat Bainbridge

Special to the Times

THOMASVILLE – Berrien's Rebelettes opened the action with a victory in the Region 1-AA (West) high school basketball tournament Thursday, and now it's the Rebels' turn in the second round tonight.

In last night's action, Berrien's sextet mowed down Bainbridge's Bearkittens, 63-46, and Bainbridge's Bearcats rolled past Crisp County's Rebels from Cordele, 68-56.

Tonight, Thomasville's Bulldogettes are scheduled to put their 14-7 record on the line against Crisp County's Rebelettes, who are 11-9. Then Berrien's boys are set to take on Thomasville's Bulldogs (6-15) at 8:30 p.m.

Both of coach Stanley Simpson's Berrien squads are seeded first in the tournament. The girls are undefeated at 23-0 while the Rebels own a 22-1 mark. The tourney is being held in the Thomasville High gym.

Last night Marla Brown came through with 26 points to spark the Rebelettes. Grace Bailey added 15. Jackie Williamson notched 31 points for the Bearkittens. The Kittens close their season with a 7-15 slate.

(Box Scores Omitted)

The Thomasville Times-Enterprise, page 8, February 21, 1970
TONIGHT IN THOMASVILLE GYM

Bulldogettes Advance to Sub-Region 1-AA Finals

By George Lassiter
T-E Sports Editor

Thomasville High's Bulldogettes finally broke a jinx and won a sub-region basketball game.

And the Bulldogettes did it in high style as they romped to a 54-39 victory over the Crisp County Rebelettes in the semifinals of the Sub-Region 1AA tournament.

The Bulldogettes play Berrien tonight at 7.

In the second half the Bulldogettes had an even 50 per cent mark, hitting on 10 of 20 shots.

Anne Rumble and Joy Alligood teamed up to pace the Bulldogettes' scoring. Rumble hit 23 points while Alligood was dropping in 22.

Rumble had a tremendous night from the field. She hit on four of five shots in each half for a torrid 80 per cent.

Rumble, who fouled out of the game with 6:06 remaining in the contest, had missed the final game against Cook County. She went to South Dakota on an exchange student program.

At the first of the week Rumble missed practice with the flu. "Ann and Joy did a fine job," said Bulldogette coach Guy Sullivan. "We haven't played in 10 days and Rumble has been out two weeks but everybody played a good game."

Alligood connected on 10 of 18 shots from the field for a better than average 55.5 per cent.

"Janet Jones did an excellent job of guarding their top scorer," added Sullivan. "And she got a lot of help from Joyce Fletcher, Yvonne Hall, Betty Sue King and Kathy Sollami."

"We did not do a good job of handling the ball," continued Sullivan. "Anytime you have 20 turnovers in a game it can hurt a team. But we were hitting well from the field."

"It's the first sub-region game to my knowledge a Thomasville girls' team has ever won," said Sullivan. "And, we have a good chance to win tonight."

The Bulldogettes have played the Berrien Rebelettes twice this season and lost both games.

The Crisp girls held an 11-7 lead with 2:53 remaining in the first quarter before the Bulldogettes scored seven straight points to take a 14-11 lead.

Susan Wine did not start the game but came off the bench and dropped in two goals in a 40 second span to tie the game at 11-11.

Alligood hit a long set shot and Rumble a free throw to give the Bulldogettes the lead.

In the second quarter the teams battled the first six minutes of the period before the Bulldogettes pulled away in the final seconds.

The Bulldogettes led 22-19. Rumble rebounded and scored and was fouled. She added the free throw and another short jump shot with nine seconds remaining to give the Bulldogettes a 27-19 halftime lead.

"The girls were real tense and nervous in the first quarter," added Sullivan. "But, they settled down and pulled away."

The Bulldogettes led by 10 points most of the third quarter and held a 12-point, 42-30, lead going into the final period.

The THS girls built a 15-point command in the fourth quarter and the Rebelettes cut the margin to 10 before Alligood hit a goal and Kay Laing completed a three-point play to give the Bulldogettes the final margin.

(Box Scores Omitted)

The Thomasville Times-Enterprise, page 8, February 21, 1970

Bulldogs Stopped by Rebels, 53-45

By George Lassiter
T-E Sports Editor

Thomasville High finished the season last night on their home court — but the Bulldogs made an impressive showing before a large crowd.

The Bulldogs battle the top-seeded Berrien County Rebels to the final buzzer before losing a 53-45 contest in the semi-finals of the Sub-Region 1AA basketball tournament.

Tonight in the finals the Thomasville High Bulldogettes go against the Berrien County Rebelettes at 7 while the Rebels battle the Bainbridge Bearcats at 8:30.

All four teams will advance to the Region 1AA tournament next week at the Crisp County gym in Cordele.

The Bulldogs performed as well as could be expected last night as they kept the fans on the edge of their seats.

The Bulldogs maintained the lead a majority of the first and second quarters and stayed within four points of the Rebels until the final seconds of the game.

And the officials didn't help the Bulldogs. Last night's officials reminded fans of the weather — always changing.

Surely the officials have called enough games to distinguish between an offensive and defensive foul. But, they failed to use their knowledge of the game last night.

The Bulldogs were charged with 20 fouls in the game while Berrien picked up nine. Thomasville probably fouled 20 times, but the Rebels had that many fouls that were not called.

Perhaps the officials can remember tonight that there ARE two teams in the game and stand by their original call without one overruling the other.

Back to the game. Thomasville came into the game with a 6-15 record while the Rebels were 22-1.

Kenneth Gatlin and Lavon Keadle got the Bulldogs off to a 4-0 lead with field goals. Berrien bounced back and took a 7-4 lead with 2:11 left in the quarter.

Angelo Mathes and Gatlin netted goals, and the Bulldogs were back in the lead, 8-7.

In the final 1:15 of the opening quarter the Rebels hit a free throw and goal and led 10-8 going into the second period.

The game was tied twice before the Bulldogs began to pull away. Keadle, Mathes, Lloyd Austin all hit goals to give Thomasville an 18-15 lead.

The teams exchanged goals and Thomasville led 20-17 with 4:02 remaining until halftime. Austin picked up his third foul with 3:51 remaining in the second quarter while Bubba Wadley was charged with a third with 2:10 left.

Berrien scored on a free throw before Gatlin connected for another goal and Keadle hit a free throw to give Thomasville a five-point, 23-18, halftime lead.

Austin sat out the third quarter with four fouls. He was charged with the fourth with 1:12 remaining until halftime.

Berrien took the lead with 4:20 left in the third quarter and from that point the game was tied or the lead exchanged hands 11 times before the Rebels gained the lead early in the fourth quarter.

The Rebels led by two and four points the remainder of the game as Wadley and Austin sat the bench after fouling out. Berrien was playing with four juniors in the starting lineup last night while the Bulldogs had three sophomores and junior.

Both teams shot well from the field. Thomasville hit 15 of 40 shots for 37.5 percent.

The Rebels shot a blazing 66.7 per cent from the field in the second half, hitting on 12 of 18 shots. Most of the goals were hit from close range.

Gatlins paced the Bulldogs with 18 points, Mathes added 13, Keadle hit eight, Austin four and Sammy Drake two.

George Sorrell dropped in 19 points to lead the Rebels, Roger Guess hit 15, Bobby Taylor 12 and Charles Wright seven.

THOMASVILLE (19-7-45) – Drake 1-0-2; Keadle 3-2-8; Austin 1-2-4; Mathes 6-1-13; Gatlin 8-2-18; Wadley 0-0-0.

BERRIEN COUNTY (19-15-53) – Sorrell 7-5-19; Wright 2-3-7; Tucker 0-0-0; Taylor 6-0-12; Guess 4-7-15; Slaughter 0-0-0; Conway 0-0-0.

Berrien: field goals, 19; free throws, 15-29; personal fouls, 19. Thomasville: field goals, 19; free throws, 7-9; personal fouls, 20.

THOMASVILLE	8	15	11	11	– 45
BERRIEN	10	8	20	15	– 53

The Tifton Gazette, page 3, February 21, 1970

Berrien Boys Get Scare in Triumph

Special to Gazette

THOMASVILLE – A highly-favored Berrien County boys' team found itself behind at halftime by five points in the Region 1-AA West Tournament here Friday night, but the Rebels got off the floor to defeat Thomasville, 53-45.

Consequently, the Berrien boys join the school's girls in tonight's finals. The girls face host Thomasville at 7 o'clock, with the boys facing Bainbridge in an 8:30 o'clock encounter.

In Friday night's matinee, the Thomasville girls coasted past Crisp County, 54-39.

Berrien's boys trailed Thomasville at intermission, 18-23. Then, the Rebels came back with a decisive 20-11 third quarter advantage for a 38-34 lead. During the fourth period, the Bulldogs were within one point.

George Sorrell, Roger Guess and Bobby Taylor spearheaded the Berrien attack with 17, 15 and 12 points, respectively. Kenneth Gatlin scored 18 and Angelo Mathes 13 for Thomasville.

In the girls contest, Thomasville's one-two punch of Ann Rumble and Joy Alligood was devastating. The former bucketed 23 points and the latter 22. Candy Eason got 24 for Crisp.

(Box Scores Omitted)

The Valdosta Daily Times, page 11, February 21, 1970

Berrien Cagers in Final Round

Special to the Times

THOMASVILLE – Berrien's Rebels held true to the style they have set all season by defeating Thomasville's Bulldogs, 53-45, here Friday to secure a seat in the finals of the Region 1-AA (West) high school basketball playoffs tonight.

In the girls action Friday, Thomasville's Bulldogettes rolled past Crisp County's Rebelettes, 54-39.

Berrien's Rebelettes gained the finals Thursday night by defeating Bainbridge, 63-46, to push their undefeated record to 23-0. They are set to go against the Bulldogettes at 7 p.m. tonight.

Meanwhile in the boys action, the Rebels are to meet Bainbridge's Bearcats for the title at 8:30 o'clock tonight.

Both coach Stanley Simpson's Berrien teams were seeded number one in the tournament. The girls were undefeated at 22-0 while the boys had a 22-1 mark and a 22-game winning streak with no region losses.

George Sorrell was the high point man for the Rebels Friday, hitting 17 points. Ed Gatlin was the top Bulldog with 18. In the girls action Ann Rumble and Joyce Allegood paced the Bulldogettes with 23 and 22 points respectively.

Since both champions and runners-up earn the right to represent the region in further tournaments, all four teams playing tonight will gain a berth in the 1-AA playoffs in Cordele next week.

(Box Scores Omitted)

The Thomasville Times-Enterprise, page 8, February 23, 1970

Rebels, Rebelettes Win West Sub-Region 1AA Basketball Titles

By George Lassiter
T-E Sports Editor

Berrien County's Rebels and Rebelettes took both first place West Sub-Region 1AA basketball tournament trophies home to Nashville Saturday night after rolling up victories in the Thomasville gym.

The Rebelettes' guards held Thomasville's Bulldogettes to only 27 points as they rolled to a 53-27 triumph and the Rebels used a balanced scoring attack to whip Bainbridge's Bearcats, 65-45.

All four teams advance to the Region 1AA tournament to be held in the Crisp County gym in Cordele Thursday, Friday and Saturday.

The Bulldogettes trailed 4-1 in the opening minutes of the game and tied the contest at 6-6. All six points came on free throws for the Thomasville girls.

Berrien then scored six straight – with Marla Brown scoring all six – to lead 12-6 at the end of the first quarter.

The Rebelettes then upped their halftime lead to 32-14. The Bulldogettes did not score a field goal until 3:06 was remaining in the second quarter when Joy Alligood hit a long set shot.

The THS Girls only managed two field goals in the first half and shot only eight per cent while the Berrien girls were hitting on 61 per cent of their shots from the floor.

And the Bulldogettes shot 30 per cent from the field in the second half while the Rebelettes hit 60.

The Rebelettes outscored Thomasville 11-6 in the third quarter and led, 43-20. Alligood scored all six of the Bulldogettes' points.

Alligood scored four in the fourth quarter and Susan Wine three as Rebelettes held a 10-7 edge.

Alligood led the Bulldogettes with 17 of their 27 points. Anne Rumble – who was leading Thomasville with a 22.5 average – managed only five points, all on free throws in the first half. Wine also added five points.

Brown led the Rebelettes with 29 points – 18 in the first half. She hit on nine of nine attempts from the free throw line.

Donna Jernigan added 12 and Grace Bailey 10.

The victory was the 24th of the season for the Berrien girls and the loss left the THS girls with a 15-8 mark.

The Berrien boys had a night from the field. The Rebels hit on nine of 20 shots in the first half for 45 per cent and bombed the nets with 15 of 25 for 60 per cent in the second half.

The Rebels led 30-24 with 6:03 remaining in the third quarter and in a one-minute span dropped in six points to up their lead to 12 points, 36-24.

Berrien opened the fourth quarter with four straight goals – and it took only four shots – to open up a 52-33 lead.

Bainbridge came back with five points before Berrien hit another hot streak and scored six to lead the Bearcats, 60-38 with 2:04 remaining.

(Box Scores Omitted)

The Tifton Gazette, page 3, February 23, 1970
Region 1-AA West

Berrien Has Two Crowns

Special to Gazette

THOMASVILLE – Berrien County claims today a pair of Region 1-AA West Tournaments championships following Saturday night activity here.

The unbeaten girls smashed host Thomasville, 53-27. The boys, a loser only once all year, upended Bainbridge, 65-45.

In the girls' triumph, Berrien grabbed a 12-6 quarter lead and increased the margin to 32-14 by halftime. The Nashville representative coasted home free.

Marla Brown got 29 points to outscore the Thomasville team herself, while Donna Jernigan chipped in 12 and Grace Bailey 10. Joy Alligood scored 17 to lead the losers.

Berrien's guards played tremendous against the high-powered Thomasville offense, namely Lenna Carey, Peggy Barber and Brenda Rudeseal.

Berrien's boys were on the short end of an 11-9 first quarter count. However, the Rebels stormed to a 26-21 halftime lead and stretched the advantage to 44-33 heading into the final stanza.

Bobby Taylor and Roger Guess share scoring honors for the victors with 14 points apiece. While George Sorrell contributed 11. Roger Robinson emerged the Bulldogs' only double-digit scorer via 13.

Coach Stanley Simpson will take his powerful Berrien squads into Region 1-AA Tournament play Thursday, Friday and Saturday at Cordele.

Girls' Championship	
Berrien (53)	**Thomasville (27)**
Brown 29	Rumble 5
Jernigan 12	Wine 5
G. Bailey 10	Alligood 17
Carey	Hall
Barber	Jones
Rudeseal	Fletcher

Berrien subs – Langford (2), McMillan, Williams, Bennett, Mathis, C. Bailey, Carter, Swain, Harrell. Thomasville subs – Laing, Sollami.

Berrien 53	12	20	11	10	–
Thomasville 27	6	8	6	7	–

Berrien: field goals, 19; free throws, 15-18; personal fouls, 11. Thomasville: field goals, 8; free throws, 11-12; personal fouls, 15.

Boys' Championship	
Berrien (65)	**Bainbridge (45)**
Guess 14	Boyd 8
B. Taylor 14	Boyett 4
Tucker 8	Nelson 5
Wright 8	Robinson 13
Sorrell 11	Thigpen 7

Berrien subs – Harnage (5), W. Taylor (3), Harrell (2). Bainbridge subs – Love (4), Spears (4).

Berrien 65	9	17	18	21	–
Bainbridge 45	11	10	12	12	–

Berrien: field goals, 24; free throws, 17-24; personal fouls, 17. Bainbridge: field goals, 15; free throws, 15-22; personal fouls, 15.

The Valdosta Daily Times, page 13, February 23, 1970

Berrien's Cagers Make Title Sweep

By Julian Miller
Times Staff Writer

THOMASVILLE – Berrien's Rebels and Rebelettes made a clean sweep of championship honors as the Region 1-AA (West) basketball tournament came to a close here Saturday night.

Coach Stanley Simpson's Berrien girls took a six-point lead in the first stanza and went from there to a 52-7 (typo) victory over Thomasville's Bulldogettes. Simpson's Rebels posted a 65-45 victory over Bainbridge, Bearcats after trailing by two points in the first quarter.

The cagers from Nashville, Ga., now move into the Region 1-AA playoffs, which are slated to begin Thursday at Cordele. The Berrien girls will be playing Appling County and the Berrien boys will be facing Dudley Hughes of Macon in the first round. Meanwhile, Thomasville's sextet and Bainbridge's quintet will be facing a pair of teams from Waycross.

Although the T'ville girls never did take the lead, they managed to stay with the Rebelettes for the first seven minutes of play.

Then Berrien forward Donna Jernigan sank a field goal to break a 6-6 tie and teammate Marla Brown hit for four more points to put Berrien ahead 12-6 at the end of the quarter. After that, the Bulldogettes never came close to the Berrien girls.

Rebelette guards Lenna Carey, Peggy Barber and Brenda Rudeseal stopped the Bulldogettes cold, allowing only six points in the first and third stanzas and seven in the second and fourth.

The victory left the Berrien girls still undefeated after 24 starts, while the Bulldogettes of coach Guy Sullivan are now 15-8.

Marla Brown led the scoring for Berrien with 29 points followed by Jernigan with 12 and Grace Bailey 10. Joy Alligood was the top Bulldogette with 17.

The boys game was nip-and-tuck for the first quarter with the score either changing hands or being tied five times. The 'Cats finally went ahead 11-9 as the quarter end.

Berrien caught the 'Cats on a two-pointer by George Sorrell and went ahead on another field goal by Roger Guess. Bainbridge made one more attempt at the lead and caught Berrien 13-13.

But field goals by Charles Wright and Guess gave Berrien the lead again. Although they came as close as one point several times before the half, the Bearcats never could catch up after that.

Roger Guess and Ben Taylor [Correction: Bobby, not Ben] scored 14 points each to lead Simpson's Rebels, who have won 24 straight since losing their season opener to Region 1-AAA foe Tift County, 46-45.

Roger Robinson led coach Lynwood Mock's Bearcats with 13 points. The 'Cats now own a 15-9 overall record.

(Box Scores Omitted)

Photo caption:
Berrien's David Harnage (40) Fights With Bainbridge Defender For A Rebound — Times Staff Photo

The Tifton Gazette, page 3, February 24, 1970
Berrien Squads Compete

Berrien County's powerful basketball teams will compete Thursday through Saturday in the Region 1-AA playoffs at Cordele.

The Berrien girls enter the competition Thursday against Appling County at 7 p.m. The boys face Dudley Hughes in 8:30 p.m. Friday activity.

Other opening play Thursday sends the Bainbridge boys against Waycross at 8:30 p.m. The opening contest Friday finds the girls' teams of Waycross and Thomasville colliding.

The finals will be Saturday night. The girls play at 7 o'clock and the boys 8:30 o'clock.

Berrien's boys and girls recently captured the Region 1-AA West Tournament championships at Thomasville. Their teams now stand 24-1 and 24-0, respectively.

Waycross captured both the boys' and girls' titles in Region 1-AA East. Dudley Hughes was the boys' runnerup and Appling second for the girls' division.

The Bainbridge boys and Thomasville girls were second for the Region 1-AA West competition behind the Berrien squads.

The Thomasville Times-Enterprise, page 10, February 25, 1970
THS Girls Open Region Bid Against Waycross Friday
By George Lassiter
T-E Sports Editor

Thomasville High's Bulldogettes face their biggest challenge of the season Friday night and a victory would gain a berth in the first round of the State AA playoffs March 13-14.

The Bulldogettes go against a tough Waycross girls team at the Crisp County gym in Cordele Friday at 7 p.m.

The Region 1AA tournament opens play in the Crisp gym Thursday night with Berrien County Rebelettes battling the Appling County girls at 7 and Waycross' Bulldogs taking on the Bainbridge Bearcats at 8:30.

Friday night the Bulldogettes and Waycross girls play at 7 followed by the Berrien County Rebels and Dudley Hughes at 8:30.

The Bulldogettes are 15-8 for the season while the Waycross girls – also the Bulldogettes – are 19-3.

The THS girls beat Crisp County to gain the finals of the West Sub-Region tourney and was runner-up to Berrien County in the final contest.

The Berrien girls are favored to win the Region crown again this season. The Rebelettes have a 24-0 record.

The Waycross girls beat Appling County in the East Sub-Region finals, 47-37. One of the three losses suffered by Waycross was to Appling earlier in the season.

"Waycross has some big guards and depend on a balanced scoring attack from the forwards," said Thomasville coach Guy Sullivan.

Leading the Waycross guard is 5-11 Dale Baker and 5-9 Ava Williams. Two other girls, both 5-7, alternate at the other position. They are Brenda Miles and Melissa Parker. All the guards are juniors except Parker.

"They have fair speed," added Sullivan, "but, play a strong man-to-man defense."

At the forward end, Vicki Cason paces the scoring attack with a 22.9 point per game average. The 5-6 senior is an excellent player according to Sullivan.

Christine Garner and Gail Baker, both 5-8 seniors, are good outside shooters. Garner hit six of seven shots from the field against Appling in the sub-Region final while Baker connected on nine of 15 shots.

Thomasville's forwards had a bad night against the Berrien girls Saturday night.

"I have coach Anne Rumble for five years," said Sullivan, "and, that is the worst night I've ever seen Anne have."

Rumble failed to hit a field goal Saturday night and scored only five points – which is well below her sparking 22.5 average a game.

The Bulldogettes shot only eight per cent from the field in the first half and only 30 per cent in the second.

"I was pleased with the play of the guards against Berrien," added Sullivan. "We did what we planned but the forwards could not score."

"Betty Sue King probably played one of her best games of the season," said Sullivan. "Kathy Sollami turned in a fine performance in her first starting role, Janet Jones and Joyce Fletcher also did fine jobs."

"The guards handled the ball well and cut down on the number of turnovers."

"According to the information on our scouting report," said Sullivan, "we are two teams which are equal and the team that plays the best game Friday night should win."

The Valdosta Daily Times, page 15, February 25, 1970

Berrien Cagers Eye Third Title

By Times Staff Writer

CORDELE – Berrien's high-riding Rebels and Rebelettes from Nashville, Ga., will be going for their third title sweep this season when the battle for Region 1-AA's hoop crowns begins here Thursday night.

The Rebs and Rebelettes, both coached by Stanley Simpson, are rolling along with 24-game victory streaks intact. The Rebs are 24-1 overall and the Rebelettes are unbeaten at 24-0.

Berrien's cagers have played in a pair of tournaments so far and made championship sweeps in both of them. Both rang the victory bell in the Lowndes Christmas tourney back in December. And both emerged as champs from the Region 1-AA (West) tourney last week at Thomasville.

Records of other teams in the 1-AA playoffs, which will run for three days at the Crisp County High gym, are as follows:

Girls – Appling County (Baxley), 16-5; Thomasville, 15-8, and Waycross, 19-3. Boys – Waycross, 19-3, Bainbridge, 15-9, and Dudley Hughes (Macon), 18-3.

Thursday's schedule calls for Berrien to face Appling at 7 p.m. in a girls game and for Bainbridge to face Waycross at 8:30 p.m. in a boys contest.

On Friday the Thomasville and Waycross girls are to play at 7 p.m. and the Berrien and Dudley Hughes boys are to clash at 8:30 p.m.

Finals in both divisions are scheduled for Saturday, with the girls game at 7 p.m. and the boys tilt at 8:30.

Region 1-AA's winners and runners-up will advance into the state Class AA playoffs.

The Berrien Press, front page, February 26, 1970

Berrien Basketball Teams Advance to 1-AA Playoff

By Tim Moore

The Berrien High Rebels and Rebelettes both finished this past Thursday, Friday, and Saturday night.

The Rebelettes put Bainbridge Kittens out in the first round Thursday night with a convincing 63-46 final decision. The Rebelettes were trailing 13-15 at the end of the first quarter, but really "turned on" in the three remaining periods. Brown pumped in 26 points to lead Berrien's scoring followed by Jernigan with 22, and Bailey with 15.

This victory put them in the finals against Thomasville Bulldogettes Saturday night when they slapped a surprisingly big defeat on them. The Bulldogettes, a team in Berrien's same caliber, could count only 27 points for the entire game. The Rebelettes almost doubled this score with 53 points. Brown again starred at the head of Berrien's scoring with 29 points. Jernigan had 12, Bailey ten, and Langford two. On defense for Berrien were Carey, Barber, Rudeseal, Carter, Harrell, and Swain.

The Rebels started their play Friday night as they slipped by the Thomasville Bulldogs with a scary 53-45 win. The Rebels had a slight 10-8 lead over the Bulldogs at the end of the first period, but by the end of the second they had fallen behind 18-23. The end of the third put Rebels back in front 38-34, and during the fourth they built up an eight point lead to carry them through.

Sorrell netted 17 points and pulled down 17 rebounds to spark the Rebels on. Guess got 15 points, Taylor 12, and Wright nine.

The Rebels started their Saturday night game against Bainbridge about the same way. They were trailing 9-11 at the end of the first, and were leading only 26-21 at the half. They came back and played a tough second half, though, to take an easy 65-45 victory from the Bearcats. Guess, B. Taylor, and Sorrell all scored in the double figures for Berrien with 14, 14, and 11 points respectively. Tucker and Wright both got eight points, Harnage five, W. Taylor three, and Harrell two.

The Rebelettes will have a 24-0 record and the Rebels a 24-1 record to take to the 1-AA play off in Cordele this coming weekend.

The Thomasville Times-Enterprise, page 8, February 26, 1970

Region 1AA Tournament Opens Play

CORDELE – The Region 1AA basketball tournament opens here tonight in the Crisp County gym.

Two games are scheduled with Berrien County's Rebelettes battling the girls from Appling County at 7 p.m. and the Waycross Bulldogs and Bainbridge Bearcats playing at 8:30.

Friday night the Waycross girls go against the Bulldogettes of Thomasville at 7 and Berrien County's Rebels play at 8:30. The finals are set for Saturday night.

The Berrien County Rebelettes have a 24-0 record and are the champions of West sub-Region 1AA. The Appling girls were the runners-up in the East sub-Region.

The Bulldogs of Waycross made a sensational comeback to win the East 1AA title. The Bulldogs trailed Dudley Hughes, 40-26, at halftime and hit a goal in the final seconds for a 72-71 victory.

Bainbridge takes a 15-9 record into the game against the Bulldogs 19-3 mark. Bainbridge was defeated in the finals of the sub-region by Berrien, 65-45.

The Thomasville girls own a 15-8 mark while Waycross is 19-3. The Waycross girls defeated Appling, 47-37, to win the East sub-Region crown.

The Bulldogettes were runners-up to Berrien in the West.

The Waycross girls have three big guards, led by 5-11 Dale Baker.

Vicki Cason, a 5-6 senior, leads the better than average forwards. Cason is the leading scorer on the team with a 22.8 average.

Christine Garner and Gail Baker, both 5-8 seniors, are good outside shooters. In the finals Waycross shot 51 per cent from the field.

Dudley-Hughes was seeded No. 1 in the sub-Region and now must face the West's top-seeded Berrien. Berrien takes a 24-1 record into the Region contest.

The Thomasville Bulldogs are the defending Region 1AA champions but they were defeated by the Rebels in the first round of the sub-Region.

The Tifton Gazette, page 2, February 26, 1970
Berrien, Atkinson Go in Tournaments

Two powerful Tiftarea girls' basketball teams will compete in region tournaments tonight.

Unbeaten Berrien County is facing Appling County in the Region 1-AA Tournament tonight at Cordele, 7 o'clock. Meanwhile, Atkinson County will be opposing Patterson at the South Georgia College gym in Douglas, 8:30 o'clock.

Following the Berrien-Appling girls' contest, the Bainbridge and Waycross boys' teams battle. The Atkinson-Patterson duel follows a 7 o'clock girls game between Brantley County and Clinch County.

Berrien's boys enter the Region 1-AA competition Friday night against Dudley Hughes at 8:30 o'clock.

Both Berrien squads claim Region 1-AA West championships. The Atkinson girls boast the Region 1-B West crown.

Elsewhere, Abraham Baldwin College will host sectional State AAA boys' play this weekend. Valdosta opposes Ballard-Hudson in Friday night action, and Albany goes Saturday night against Carver of Columbus. Both tilts have 8 o'clock tip-offs.

The Thomasville Times-Enterprise, page 6, February 27, 1970
BEARCATS, BERRIEN GIRLS ADVANCE TO REGION FINALS
THS Girls, Waycross Meet in 1-AA Tourney Tonight

CORDELE – The Thomasville High Bulldogettes won their first sub-Region game in the history of the school last week and have a chance to gain a berth in the state tournament with a triumph tonight.

The Bulldogettes battle the Waycross girls at 7 tonight in the Crisp County gym while the Berrien County Rebels take on Dudley Hughes at 8:30 in the semi-finals of the Region 1AA basketball tournament.

In semi-final action last night, Bainbridge's Bearcats rolled over Waycross 69-59, and the Berrien Rebelettes routed Appling County, 46-28.

The Bulldogettes eliminated Crisp County from the West sub-Region tournament last week and gained a spot in the Region meet, although losing to Berrien County in the sub-region finals.

If the THS girls win tonight they will face Berrien's girls in the finals Saturday night at 7. The Bainbridge boys meet the winner of the Berrien – Dudley Hughes game at 8:30. The top two teams in girls and boys division advance to the state tourney.

The Bulldogettes take a 15-8 record into the game while the Waycross girls are 19-3.

Thomasville coach Guy Sullivan plans to start Anne Rumble, Joy Alligood and Susan Wine at forwards tonight and Betty Sue King, Janet Jones and Joyce Fletcher or Kathy Sollami.

Rumble is the leading scorer on the team with a 21-9 average. In the two sub-region games Rumble scored 30 points.

She hit 25 against Crisp County and only five in the Berrien contest.

Joy Alligood upped her average from 15.7 to 16.1 in the two sub-region games. Alligood scored 22 against Crisp and 17 in the Berrien game.

Wine is averaging 9.4 a game.

Vicki Cason paces the Waycross scoring with a 22.5 average. Christine Garner and Gail Baker are the other forward starters and handle most of the outside shooting for Waycross.

The Bulldogettes averaged better than 50 points a contest this season.

"Our guards are capable of holding Waycross under 45, so it's up to the forwards," Sullivan added.

In last night's action, the Bearcats and Bulldogs were deadlocked at 18-18 at the end of the first quarter.

Bainbridge pulled to a six-point 34-28 halftime lead and then romped to a 20-20 margin the third quarter to lead, 54-38.

Waycross managed to outpoint Bainbridge, 21-15, in the final period but could not get back into contention.

Waycross, now 19-4, made a sparkling comeback in the East sub-Region to win the title from Dudley Hughes. The Bulldogs trailed, 40-26, at halftime and finished the game with a 72-71 triumph.

"We shot well from the field," said Bainbridge coach Lynwood Mock. "We didn't play good defense and gave up too many easy shots."

The Bearcats did shoot well from the field with a 53 per cent mark from the field, hitting on 29 of 55 shots.

Rodger Robinson led the Bearcats' scoring with 16 points, Ivey Thigpen and James Spears each chipped in 14 points, Paul Boyd added eight and Jerry Boyett seven.

In the girls' game, Appling County took a 12-7 first quarter lead but the Berrien guards proved to be a little tough in the second quarter and shutout the Appling girls.

Berrien outscored Appling 11-0 in the second quarter and held an 18-12 margin at halftime.

The Rebelettes then romped to a 28-16 second half margin to post their 25th victory without a loss.

(Box Scores Omitted)

The Tifton Gazette, page 3, February 27, 1970

Girls Shine at Berrien

Special to Gazette

CORDELE – Berrien County High's boys hope tonight to join the school's girls in the Region 1AA Tournament basketball finals.

In Thursday night's activity here, the unbeaten girls rolled past Appling County, 46-28. Other play found the Bainbridge boys decisioning Waycross, 69-59.

By virtue of their victory, the Berrien girls qualified for Saturday night's finals. The boys can also gain a berth if they beat Dudley Hughes tonight in their 8:30 o'clock contest.

Tonight's 7 o'clock matinee will pit the Waycross girls against Thomasville. Berrien takes on the winner Saturday night for the title.

In the Berrien girls' triumph, Donna Jernigan led the attack with 20 points. Marla Brown and Grace Bailey contributed 13 each.

The tremendous defensive trio of Lenna Carey, Peggy Barber and Brenda Rudeseal held Appling scoreless in the second period. Berrien had trailed at the first quarter turn, 7-12, but the Rebelettes held an 18-12 intermission advantage and never trailed after that.

Beth Morris, who tallied 14 points, was the only Appling performer hitting in double digits.

In the boys' skirmish, Ivey Thigpen and Roger Robinson were the top guns for Bainbridge with 16 points each. Waycross' Harry Killens took game honors on a 19-point performance.

Girls' Game

Berrien (46)	Appling (28)
Brown 13	Morris 14
Jernigan 20	Snipes 9
Bailey 13	Leggett 5
Carey	Warren
Barber	McDonald
Rudeseal	Ballenger

Berrien subs – Carter, Mathis, Harrell, Swain. Appling subs – None.

Berrien	7	18	34	46
Appling	12	12	20	28

Berrien: field goals, 17; free throws, 12-17; personal fouls, 7. Appling: field goals, 11; free throws, 6-10; personal fouls, 12.

Boys' Game

Bainbridge (69)	Waycross (59)
Robinson 16	Stovall 8
Nelson 10	Killens 19
Thigpen 16	Dubberly 4
Boyd 8	Jackson 13
Boyett 7	Moore

Bainbridge subs: Speers (12), Love. Waycross subs – Gail (6), Wells (4), Miller (5), Young, Lee.

Bainbridge: field goals, 29; free throws, 11-18; personal fouls, 14. Waycross: field goals, 25; free throws, 9-21; personal fouls, 13.

The Valdosta Daily Times, page 13, February 27, 1970

Berrien's Sextet Gains 1-AA Finals

Special to the Times

CORDELE – Berrien's Rebelettes and Bainbridge's Bearcats took opening round victories in the Region 1-AA high school basketball playoffs here Thursday night to assure themselves a berth in the finals Saturday.

Coach Stanley Simpson's Rebelettes kept their record unblemished by surging ahead in the second quarter and staying there for a 46-28 victory over Appling County (Baxley). The 'Cats went ahead in the second quarter and posted a 69-59 win over Waycross' Bulldogs.

Tonight, Waycross' Bulldogettes take on Thomasville's Bulldogettes at 7 p.m. in a girls game while Simpson's Berrien Rebels take on Dudley Hughes of Macon at 8:30 p.m. in a boys contest in the Crisp County high gym.

The winners of all first-round games earn seats in the finals and berths in the state Class AA playoffs as either region champions or runners-up.

At the end of the first quarter last night, Appling had a 12-7 lead. But in the second stanza Berrien forwards Marla Brown, Frances Jernigan and Grace Bailey picked up 11 more points, while Rebelette guards Lenna Carey, Peggy Barber and Brenda Rudeseal held Appling scoreless.

Jernigan got 20 points for the Rebelettes, followed by Brown and Bailey with 13 apiece. Ann Morris led the field for Appling with 16 points.

The victory brought the Rebelettes' undefeated record to 25-0, while the Appling girls are now through for the season with a 16-6 record.

The boys game was a nip-and-tuck affair for the first quarter but the Bearcats went ahead early in the second period. After that they never trailed again.

Roger Robinson and Ivey Thigpen turned in equal 16-point performances for Bainbridge, while Harry Killens paced the Bulldogs with 19.

The victory brought the 'Cats to a 16-9 record, while Waycross, the east section champ, is now out of the running with a 19-4 mark.

(Box Scores Omitted)

The Thomasville Times-Enterprise, page 6, February 28, 1970

Bulldogettes Eliminated From Region 1AA Tourney

By George Lassiter
T-E Sports Editor

CORDELE – "If you don't score there is no way to win," said Thomasville High girls' coach Guy Sullivan after his Bulldogettes were defeated by Waycross, 52-35, in the semifinals of the Region 1AA basketball tournament last night in the Crisp County gym.

In other action last night, Berrien County's Rebels advanced to the finals with a 60-48 triumph over Dudley-Hughes of Macon.

In tonight's Region finals Berrien County's Rebelettes take on Waycross girls at 7 in the Crisp gym and Bainbridge's Bearcats battle the Berrien boys at 8:30.

All four teams will advance to the state tournament.

It was the second straight game the Bulldogettes have failed to produce any points. In the sub-Region final against Berrien County the THS forwards managed only 27 points.

The Bulldogettes trailed three points at the end of the first quarter, 11-8.

Thomasville led 8-7 with 1:42 remaining in the period but Waycross regained the lead 30 seconds later and the Bulldogettes trailed the remainder of the contest.

In the second quarter Waycross rolled to a 14-8 margin behind the scoring of Vicki Cason.

Cason led the Waycross girls with 26 points – including 12 of the 14 in the second quarter.

The two teams exchanged two goals each before Cason dropped in two straight and Waycross held a 19-12 lead.

Anne Rumble scored for the Bulldogettes and Cason bombed in three long range set shots to give Waycross a 25-14 margin.

Rumble scored on a driving layup with eight seconds remaining until half to cut the Waycross lead to nine points, 25-16.

Waycross opened up the third quarter with a goal to up the leading margin to 11 points. Joy Alligood, Rumble and Susan Wine then began to cut the Waycross lead.

With 2:08 remaining in the third quarter Rumble scored after grabbing a rebound and was fouled.

Rumble hit the free throw to complete the three-point play. The Bulldogettes stole the ball and Rumble dropped in another goal to cut the deficit to five points, 33-28, with 1:52 left in the period.

But the Bulldogettes could not stop Cason and Gale Baker from scoring baskets in the final minute of the third quarter and Waycross held a nine point, 37-28, command going into the final quarter.

The Bulldogettes could not get back into the ball game and Waycross grabbed a big command after the THS girls had several fouls called attempting to steal the ball.

Gale Baker dropped in 18 points for Waycross while Christine Garner added eight points.

The Waycross girls shot 48 per cent from the field in the first half, hitting on 12 of 25 shots while the Bulldogettes dropped in 38 per cent of their attempts – connecting on eight of 21.

The winners managed 10 of 24 for 41 per cent in the second half while Thomasville hit only seven of 25 shots for 28 per cent.

Alligood paced the Bulldogettes with 15 points – 11 in the second half – Rumble added 12 and Wine eight.

The Bulldogettes finished the season with a 15-9 record and the Waycross girls are now 20-3.

The Berrien boys won their 25th straight game of the season last night.

George Sorrell paced the Rebels with 19 points, Bobby Taylor added 16 and Roger Guess 16.

The Rebels held an 11-9 first quarter and led four points at halftime, 25-21.

Berrien managed to add two points to the lead in the third quarter and led 40-34 going into the final period.

With three minutes remaining in the game the Rebels began to pull away as they outscored Dudley Hughes 20-14 in the fourth quarter.

The Berrien boys take a 25-0 record into tonight's game while Bainbridge is 16-9.

(Box Scores Omitted)

The Tifton Gazette, page 4, February 28, 1970

<u>Join School's Girls</u>

Berrien's Boys Set for Finals' Berth

Special to Gazette

CORDELE – Berrien County High's boys will be joining their school's girls in the Region 1-AA Tournament basketball finals here tonight.

The Berrien boys gained the finals with a 60-48 victory Friday night over Dudley Hughes. In other action, the Waycross girls easily turned back Thomasville, 52-35.

In tonight's finals, the Berrien girls take on Waycross at 7 o'clock. The 8:30 o'clock boys' contest matches Berrien and Bainbridge.

George Sorrell sparked the Berrien boys' victory over Dudley Hughes with 19 points. Bobby Taylor pitched in 16 and Roger Guess 11.

In the Dudley Hughes' cause, William Jordan scored 14 markers and Larry Willis 13.

Berrien gained an 11-9 first quarter lead and held 25-21 and 40-34 advantages after the next two turns.

Vicki Carson bucketed 23 points and Gale Baker 21 as Waycross displayed a tremendous one-two scoring punch. Joy Alligood netted 15 and Ann Rumble 12 for Thomasville.

Boys' Game				
Berrien (60)	**D. Hughes (48)**
Guess 11	Willis 13
Taylor 16	Raines 8
Tucker 6	Jordan 14
Wright 8	Henry 4
Sorrell 19	Outlaw 9

Berrien subs – Harnage. Dudley Hughes subs – None.

Berrien	11	25	40	60
D. Hughes	9	21	34	48

Berrien: field goals, 22; free throws, 16-29; personal fouls, 9. D. Hughes: field goals, 21; free throws, 6-12; personal fouls, 18.

Girls' Game	
Waycross (52)	**Thomasville (35)**
Carson 23	Rumble 12
Garner 8	Wine 8
G. Baker 21	Alligood 15
Miles	King
B. Baker	Jones
Williams	Sollami

Waycross subs – None. Thomasville subs – None.

Waycross	11	25	37	52
Thomasville	8	16	28	35

Waycross: field goals, 22; free throws, 8-20; personal fouls, 12. Thomasville: field goals, 15; free throws, 5-11; personal fouls, 14.

The Valdosta Daily Times, page 10, February 28, 1970

Berrien's Quintet In Region Finals

Special to the Times

CORDELE – The Berrien Rebels became the second Nashville, Ga., team to reach the finals of the Region 1-AA high school basketball playoffs by defeating Dudley Hughes of Macon, 60-48 here Friday night.

In girls division action, Waycross' Bulldogettes overpowered the Thomasville's Bulldogettes, 52-35 to earn their seat in the finals.

Coach Stanley Simpson's Rebels joined the Rebelettes, also coached by Simpson in the game winning streaks. The girls championship action tonight. Both Nashville teams own 25-game winning streaks. The girls are still undefeated this season with a 25-0 slate while the boys are 25-1.

The Rebelettes are now scheduled to put their record on the line against Waycross' girls, who are 20-3, in the championship game at 7 o'clock tonight. Then the Rebels are scheduled to go against sub-region runners-up, Bainbridge's Bearcats at 8:30 p.m. in the Crisp County High gym.

The Rebs defeated the 'Cats, 65-45, in the west sub-region championship game in Thomasville last week.

In last night's action, Berrien took an 11-9 lead coming out of the opening quarter and expanded it the rest of the game.

George Sorrell scored 19 points to lead the Rebs followed by Bobby Tucker, 16, and Roger Guess 11. William Jordan and Larry Willis led the way for Dudley Hughes with 14 and 13 points respectively.

In the girls game, Vickie Carlson and Gail Baker got 23 and 21 points respectively to lead the Waycross girls. Joyce Alligood and Ann Rumble scored 15 and 12 points respectively, while Susan Wine added the other eight for Thomasville.

Thomasville's girls and Dudley's boys are now through for the season. The Bulldogettes go out with a 15-9 mark while Dudley leaves, 18-4.

Regardless of the outcome of tonight's games all four teams in the 1-AA finals will advance into the Class AA playoffs.

(Box Scores Omitted)

March 1970

The Berrien Press, front page, February 26, 1970

Calendar Girl For March

The Berrien High School Rebels play Dudley Hughes of Macon and the Rebelettes battle Appling County in the opening round of the Region 1-AA playoff in Cordele this week. Guard Lenna Carey, The Berrien Press Calendar Girl for March, checks the roadmap to the tourney town – and the map also shows the way to Atlanta where the state finals will be held next week. A senior at Berrien High, Lenna has played guard on the varsity for three years after two years on the Enigma team. She is vice-president of the B Club and a member of the tennis team, Pep Club and Senior Tri-Hi-Y. She is the daughter of Mrs. Louise Cranford of Enigma.

The Tifton Gazette, page 3, March 2, 1970

Berrien Has Two Crowns

Special to Gazette

CORDELE – Berrien County boasts a pair of Region 1-AA Tournament championships following play here Saturday night.

The unbeaten Berrien girls racked up their 26th victory by taking the measure of Waycross, 41-35. The boys followed with a near identical 41-36 score over Bainbridge.

All four finalists will compete in State AA activity. Both Berrien teams face Lakeshore squads which finished as Region 2-AA runners-up.

The Berrien boys play either Friday or Saturday at a time and place to be announced. The girls go next week.

Ironically, both Berrien teams trailed at the first quarter turns. However, they rebounded in fine style.

"We didn't shoot the ball well at all," Berrien Coach Stanley Simpson said of his boys' victory. "We had already beaten them three times (two 20-point victories and once by 17), but Bainbridge changed their plans a little … They defensed us differently, and they had a little different attack."

Simpson, who also guides the Berrien girls, praised, "Our defensive people … particularly Peggy Barber and Lenna Carey … did a tremendous job. Grace Bailey took hold on the offensive end … They (Waycross) played (Marla) Brown and (Donna) Jernigan real tough."

Bailey was the game's leading scorer with 24 points. Gail Baker scored 18 to pace Waycross.

*****

Girls' Game		Boys' Game	
Berrien (41)	**Waycross (35)**	**Berrien (41)**	**Bainbridge (36)**
Bailey 24	Cason 15	Guess 6	Robinson 11
Jernigan 12	Garner 2	B. Taylor 9	Nelson 2
Brown 5	G. Baker 18	Sorrell 12	Thigpen 16
Carey	Miles	Tucker 2	Boyd 5
Barber	D. Baker	Wright 7	Spears 2
Rudeseal	Williams		

Berrien subs – Carter. Waycross subs – None.

Berrien subs – W. Taylor (5). Bainbridge subs – None.

Berrien	8	21	32	41
Waycross	11	14	21	35

Berrien	7	14	32	41
Bainbridge	12	20	27	36

Berrien: field goals, 18; free throws, 5-10; personal fouls, 12. Waycross: field goals, 15; free throws, 5-14; personal fouls, 10.

Berrien: field goals, 13; free throws, 15-18; personal fouls, 12. Bainbridge: field goals, 13; free throws, 10-15; personal fouls, 13.

The Valdosta Daily Times, page 11, March 2, 1970

Berrien Is Ruler in 1-AA Playoffs

Special to the Times

CORDELE – Berrien's Rebels and Rebelettes proved they were the best Class AA basketball teams in this section by capturing both ends of the Region 1-AA playoffs here Saturday night, and now they're going after the state crowns.

Coach Stanley Simpson's Rebelettes handed Waycross' Bulldogettes 41-35 licking which his Rebels defeated Bainbridge for the fourth time this season, 41-36, in the playoff finals.

The victories bring the winning streaks of both Nashville, Ga., teams to 26 games. The girls are still undefeated at 26-0 while the Rebs own a 26-1 mark. They are scheduled to take on Lakeshore High teams from College Park in the first round of the state playoffs.

In Saturday's girls game, the Bulldogette guards went after Berrien's two top scoring forwards, Frances Jernigan and Marla Brown, holding them to 12 and 5 points respectively. But they didn't figure on the third member of the trio, Grace Bailey, who celebrated by pumping in 24 points.

The Waycross sextet carried an 11-8 lead into the second quarter, but while the Berrien forwards were hitting 13 points, guards Lenna Carey, Peggy Barber and Brenda Rudeseal stopped the Bulldogette forwards almost cold, holding them to only three points to give the Nashville girls a 21-14 lead at the half.

Berrien managed to keep this distance for the rest of the game.

Gail Baker and Vickie Cason led the way for the Waycross girls with 18 and 15 points respectively.

Some nifty shooting at the free-throw line proved (to) be the deciding factor in the Rebels' 41-36 victory over Bainbridge's Bearcats.

Both teams totaled 13 field goals, but Berrien sank 15 of its 18 free throws while the Bearcats hit only 10 of 15 to make the difference in the final totals.

The Bearcats of coach Lynwood Mock took a 20-14 lead into the second half, but again the Berrien offense and defense stepped in to change things.

The Rebels picked up 18 points while allowing only seven in the third stanza to take a 32-27 lead and kept that margin for the rest of the game.

George Sorrell was the only Rebel in double figures with 12 points while Ivey Thigpen led the Bearcats with 16 points.

The Bainbridge boys (16-10) and Waycross girls (20-4), as 1-AA runners-up, also advance into the state Class AA playoffs.

(Box Scores Omitted)

Photo Caption:
Peggy Barber grabs a rebound and pushes the ball down toward the offensive end of the court in Berrien's 41-35 win over Waycross in the Region 1-AA final.

The Waycross Journal-Herald, page 6, Monday, March 2, 1970

Berrien Cops 1-AA Cage Titles; Bulldogettes Lose

CORDELE – Berrien County's defense-minded basketball teams notched twin championships here Saturday night in the finals of the Region 1-AA tournament.

Coach Stanley Simpson's Berrien sextet displayed unusual accuracy from the field to best Waycross girls 41-35 in a game marked by excellent defensive play.

Simpson's Rebel quintet rallied from a halftime deficit to defeat Bainbridge 41-36.

ALL FOUR teams enter state tournament sectional playoffs next week.

Berrien girls face the Lakeshore-South Fulton loser and Waycross meets that playoff winner. Berrien boys battle the Lakeshore-Newnan Central loser and Bainbridge the winner.

Neutral sites near the homes of the winners will be named for the playoffs.

Sectional winners gain berths in the state tournament quarter-finals in Atlanta.

SIX OF THE finest guards in South Georgia showed a near-capacity crowd here Saturday night how defense is supposed to be played.

Lenna Carey, Peggy Barber and Brenda Rudeseal of Berrien threw up a defense that stymied Waycross' offense. Miss Barber turned in one of the finest individual defensive exhibitions seen in South Georgia in many years, sticking like a leach to Vicki Cason all evening.

Dale Baker, Brenda Gaile Miles and Ava Williams were just as tough for the Bulldogettes. Miss Baker held Berrien's Marla Brown scoreless in the first half and Miss Williams was almost as effective in the last half although the usual scoring leader for the Rebelettes got open for two field goals during the final 14 minutes of action.

Miss Miles checked Donna Jernigan of Berrien on 12 points for the evening, another brilliant guarding job.

But while the defense was stopping two of the Berrien sharp-shooters, Grace Bailey was leading the Rebelettes to the victory.

Berrien hit 18 of 31 field goals in a fine exhibition of shooting for 58 per cent of their floor shots. Waycross, kept off balance most of the evening by the Berrien defense, connected on 33.3 per cent, getting 15 of 45 from the field.

THE Bulldogettes regained the lead at 7-6 but Berrien scored to take an 8-7 edge. Waycross then scored twice as Cason and Gale Baker tallied to make it 11-8 for the Bulldogettes at the end of the initial stanza.

Jernigan and Bailey each hit two apiece from the field at the start of the second period and Berrien raced ahead 16-11 as Waycross could not find the basket. The Rebelettes led 21-14 at halftime.

Berrien widened the gap to 11 points early in the third quarter and led 32-21 at the start of the final canto. Waycross pulled to within six points at 39-33 with 1:21 left but that was the final margin as Berrien won 41-35.

Miss Bailey's 24 points took game honors for Berrien. Gale Baker bagged 18 to pace Waycross and Miss Cason added 15. Christine Garner led in offensive rebounds as Waycross out-rebounded Berrien 22-18.

UPSET MINDED Bainbridge boys, losers to Berrien three times previously this year including a 20-point setback in the Subregion finals, led the Rebels for more than two periods here Saturday.

The Bearcats led 12-7 after the first period and were out front 20-14 in the low-scoring affair by halftime. An 18-7 scoring edge in the third stanza gave Berrien a 32-27 lead at the three-quarter mark and the Rebels matched baskets with the Bearcats in the last eight minutes to win 41-36.

Accuracy at the charity line gave Berrien the victory. Both teams shot 13 field goals but Berrien was 15 of 18 at the foul stripe to 10 of 16 for Bainbridge. The Bearcats led in rebounding 28-27.

George Sorrell led Berrien with 12 points and Ivey Thigpen had 16 for Bainbridge.

(Box Scores Omitted)

The Tifton Gazette, page 5, March 4, 1970
<u>Boys Face Lakeshore</u>

Berrien Has Friday Game

By Staff Writer

Berrien County High will compete in the State AA boys' sectional play Friday night against Lakeshore at Cordele, 8 o'clock.

The Berrien and Atkinson girls, the only other two Tiftarea basketball-playing representatives still surviving, do not go in state sectional play until next week.

Abraham Baldwin College will host doubleheader State AAA girls' sectional action Friday night. Lowndes faces Ballard-Hudson at 7 o'clock, with Warner Robins playing Monroe of Albany at 8:30 o'clock.

Berrien's boys enter the Friday night competition at Cordele as the Region 1-AA champion. Lakeshore is the Region 2-AA runner-up.

The Friday night survivist (survivalist) will be among eight teams competing for state AA honors March 12-14 in Atlanta.

Ironically, the Berrien girls – who also claim a Region 1-AA crown – will also be facing Lakeshore, the Region 2-AA runnerup.

The Georgia High School Association has not determined the date and site of their next week's collision.

Meanwhile, the Atkinson girls lay claim to the Region 2-A crown. They will be playing region 1-B runnerup Mitchell County at a date and site to be announced.

Lowndes recently captured the Region 1-AAA Tournament championship at the Tift County High gymnasium. Monroe of Albany took the runnerup position.

Warner Robins claims the Region 2-AAA crown. Ballard-Hudson finished in the No. 2 spot.

The Valdosta Daily Times, page 16, March 4, 1970

Berrien, Clinch Get Playoff Info

By Times Staff Writer

Two more area teams, the Berrien Rebels and Clinch County Panthers, have received the word on when and where they will be playing state basketball playoff games this weekend.

Dates and sites for all state playoff games are selected by the Georgia High School Association.

Coach Stanley Simpson's Rebels from Nashville, Ga., are to face the Lakeshore (College Park) Lancers in a game set for 8 p.m. Friday at the Crisp County High gym in Cordele.

The Rebs, who have a 26-1 record, are the champions from Region 1-AA, while the Lancers, who have a 21-5 mark, are the runners-up from 2-AA.

Also on Friday coach Austin DeLoach's Clinch Panthers from Homerville will be coming here to meet the Seminole County Indians from Donalsonville.

Clinch, the Region 2-B runner-up, and Seminole, the 1-B victor, are to meet at 7 p.m. here at the gym on the Valdosta Junior High campus.

The Clinch-Seminole tilt will be the first game of a twin-bill. At 8:30 p.m., the 2-B title-holder Blackshear is to meet 1-B runner-up Pelham.

Earlier it was announced that Lowndes' Vikettes and Ballard-Hudson's Tigerettes from Macon are to clash at 7 p.m. at the Abraham Baldwin (Junior) College gym at Tifton. The Vikettes are the Region 1-AAA winners, while Ballard-Hudson is the runner-up from 2-AAA.

On Saturday Georgia Christian School's Generals, the newly crowned Region 1-C champs, are to face Calhoun County (Edison), the 2-C runner-up at 7 p.m. at the Westover High gym at Albany.

Winners of all playoff games will continue in state tourney competition in their respective classifications.

[Compiler's note: Typesetting errors in the article were corrected here.]

The Berrien Press, front page, March 5, 1970

Berrien Basketball Teams Advance to State

By Tim Moore

The Berrien County Rebels and Rebelettes continued to roll on as they made their latest "waves" this past Saturday night when they took two almost identical wins from the Waycross Bulldogettes and the Bainbridge Bearcats.

The Rebelettes got into the finals at the expense of the Appling County girls team Thursday night. They had a rough time in the first half of the game as they were behind 7-12 at the end of the first quarter, and had only a six-point lead at half time; but they pulled farther and farther ahead in the final half to slip by Appling, and into the finals by the score of 46-28.

Donna Jernigan led Berrien's scoring with 20 points. Marla Brown and Grace Bailey both added 13 points to aid them in their victory. Berrien's guards were Lenna Carey, Peggy Barber, Brenda Rudeseal, and Andrea Carter.

The Rebels slapped a 60-48 defeat on the Dudley-Hughes Wolverines Friday night to put them in the finals the following night. The Rebels led the entire game, but didn't get more than a 10-point lead until late in the fourth quarter. Sorrell took Berrien's high score honors with 19 points, and also snagged 15 rebounds. Bobby Taylor added 16 points, Guess 11, Wright eight, and Tucker six.

In the finals Saturday night, the Rebelettes upset the Waycross Bulldogettes 41-35, followed by the Rebels putting Bainbridge down, 41-36.

Grace Bailey netted 24 points for Berrien's high score of the night. Jernigan added 12 points and Brown five. Berrien's defenders were Carey, Barber, Rudeseal, and Carter.

The Rebels won their first-place marble with George Sorrell leading the way with 12 points and 11 rebounds. Bobby Taylor made nine points, Wright made seven and got ten rebounds, Guess made six, Wayne Taylor five and Tucker two.

These wins put both Berrien teams in the first round of the State tournament with both Lakeshore teams.

The Berrien Press, front page, March 5, 1970

State Play Off Basketball Game

1AA winner Berrien County High School will play 2AA loser, Lakeshore, of College Park, Friday night, March 6 at 8 p.m. in Cordele. Admission will be $1.00.

The winner of this game will play the winner of the Carver-Murphy game in Atlanta, at Georgia Tech Coliseum on Thursday, March 12 at 4:30 p.m. this will be a game in the state quarter finals.

The Tifton Gazette, page 3, March 5, 1970

Face Lakeshore

Berrien Set for Toughie

By Doug Hawley
Gazette Sports Editor

From all indications, Berrien County can expect a titanic struggle in its State AA Tournament sectional game Friday night.

Berrien will be taking on Lakeshore in the Friday activity at Cordele. The contest is ticketed for an 8 p.m. start.

Lakeshore, a College Park school of the Atlanta area, took third in last year's State AA Tournament. Only champion Carver of Atlanta and Brown finished higher.

Back from that team are three full-time starters. A fourth member saw part-time starting duty last year.

"I would think we're about equal (to last year)," Lakeshore Coach John Vaughn has told the Gazette. "We just try to stay in there and battle."

Lakeshore visits Cordele with a 21-5 record, two of the defeats coming by one point. No team has beaten the College Park representative more than six points.

The North Georgia team has excellent height with the likes of Johnny Lowe (6-3), Willie Reeves (6-3) and Steve Foster (6-6). The backcourt performers are Charlie Fleming (5-10) and Chucke Fowke (5-10).

Stanley Simpson, the Berrien head coach – who has seen Lakeshore play – observes, "They try to run the basketball … They don't run as much as some times … but they play together better as a team than a lot of ballclubs who run." Defensively, the opposition employs primarily a "pressing game," and it also uses a 1-3-1 zone.

"This may be the strongest AA field ever," Simpson says. "It boils down to the effort." We realize it will take our best effort."

In Berrien's bracket, the rivals include defending state champion Carver and perennial power Newton County.

If Berrien can hurdle Region 2-AA runnerup Lakeshore, it will then enter further State AA competition at Georgia Tech's Alexander Dome in Atlanta Mar. 12-14.

Berrien would play an opening day against the Carver-Murphy winner. That contest has a 4:30 p.m. tipoff.

Simpson's Rebels seemingly have the potential to ride the rough storm. The Region 1-AA champions have posted 26 consecutive victories since an opening game loss to Tift County.

Surprisingly, forward George Sorrell (6-5) is the only Rebel averaging in double figures at 17 per outing. However, the disciplined team – which has been hitting 46 per cent of its field goal attempts – does not shoot a lot.

Berrien is averaging 52.2 points per contest. The sticky defense, which has been instrumental in the great record to date, shows a mere 39.6 record.

Sorrell and center Charles Wright (6-5) provide a tremendous one-two rebounding punch. Guards Bobby Taylor (6-0) and Roger Guess (6-0), together with forward Richard Tucker (6-2) are all consistent performers.

Photo caption:
AWAIT STATE OPENER – George Sorrell (left), Berrien County's leading scorer, awaits with Coach Stanley Simpson the sectional State AA Tournament game Friday night against Lakeshore at Cordele. (Staff Photo).

The Valdosta Daily Times, page 20, March 5, 1970
Berrien, Lancers Meet at Cordele
By Times Staff Writer

NASHVILLE, Ga. – The basketball fur is sure to fly when Berrien's Rebels and the Lakeshore Lancers hook up in a state Class AA boys basketball playoff game at Cordele on Friday night.

Coach Stanley Simpson's Rebs, the Region 1-AA champs, will carry a 26-1 record into the all-important duel. All of their triumphs have come in a row.

Coach John Vaughn's Lancers from College Park, the 2-AA runner-up, have a 21-5 mark. They finished third in the 1968-69 state "AA" tourney and are well stocked with returning regulars from that team.

Tomorrow night's meeting between the Rebs and Lancers is slated for 8 p.m. at the Crisp County High gym in Cordele. The winner will join seven other playoff victors at Atlanta on March 12 for the start of three days of tourney action which will decide this year's state Class AA championship.

With a balanced attack, the Rebs have been averaging 52.2 points a game this year. But it has been Berrien's amazing defense which has been the major factor in the Rebs' run of success. They've limited 27 foes to an average of just 39.6 points per game.

The Rebels probable starters, according to Simpson, are Roger Guess (6-0, jr.), Bobby Taylor (6-0, jr.), Charles Wright (6-5, jr.), George Sorrell (6-5, jr.) and Richard Tucker (6-2, sr.).

Lakeshore's probable starters are Johnny Lowe (6-2, sr.), Willie Reeves (6-0, jr.), Steve Foster (6-6, jr.), Charlie Flemming (5-10, sr.) and Chuck Fawke (5-10, jr.). The Lancers' top gun is Lowe, who is averaging 19 markers per outing.

Berrien's Rebelettes also swept to the Region 1-AA girls title. They own a perfect 26-0 record. Next week they'll be meeting the Lakeshore sextet in the playoffs on a date and at a site which hasn't been determined yet.

The Tifton Gazette, page 3, March 6, 1970

Berrien Plays Lakeshore

By Johnny Futch
Special to Gazette

NASHVILLE – Down in the pine flats, where the streets roll up at 6 p.m. and the thrill of the week is watching "Hee Haw," the lure of the city lights can be mighty strong.

Ramrod Simpson and his Berrien High Rebels are hoping to get a look at those city lights and a shot at the Georgia State AA title, but first they have to get past tough Lakeshore of College Park this weekend in the first round of the state tourney.

A victory over Lakeshore would give the Rebs a chance to plead their case for deliberate, defensive basketball before Atlanta audiences. The at large game between Berrien and the Lancers, the runners-up from 2-AA , is set for 8 p.m. Friday at Crisp County High School in Cordele.

Simpson's Rebels don't mind the country cousin role in state basketball – the kids from Alapaha and Nashville and Enigma and other exotic points of interest in Berrien County already own South Georgia.

After a 45-46 false start against AAA Tift County in the opener, the Rebs went on to win 26 straight including three victories over 1-AAA champion Valdosta, a pair of wins over 1-A champ Cairo and an unblemished region record. On the way they picked up championship trophies at the Lowndes-Hahira Invitational Tournament, the 1-AA (West) Tournament and the 1-AA meet.

"It'll take one of our best efforts to get by Lakeshore," said Simpson, who figures there aren't any easy victories left. "They have one of the finest, fastest teams we'll see."

Lakeshore, playing in tough company, bowed to Central of Newnan in the 2-AA finals, 63-53. Central will meet Bainbridge, the runner-up from 1-AA.

Berrien got a look at the high-flying offense they'll have to stop at state when they met Dudley-Hughes in the first round of the region. Hughes, used to hitting in the 70-80 point range, could manage only 48 as Berrien won, 60-48.

The Rebel defense has been giving up an average of 38.9 points an outing while the offense has been putting them back in at a 53.5 pace.

Co-captain George Sorrell, a 6-5 center, has been the Rebel ringleader. Sorrell, a junior, is hitting 16.4 points a game and has been hauling down 15-plus rebounds.

Sorrell and his supporting cast – 6-5 Charles Wright, 6-2 co-captain Richard Tucker, 6-0 Bobby Taylor and 6-0 Roger Guess along with top subs David Harnage (6-2), Bobby Conway (6-0) and Wayne Taylor (5-10) – spread the scoring honors around and any player is capable of bombing an unwary opponent.

The last Rebel appearance in the state tournament came in 1968 when they finished third.

Meanwhile back at the gym, Simpson's undefeated Rebelettes will have to wait a week before they meet the Lakeshore ladies in the first round of the girls state AA tournament.

The Valdosta Daily Times, page 11, March 6, 1970

Area Teams See Tourney Action

By Times Staff Writer

Basketball teams from four area high schools are scheduled to take part in games at various sites tonight which will determine if they are to continue in the running for state titles.

That list includes the Lowndes Vikettes, Berrien (Nashville, Ga.) Rebels, Clinch County (Homerville) Panthers and Hamilton County (Jasper, Fla.) Rebels.

Coach Steve Kebler's Lowndes Vikettes, who rule as the Region 1-AAA champs and own a 20-5 record, are to meet the Ballard-Hudson Tigerettes from Macon in a game slated for 7 p.m. at the Abraham Baldwin (Junior) College gym at Tifton. Ballard-Hudson, the runner-up from 2-AAA, has a 6-4 mark.

The winner will move onto Thomaston on March 12 where the final three rounds of the state Class AAA girls tourney are to be played on consecutive nights.

At the Crisp County High gym in Cordele tonight coach Stanley Simpson's Berrien Rebels have an 8 p.m. basketball date with the Lakeshore (College Park) Lancers. The Rebs are the boys champs from Region 1-AA and own a 26-1 record. The Lancers are the runners-up from 2-AA and have a 21-5 mark.

Next stop for the winner will be Atlanta on March 12 where the three-day showdown for the state Class AA boys championship will begin.

This section's four most successful Class B quintets are to take part in a playoff double-header slated here tonight at the Valdosta Junior High gym. Coach Austin DeLoach's Clinch Panthers are to face the Seminole County (Donalsonville) Indians at 7 p.m. and Blackshear's Tigers are to duel Pelham's Hornets at 8:30 p.m.

The Panthers are 16-8 and were runners-up in the recent Region 2-B tourney. The Indians own the 1-B title and have an 18-8 record. Blackshear is 21-3 and Pelham has a 19-8.

The two teams which win here tonight will join six other playoff victors at Macon next week where the final three rounds of the state Class B tourney are to be played.

Coach Ray Rollyson's talented Rebels from Hamilton County will be at Daytona Beach tonight for the opening of the four-team duel for Florida's Region 2-B title and a berth in the state Class B tourney slated next week at Jacksonville.

The Tifton Gazette, page 3, March 7, 1970

Berrien Solves Lakeshore Press

By Johnny Futch
Special Correspondent

CORDELE – Berrien High's Rebels found the solution to Lakeshore's full court press puzzle at the free throw line here Friday night and spilled the Lancers' from College Park, 57-46, in the opening round of the State Class AA tournament.

And in Dublin, play began toward the state Class B and C titles. East Laurens defeated Vidalia 61-51 and Johnson County downed Reidsville 77-61 in first rounds of Class B play. Stratford Academy won a 78-66 decision over Bryan County and advanced to Class C quarterfinals.

The Rebel victory set up a meeting between Berrien and pre-tournament favorite Carver, a team that throttled Murphy, 114-77 in their tourney opener at 4:30 p.m. Thursday in Alexander Memorial Coliseum in Atlanta.

Lakeshore, runnerup from Region 2-AA and highly regarded in state circles, baffled Coach Ramrod Simpson's Rebels for a half and led by as much as 8 points midway in the second period as they pressured the Rebels all over the court.

Only the free throw and field shooting of Bobby Taylor, who picked up 10 of his 13 points in the first half, kept the Rebs in contention.

The Lancers led 26-24 at intermission, but the 6-5 duo of George Sorrell and Charles Wright took charge and dominated the boards and the scoring. Berrien then won going away.

Wright turned in a season-best 19 point performance and hauled down 13 rebounds. Sorrell took rebounding honors with 18 and chalked up 16 points with a perfect six-of-six from the floor.

The Rebels outrebounded Lakeshore 43-23, while allowing the Lancers only 17 of 64 shots from the floor, a miserable 26 per cent. Lakeshore usually hits in the high 70s.

Berrien could do very little right in the first half, as they turned the ball over 19 times.

Charles Fleming, who ended the evening with 12 points put together the Lancer attack to give Lakeshore a 26-19 edge just before the half.

Taylor hit for from the line. Sorrell dumped in a layup and Wright cashed two free throws to cut the deficit to 24-26 at the half.

Sorrell muscled in a layup with 29 seconds gone in the third period to tie the score at 26-26, but Lakeshore matched his next two field goals to tie the score again at 30-30.

Wright nearly broke the game open, pumping a pair of medium jumpers, Sorrell and Guess added a field goal each and Berrien led 38-32 at the end of the period.

Fleming and his buddies refused to roll-over and play dead and a Steve Foster jumper made it 40-40 with 6:03 left in the game.

Then foul problems caught up with the Lancers. Wright hit a looper, and Richard Tucker hit from the corner to give the Rebs a four-point lead and Lakeshore had to play catch up with 2:30 remaining.

Sorrell and Wright salted away the game at the line and ended things on a spectacular note as a Taylor shot bounced off Sorrell's hand into the basket as the buzzer sounded.

The win extended the Rebel victory string to 27 games after an opening loss to Tift County. Coach John Vaughn's Lancers went home 21-6 for the season.

Berrien (57)	Lakeshore (46)
Sorrell 16	Fleming 12
Tucker 3	Lowe 7
Guess 5	Foster 8
Wright 19	Reeves 9
Taylor 13	Fowke 4

Berrien subs: Taylor, W., Conway 1.
Lakeshore subs: Shaws 4, Lanham 2.

Berrien	12	24	38	57
Lakeshore	13	26	32	46

The Valdosta Daily Times, page 10, March 7, 1970

Berrien's Quintet Trips Up Lancers
Special to the Times

CORDELE – Berrien's Rebels earned themselves a coveted trip to Atlanta by handing Lakeshore's Lancers a 57-46 defeat in a state Class AA boys high school basketball playoff game here Friday night.

The victory brought coach Stanley Simpson's Rebels to a 27-1 record, with a 27-game winning streak, and earned them a seat in the quarter finals of the state tournament when action resumes next Thursday in Atlanta.

But for coach John Vaughn's Lancers, the defeat sent them to the sideline with a 21-6 record. The Lancers battled their way to the number three spot in the state during the 1968-69 season and returned four of five starters.

Charles Wright, George Sorrell and Bobby Taylor led the way for the Rebels with 19, 16 and 13 points respectively. Charlie Flemming was the leading scorer for the Lancers with 12 points and was the only Lakeshore player the tough Berrien defense allowed into double figures.

The Lancers took an early lead but a scoring surge in the second period chopped Lakeshore's lead to two points at 26-24 by the time intermission rolled around.

Berrien continued in high gear as the third period started, grabbed the lead and then stayed out front to the finish.

Berrien's Rebelettes, who own a 26-0 record, are also in the state Class AA playoffs as the girls champions from Region 1-AA.

They are still awaiting word on when and where they are to meet the Lakeshore girls in playoff action next week.

Individual scoring and team totals in the game here Friday night are as follows:

(Box Scores Omitted)

The Tifton Gazette, page 2, March 10, 1970

Berrien's Boys Tackle Defending State Champ
By Staff Writer

A tremendous challenge is on tap for the Berrien County boys Thursday in the State AA Tournament at Atlanta.

Berrien (27-1) faces defending State AA champion Carver of Atlanta (23-2) in Thursday's 4:30 p.m. game which kicks off three days of activity. Other opening play pits Sandy Springs (20-4) against Newton County (26-3), 6 p.m.; East Rome (24-3) vs. North Springs (20-5), 7:30 p.m.; East Atlanta (25-3) vs. Central of Newnan (22-1) 9 p.m.

If Berrien manages to take rugged Carver, it would then face the Sandy Springs-Newton victor in semi-final play Friday. The other two survivists also play that night.

There is championship action slated Saturday night. A consolation game will also be staged.

Meanwhile, the Berrien girls are making plans for State AA sectional play next Monday against Lakeshore at Vienna. This has an 8 o'clock tipoff.

The unbeaten Berrien girls reign as Region 1-AA champions. Lakeshore lays claim to the Region 2-AA runnerup spot.

The Valdosta Daily Times, page 10, March 10, 1970

Six Area Teams Still In Running
By Sammy Glassman
Times Sports Editor

After another week of fast-paced high school basketball action this area still has six teams in the running for state championships.

The cage outfits on this list are equally divided with three of them being boys teams and three of them sextets.

Let's take a look at them one at a time, see what they've done and consider what is in store for them in the immediate future.

We'll lead off with coach Steve Kebler's Lowndes Vikettes. They own a 21-5 record after winning the Region 1-AAA girls title and whacking down Ballard-Hudson of Macon, 52-40, in a first-round game of the state "AAA" playoffs this past Friday at Tifton.

They will move on to Thomaston on Thursday where the final three rounds of the State Class AAA girls meet are to be played on consecutive nights. In the quarter-finals the Vikettes are to face Cherokee (Canton) at 4:30 p.m. Cherokee is the defending state champion.

Coach Stanley Simpson's Berrien Rebels from Nashville, Ga., are 27-1. They've picked off the 1-AA (West) and 1-AA crown and last Friday beat Lakeshore (College Park), 57-46, in a first-round state playoff duel.

Their state tourney is to resume Thursday at the Alexander Memorial Coliseum in Atlanta with Berrien to face Carver (Atlanta) at 4:30 p.m.

GCS Going to Macon

Berrien's girls, who have a perfect 26-0 record, also rule as champs in 1-AA (West) and 1-AA. They are to meet 2-AA runner-up Lakeshore in a state Class AA playoff game slated for 8 p.m. Monday at Vienna.

At Dasher coach Jon Hazelip's Georgia Christian School Generals have a 20-4 mark and a 10-game victory streak going. They're the Region 1-C boys champs and whacked Calhoun County (Edison), 87-69, this past Friday at Albany in a state Class C playoff duel.

When the state "C" title competition resumes on Thursday at Macon's Coliseum, the Generals are to face Glascock County (Gibson), which has a 22-6 record, at noon.

Meanwhile, coach Angie Devivo's Lanier County (Lakeland) Bulldogettes are in the state Class C girls playoffs as the runner-up from 1-C.

Pulled Surprise

The Bulldogettes have a 12-11 record, but they pulled of one of the area's biggest surprises by knocking off Whigham's top-seed Squaws to reach the finals of the Region 1-C girls meet.

The Lanier sextet is to tackle Calhoun at 8:30 p.m. in the Westover High gym in Albany in a first-round state playoff duel.

Coach Ray Rollyson's Hamilton County (Jasper, Fla.) Rebels have a 10-game victory streak going, they own a 23-3 record and they've won the Suwanee Conference, District 5 and Region 2 tournament in Sunshine State competition.

Hamilton will be in the four-team field that will battle it out for Florida's state Class B crown this coming Friday and Saturday at Jacksonville.

It has been an amazingly successful season for prep cage teams in the area and as you can see, it isn't over yet.

The Tifton Gazette, Doug's Digest, page 4, March 11, 1970

This Lady Coach Humiliated Berrien Headmaster 'Ramrod'

Stanley (Ramrod) Simpson continually amazes those in the coaching fraternity and prep sports world.

While coaching the Berrien County varsity basketball boys and girls this year, Simpson has compiled an incredible 53-1 record.

The boys, who enter the State AA competition Thursday in Atlanta, have won one more game (27-1), but they also show the only loss. The girls are unbeaten (26-0).

Over the years, few coaches have gotten the best of Simpson. Yet, there's one who might have inflicted the worst defeat ever on a Ramrod-coached outfit.

Believe it or not, the shellacking was administered by a woman. Naturally, that can hardly help but hurt the pride of the "stronger sex" (?).

Actually, this occurred before Simpson came onto the scene for his legendary years at Berrien. He was practice teaching and coaching at Montgomery County in Mt. Vernon.

One of his duties there was coaching the girls' junior varsity basketball team. It seems that a school official decided in December, 1960, at the spur of the moment to have his team play Wheeler County from Alamo, a community just down the road.

Simpson relates that the lady coach, who was to administer such a sound licking, "brought a bunch of overaged girls … and also big girls. She beat me, 56-12."

The lanky Simpson interjected, "She didn't pull her first string. She left them in the whole game … It was 33-3 at one point."

This particular coach happened to be Betty Jean Simpson. Now, isn't that a coincidence – a woman coach with the same last name as the man victim?

In reality, that lady happens to be Stanley's wife. What was her husband's feeling on such a debacle?

"That's the last game she coached," Ramrod asserted. "I made a proposal to her … It was either to the kitchen or get out."

Mrs. Simpson will tell you that Stanley was only being a poor loser. Her girls just happened to be "better-coached."

Stanley added with tongue in cheek, "I guess it was three months later that I spoke to her." At the time, they lived in Wheeler County.

How does his wife react to his coaching these days?

"She's a typical fan," Ramrod discloses teasingly. "I can't please her."

Mrs. Simpson might be "a typical fan." Yet, how many basketball coaches can claim 1.000 records against Stanley (Ramrod) Simpson – by an average spread of 44 points?

The Tifton Gazette, page 4, March 11, 1970
State AA Boys' Tournament

Can Berrien Stop Defending Titlists?

By Doug Hawley
Gazette Sports Editor

To say that Berrien County has a stern test Thursday in the State AA boys' Tournament at Atlanta, would be putting it mildly.

Berrien takes on defending State AA champion Carver of Atlanta in the first of four games Thursday at the Alexander Dome, 4:30 p.m. What more formidable foe do you play than the reigning titlist?

"Their game is press and running," Berrien Coach Stanley Simpson was evaluating Tuesday. "I'm sure they'll try to play their game, and we'll try to play ours."

Simpson's "game" this year is a deliberate style offense. The formula has worked to the tune of 27 consecutive victories since an opening game upset loss to Tift County.

"If you beat Carver," Simpson pointed out, "No. 1, you've got to get it up the floor … No. 2, you've got to get it under the bucket."

Due to this full court press applied by Carver, the Berrien headmaster is understandably concerned about "setting up" on offense.

Offensively, the run-and-gun Carver team is averaging some 80 points per game. On numerous occasions, the team has exceeded the century mark.

Regarding the Carver personnel, Simpson noted, "They are real tough … probably they don't have the number of shooters that they had last year. It's more concentrated in two boys."

Supplying this major firepower are George Anderson (6-2) and Rabbit Hall (5-10) hitting at the rate of 26.7 and 21.6 points per game, respectively.

Simpson says that Carver Coach Calvin Jones utilizes three subs into the lineup for the equivalent of eight starters. This means that the team can run and gun from start to finish.

Jones' school has captured the State AA championship twice in the last three years. The "lean" season went as far as the State quarter-finals.

Berrien's probable starters include George Sorrell (6-5), Charles Wright (6-5), Richard Tucker (6-2), Bobby Taylor (6-0) and Roger Guess. The former has been the leader with 16 points and 15 rebounds per contest.

Following the Berrien-Carver contest Thursday the Georgia Tech gym will host Newton County vs. Sandy Springs, 6 p.m.; East Rome vs. North Springs, 7:30 p.m.; East Atlanta vs. Central of Carrollton, 9 p.m.

If Berrien can slip past Carver, it would go in Friday's semi-finals against the Newton-Sandy Springs winner.

Based on tradition, Newton would appear a slight favorite. Coach Ronald Bradley has posted an incredible 331-38 record in his 12 campaigns at that school.

There's little to choose among the eight teams record-wise. All possess loaded looks.

Berrien has a slightly better mark percentage-wise than the field at 27-1. However, it's minimal.

The other records include Central, 22-1; Newton, 25-2; Carver, 23-2; East Rome, 24-3; East Atlanta, 22-4; North Springs, 20-5; Sandy Springs, 18-5.

What are Berrien's chances against Carver and the star-studded field?

"These are the eight toughest 'AA' teams left in the state," Simpson informs. "It depends on who has the effort and the coolest head."

The Tifton Gazette, page 5, March 11, 1970
All-Tiftarea Cage Scholars
Undefeated Berrien Paces All-Academic
By Doug Hawley
Gazette Sports Editor

Those people who contend that athletics and academics do mix, can point with pride at the unbeaten Berrien County High girls' basketball team.

The Gazette's annual All-Academic Tiftarea basketball teams, which are exclusively for seniors, show five Berrien girls incredibly holding minimum high school four-year averages of 90.

The elite group includes Pat Williams, Andrea Carter, Peggy Barber, Sandra McMillan and Jo Ann Langford.

Three other Tiftarea girls' cagers join the elite '90' class. Included are Bonnie Evans and Glenna Taylor, both Tift County; Gail James, Worth County.

On the boys' scene, the squad has no school with more than one representative.

Heading the boys' team include Bill Thombs, Atkinson County; Riley Cates, Tift County; Bobby Tucker, Cook County; Gary Raines, Fitzgerald; Wade Monk, Worth County. All are in the '90' class except the latter who missed the charmed circle by only a fraction of a point.

In the girls' sector, Berrien's Williams and Tift's Evans have the highest recorded averages at 96 and 95.56, respectively. They rate the co-captain tags for the girls' All-Academic Tiftarea squad.

Atkinson's Thombs, 94.4, and Tift's Cates, 94.39, share the boys' spotlight as All-Academic Tiftarea co-captains.

Seniors gaining Honorable mention include (minimum high school averages of 80).
Girls
Tift – Bonnie Tucker and Mary Fordham; Berrien – Marla Brown, Mary Grace Bailey and Lenna Carey; Turner – Margaret Scott, Linda McSwain and Martha Woodard; Atkinson – Linda Sue Courson, Linda Sue Nugent and Sherry Boyd.
Boys
Tift – Edd Dorminey; Fitzgerald – Mike Abell and Bobby Stewart; Berrien – Jerry Slaughter and Richard Tucker; Worth – Keith Bridges.

The Valdosta Daily Times, page 17, March 11, 1970
Berrien, Carver in 'AA' Contest
By Times Staff Writer

NASHVILLE, Ga. – Berrien's Rebels are going to match their tough defense against the Carver Panthers' potent offense when they meet in a quarter-final round game of the state Class AA boys high school basketball tournament at Atlanta on Thursday.

The duel between coach Stanley Simpson's Rebs and coach Calvin Jones's Panthers from Atlanta is set for 4:30 p.m.

It will be one of four quarter-final round games on tap that day at Georgia Tech's Alexander Memorial Coliseum. In other action, Sandy Springs (Atlanta) is to face Newton County (Covington) at 6 p.m.; East Rome is to duel North Springs (Atlanta) at 7:30 p.m. and East (Atlanta) is to meet Central (Newnan) at 8:30 p.m.

The semi-finals are slated for Friday with a consolation game and the championship battle on tap for Saturday.

Carver's Panthers are the defending state champions and have won the "AA" crown twice in the last three seasons. Currently they are the 6-AAA champs, own a 25-2 record and spanked Murphy (Atlanta), 114-77 in a first round playoff duel last week. For the season Carver has been averaging better than 80 points a game.

Berrien's last appearance in the state tourney was in 1968 and the Rebels finished third that time. Currently, they have a 27-1 record, rule as the 1-AA (West) and 1-AA champs, and beat Lakeshore (College Park), 57-46 in a first round game last Friday at Cordele.

While the Rebs have a smooth-working and balanced attack, defense is their strong suit. They've limited their foes to an average of 38.2 points a game this season.

Berrien's probable starters are Roger Guess (6-0, jr.), Bobby Taylor (6-0, jr.), Charles Wright (6-5, jr.), George Sorrell (6-5, jr.), and Richard Tucker (6-2, sr.). Sorrell, who has been averaging about 17 points a game, is the leading scorer.

Carver's probable starters are George Anderson (6-2, sr.), Claude Williams (5-11, sr.), Robert Taylor (6-2, sr.), Michael Lupoe (5-8, sr.), and Michael Hall (6-4, jr.).

Anderson is averaging 26.7 points a game and Williams has been averaging 21 markers per tilt. In their opening playoff duel against Murphy last week Anderson poured in 56 points.

The Berrien Press, front page, March 12, 1970
<u>**Today In Atlanta**</u>

Rebels Face Carver in State Basketball
By Johnny Futch

Folks in Berrien County are fanatics about their basketball, and who can blame them.

After all, their Rebels, who meet Carver of Atlanta at 4:30 Thursday afternoon in Atlanta in the quarterfinals of the state class AA tournament, are easy to become a fanatic about.

The Rebs, who sometimes play like a dribbling disaster area, still manage, like the heroes in a Saturday afternoon matinee, to snatch victory from the jaws of defeat consistently. Consistently enough, that is, for a 27-1 record.

Take their opening round bout in state against Lakeshore last week, for example. Berrien, true to form, blew an early six-point lead and went down eight midway the second quarter.

The Lancers should have blown them out of the gym, but that's not the way it works. The cavalry, better known as Charles Wright and George Sorrell, came to the rescue and while the fans howled with glee, the Rebels put Lakeshore out of their misery, 57-46, and sent the Lancers home muttering something about being glad baseball season had arrived.

Things will be different when the Rebels meet Carver as Berrien coach Ramrod Simpson sadly realizes. The days of cat-and-mouse end when his team collides with a quintet the caliber of Calvin Jones'.

"We just can't make the mistakes we made against our last two or three opponents and get away with it," Simpson moaned. "Bobby Taylor kept us in it early against Lakeshore and Charles and George bailed us out but we're going to have to get more balanced scoring to have a chance against Carver."

Carver will feature the high-tension pressing defense that Lakeshore rattled the Rebs with, except more so.

"We made too many turnovers against Lakeshore – gave them too many opportunities to score – and Carver won't mind taking advantage of gifts like that," he continued.

The Carver-Berrien game is billed as high-powered offense against stingy defense, the proverbial irresistible force meeting the immovable object. Carver consistently hits around 100 points; the Rebels are only giving up 39 a game.

Simpson figures the winner will be the team that forces their opponent out of their normal game pattern.

"We're going to have to make them come to us and we're going to have to play a nearly perfect floor game to stay with them," he said, laying out a tall order for his Rebels.

"We'll have to put it all together," he added, "or we'll be coming home Friday."

While the Rebels wait for Carver, Simpson's undefeated Rebelettes are looking for a shot at Lakeshore's ladies. The first-round girls' AA state tourney is set for 8 p.m. Monday at Vienna. The winner goes on to Atlanta later in the week for the remaining three rounds.

[Compiler's note: The article repeated the boys' team picture that appeared in the January 15, 1970 edition.]

The Berrien Press, front page, March 12, 1970
Berrien Wins In First Round
By Tim Moore

The Berrien High Rebels used free throws to stay in the game the first half and then throttled through the second to down 2-AA's runner-up, Lakeshore, this past Friday night.

After faltering the first half, the Rebels came back in the second and outrebounded Lakeshore 25-11 and outscored them 33-20. Their final decision against them was 57-46.

Charles Wright, with his season's high score, sparked the Rebels on by dumping in 19 points and jerking down 13 rebounds. George Sorrell bucketed 16 points and snagged 18 rebounds and Bobby Taylor netted 13 points.

With their record standing at 27-1, the Rebels will face Carver, of Atlanta, in the second round of AA State Tournament Thursday, March 12, in Atlanta at 4:30 p.m.

The Rebelettes begin their play in the State Tournament Monday, March 16, in Vienna at 8 p.m.

The Thomasville Times-Enterprise, Sports Line, by George Lassiter, page 8, March 12, 1970
Berrien Makes Bid
Teams from Region 1AA, 1B and 1C open bids in State Basketball tournaments tonight.

Berrien County – The Regional 1AA champion – takes on last year's defending champion, Atlanta Carver, at Alexander Memorial Coliseum on the Georgia Tech campus in Atlanta at 4:30 p.m.

The Berrien Rebels take a 27-1 record into the state tournament. The Rebs lost their opener to Tifton, then rolled to 27 consecutive victories.

In the first round of the State AA Tournament last week in Cordele, Berrien romped over Lakeshore of Atlanta, 57-46.

Berrien has the best record in the tournament. Newton County has a 25-2 mark, East Rome 24-3, Central Newnan 22-1, Carver 23-2, East Atlanta 22-4, Sandy Springs 18-5 and North Springs 20-5.

Carver is the Region 6AA champion and blasted Murphy in the first round of the state, 114-77. Carver is known as "The King of the Runners" in Georgia basketball.

[Compiler's note: The rest of the article was about the other teams and was not reprinted here.]

The Valdosta Daily Times, page 24, March 12, 1970
Area Cage Teams in State Meets
By Times Staff Writer

Three area teams, the Lowndes Vikettes, Georgia Christian School Generals and Berrien Rebels, were slated to take part in state basketball tournament contests at various sites today.

Coach Jon Hazelip's Generals from Dasher had a game scheduled for noon with the Glascock County (Gibson) Panthers in the state Class B boys tourney at Macon.

At 4:30 p.m. coach Steve Kebler's Lowndes Vikettes were to meet the Cherokee (Canton) Warriorettes in the girls state Class AAA tourney at Thomaston.

Also, at 4:30 p.m., coach Stanley Simpson's Berrien Rebels from Nashville, Ga., were to face the Carver (Atlanta) Panthers in a state Class AA tourney match in Atlanta.

All of the games involving the area teams were quarter-final round tilts.

The Vikettes, bidding for their first state "AAA" sports champion, are the Region 1-AAA title-holders and have a 21-5 record. The Cherokee team the(y) were to face today at Thomaston has a 20-4 record. It is the defending state Class AAA girls champion and has ruled that division three times in the last four years.

The Generals have a 20-4 record and rule as Region 1-C champions. The Glascock team they were to face at Macon today has a 22-6 record and reached the semi-finals in the 1968-69 state "C" tourney.

Berrien's Rebels own a 27-1 record and have already won the Region 1-AA (West) and Region 1-AA crowns. Carver's Panthers are the defending state Class AA boys champions and have a 25-2 mark this season.

The tournaments at Thomaston, Macon and Atlanta are to continue through Saturday when champions will be crowned.

The Tifton Gazette, page 3, March 13, 1970
Berrien Falls to Carver as Anderson Goes Wild
By Johnny Futch
Gazette Correspondent

ATLANTA – Berrien County ran into a whirlwind named George Anderson as the Rebels were eliminated, 70-60, in the quarter-finals of the State Class AA basketball Tournament here Thursday afternoon.

Anderson, 6-2 forward from Carver of Atlanta – the odds-on favorite to repeat as State AA champion – took charge of the sagging Panthers' offense and scored 27 of 39 points in the second half to erase a 27-24 Berrien halftime edge.

In the process, the Panthers' senior star put Carver as far as 20 points out early in the fourth quarter.

The Rebels were giving Carver plenty of opportunities to score as they turned the ball over 40 times in the game.

In other action, Newton County edged Sandy Springs, 58-56; East Rome defeated North Springs, 66-55; Central of Newnan beat East Atlanta, 82-69.

Today's play calls for Carver to face Newton and East Rome to engage Central.

Big George Sorrell, the Berrien co-captain, carried much of the load for the Rebs with 25 points and 17 rebounds, but it wasn't enough to match the gunning of Anderson and his playmates. Bobby Taylor with 10 was the only other Rebel in double figures.

The deliberate Berrien offense combined with its stingy defense to throttle Carver for the first half.

Pumping medium-range shots and shredding the proud Rebel defense with his flashy drives, Anderson hit 13 points in the third quarter and 14 during the fourth to give the Panthers a comfortable margin.

Berrien rallied late behind the first set of subs but could get no closer than 10 at the final buzzer.

Both teams ran into foul trouble. Berrien had three starters with three personals each at halftime – Sorrell, Taylor and Roger Guess – and Carver fouled out a starter, with two others carrying four at game's end.

The loss wrapped up the Rebels' season at 27-2. It also halted a 27-game winning streak.

Berrien's girls get a shot at the State AA title in the first round. They meet Lakeshore Monday at Vienna, 8 p.m., via sectional play.

The winner advances to the quarter-finals at Northside High in Atlanta on Thursday.

*****

Berrien (60)	**Carver (70)**	Rembert (2), Tothia (2).
B. Taylor 10	Williams 12	
Sorrell 25	Taylor 8	
Tucker 6	Lupoe 2	
Wright 7	Anderson 39	
Guess	Hall 1	

Berrien	14	13	11	22	–
60					
Carver	12	12	25	21	–
70					

Berrien subs – W. Taylor (6), Harrell (2), Harnage (4). Carver subs – Bridges (4),

Berrien: field goals, 19; free throws, 22-35; personal fouls, 18. Carver: field goals, 27; free throws, 16-23; personal fouls, 26.

The Valdosta Daily Times, page 12, March 13, 1970

Berrien's Quintet Beaten By Carver

ATLANTA – Berrien's Rebels from Nashville, Ga., finally met their match in the quarter-finals of the state Class AA boys basketball Thursday night.

Carver's defending state champion Panthers from Atlanta staged a second half rally to erase Berrien's three-point lead and they went on to win the opening game, 70-60.

The loss snapped a 27-game winning streak for coach Stanley Simpson's Rebels. They are now through for the season with a 27-2 overall mark.

The victory left coach Calvin Jones' Panthers with a 26-2 overall record and a berth in the semi-finals tonight.

In other quarter-final action last night, Sandy Springs (Atlanta) trimmed Newton County (Covington), 58-56; East Rome rolled over North Springs (Atlanta), 66-55; and East High (Atlanta) dropped an 82-69 decision to Central of Newnan.

In tonight's action Carver takes on Newton County at 7 p.m. with East Rome locking horns with Central at 8:30 p.m.

The losing team will meet in the consolation match at 7 p.m. Saturday, while the winners go up for the championship at 8:30 p.m.

The Rebels matched the Panthers bucket for bucket throughout the first half and managed to hold a 27-24 lead at the half.

But Carver returned under the leadership of George Anderson and managed to take a 49-38 lead by the end of the third quarter.

Berrien could trim only one point off the Panthers' lead in the final period.

Anderson was the top scorer for Carver with 39 points while George Sorrell was the leading scorer for Berrien with 25.

(Box Scores Omitted)

The Valdosta Daily Times, page 8, March 14, 1970
Berrien's Girls Set for Playoff
By Times Staff Writer

NASHVILLE, Ga. – Berrien's unbeaten Rebelettes are to face the Lakeshore Lancerettes at Vienna on Monday night in a state Class AA girls basketball playoff contest.

The game between coach Stanley Simpson's Rebelettes and coach Joe Pittman's Lakeshore sextet from College Park is slated for 8 p.m. at the Vienna High gym.

Monday's victor will join seven other playoff game winners when the duel for the 1969-70 state Class AA girls championship resumes next Thursday at the Northside High gym in Atlanta.

While clicking off 26 straight wins, the Rebelettes have claimed the 1-AA (West) and 1-AA titles.

They're making their fourth appearance in the state tourney. In 1962, 1968 and 1969 they reached the state quarter-finals before bowing out. This year they have their sights on the championship.

Lakeshore, the runner-up from Region 2-AA, owns an 18-9 record.

Berrien's probable starters are forwards Donna Jernigan (5-4, jr.), Mary Grace Bailey (5-10, sr.), and Marla Brown (5-9, sr.) and guards Peggy Barber (5-7, sr.), Lenna Carey (5-10, sr.) and Andrea Carter (5-6, sr.).

As a team the Rebelettes have been averaging 48.9 points a game and on defense allowing an average of just 30.5.

Brown is the individual scoring leader with a 17.7 average, followed by Jernigan, 16.7, and Bailey, 10.0.

The Tifton Gazette, page 3, March 17, 1970
Berrien Girls Win Easily

VIENNA – Berrien County High's girls have advanced to the quarter-finals of the State AA Tournament at Atlanta.

Coach Stanley Simpson's Rebelettes made quick work of Lakeshore by 17 points here Monday night, 43-26, in sectional play.

Unbeaten Berrien goes Thursday at the Northside High gym in Atlanta against O'Keefe at 4:30 p.m. That foe advanced with a victory Friday night over Bass of Atlanta.

"Defensively, we did an outstanding job," Simpson told the Gazette today. "We thought the forwards, considering they had to adjust some things at the last minute, did all right."

Heading Berrien's obstinate defense included Lenna Carey, Peggy Barber and Andrea Carter.

The offense was spearheaded by Donna Jernigan's 20-point performance. Joann Langford tossed in 11 markers and Mary Grace Bailey 10.

Marla Brown, the Rebelettes' leading scorer with a 17.7-point average, did not play due to an injured back. The status of the senior sharp-shooter was uncertain, with a verdict due today from a specialist.

Berrien jumped to a 16-8 first quarter lead and had minimum difficulty. The Rebelettes held 28-15 and 34-18 advantages after the next two junctures.

The Berrien squad, which now stands 27-0, entered the state sectional activity as the Region 1-AA champion. Lakeshore, which resides in the College Park area, claimed the runnerup position for Region 2-AA.

Berrien (43)	Lakeshore (26)	
Bailey 10	Brown 20	Berrien subs – McMillan (2), Williams, Swain, Rudeseal, Harrell. Lakeshore subs – Beacham.
Jernigan 20	Smith 4	
Langford 11	Rex 2	

Berrien	16	28	34	43
Lakeshore	8	15	18	26

Carey — Overten — Carver — Carter — Ezell

Berrien: field goals, 17; free throws, 9-12; personal fouls, 15. Lakeshore: field goals, 9; free throws, 8-14; personal fouls, 9.

The Valdosta Daily Times, page 9, March 17, 1970

Berrien's Sextet Thumps Lakeshore

Special to the Times

VIENNA – Berrien's Rebelettes from Nashville, Ga., put their entire team into first gear and promptly rolled past the Lakeshore Lancerettes from College Park, 43-26, in state Class AA girls basketball playoff here Monday night.

Coach Stanley Simpson's Rebelettes, operating without team captain and leading scorer Marla Brown who is out with a back injury, kept their record unblemished. They are still undefeated after 27 games.

With the victory the Rebelettes will advance to the quarter-finals of the state Class AA tourney. The final three rounds are to be played Thursday, Friday and Saturday at the Northside High gym in Atlanta.

Thursday's pairings call for Berrien to face O'Keefe (Atlanta) at 4:30 p.m.

The loss put coach Joe Pittman's Lancerettes on the sidelines with an 18-10 overall record for the season.

Although Brown was absent, Frances Jernigan, Jo Ann Langford and Grace Bailey stepped in to fill the bill. They scored 20, 11 and 10 points respectively to lead the victory, with substitute Sandy McMillan adding another 2 points.

While the Lancerettes were busy trying to stop the Rebelette scoring trio, they forgot about the Nashville guards. Lenna Carey, Peggy Barber, and Andrea Carter, who held the Lakeshore girls to only 18 points in the first three quarters.

Joy Brown was the leading scorer for the Lancerettes with 20 points.

Berrien's girls outscored the Lakeshore sextet 17 to 9 in field goals and hit on 9 of their 12 shots, compared with 8 of 14 for the Lancerettes.

Simpson said Brown's injury may keep her out indefinitely.

(Box Scores Omitted)

The Tifton Gazette, page 5, March 18, 1970
State AA Girls Action

Berrien Set for Atlanta

By Staff Writer

Unbeaten Berrien County rates as one of the favorites in the State AA Girls Basketball Tournament which starts Thursday at the Northside High of Atlanta arena.

Berrien takes on O'Keefe of Atlanta in the tournament's opening game Thursday at 4:30 p.m. Following are St. Pius X vs. Forsyth County, 6 p.m.; Franklin County vs. Wheeler (Marietta), 7:30 p.m.; East Atlanta vs. Waycross, 9 p.m.

If Berrien can defeat O'Keefe, it would go in Friday's semifinals at 7 p.m. against the St. Pius – Forsyth victor. The Franklin-Wheeler and East Atlanta – Waycross winners have an 8:30 p.m. engagement.

The finals will be staged Saturday at 8:30 p.m. A consolation game is scheduled for 7 p.m.

Team captain Marla Brown, the team's leading scorer at 18.5 points per game, seemingly holds the key to the Rebelettes' success. The 5-9 senior, who did not play in the 43-26 state sectional triumph Monday night over Lakeshore at Vienna, has been receiving treatment for a back injury.

"If Brown is ready," Coach Stanley Simpson says, "our chances are probably better (than any other team) … It looks as though she'll play some."

Simpson expects to start basically his same combination which has produced 27 victories this year. The forwards figure to include Donna Jernigan, Grace Bailey and Joann Langford or Brown; the guards are Lenna Carey, Peggy Barber and Andrea Carter.

The Berrien team was scheduled to leave today for Atlanta where it hopes to remain the rest of the week.

The Valdosta Daily Times, page 21, March 18, 1970

Berrien Is Ready

By Times Staff Writer

NASHVILLE, Ga. – Berrien's basketball Rebelettes will try to keep their record unblemished when they meet O'Keefe's fighting Irish in Atlanta Thursday.

But the task won't be made any easier with their leading scorer, Marla Brown, out with a back injury.

Coach Stanley Simpson's Nashville, Ga., girls are to meet coach Dick Duncan's Irish in the quarter-finals of the State Class AA girls high school basketball tournament at 4:30 p.m. at the Northside High gymnasium.

In the rest of the quarter-finals St. Pius X (Atlanta) will meet Forsyth County (Cumming) at 6 p.m.; Franklin County (Carnesville) takes on Wheeler (Marietta) at 7:30 p.m. and East of Atlanta locks horns with Waycross at 9 p.m.

Winners of those games earn places in the semi-finals, set for 7 p.m. and 8:30 p.m. Friday. The championship match is slated Saturday at 8:30 p.m.

The Rebelettes will put their perfect 27-0 record on the line against an 18-10 mark held by O'Keefe, the Region 6-AA champion.

Brown, a 5-9 senior, who had been averaging 17.7 points per game with 2.7 rebounds sustained a back injury last week and was not able to participate in the Rebelettes' 43-26 victory over Lakeshore (College Park) in opening round action Monday.

On offense the Rebelettes will be counting on the forward trio of Donna Jernigan (5-4, jr.), Mary Grace Bailey (5-10, sr.), and Brenda Rudeseal (5-8, jr.). It was Rudeseal who has been moved from guard to take the place of injured forward Brown. Rudeseal scored 11 points against Lakeside. Jernigan is averaging 17 points a game, followed by Bailey, who has a 10-point average.

Berrien has one of the finest defensive groups around in guards Lenna Carey (5-10, sr.), Peggy Barber (5-7, sr.) and Andrea Carter (5-6, sr.).

Leading the way for the Irish are forwards Diane Thompson (5-6, sr.), Joan Mergan (5-9, jr.) and Jean Warlick (5-7, sr.). They have been averaging 30, 16 and 12 points respectively.

O'Keefe's starting guards are Sue Peters (5-6, jr.), Brenda McCallum (5-6, sr.) and Shelia Carey (5-2, jr.).

This marks the fourth year Simpson's Rebelettes have reached the quarter-finals. They also made it to the second round in '62, '68 and '69.

Last year they were knocked out in the quarter-finals when they dropped a 40-35 decision to Wheeler of Marietta, whose girls are back in the competition this year.

The Berrien Press, front page, March 19, 1970

Berrien Basketball Teams In State Basketball

The Berrien High Rebelettes put an end to the basketball season for the girls from Lakeshore High of Atlanta on Monday night as they defeated the Lancerettes by a score of 43-26.

The tremendous defensive trio of Lenna Carey, Andrea Carter and Peggy Barber completely un-nerved the Lakeshore forwards with a tight and very sticky defense. Donna Jernigan pumped in 20 points to lead the Berrien offensive attack. Grace Bailey scored 10 and Joann Langford, who started in the place of leading scorer Marla Brown, did a good job as she scored 11 points. Joy Brown was the attack leader for Lakeshore as she scored 20 points. Berrien moved off to an early lead and was never challenged in the game.

The girls of Berrien now move to the quarter-finals of AA action in Atlanta as they meet the O'Keefe high of Atlanta at 4:30 on Thursday at Northside High. If Berrien can take O'Keefe, they would then play on Friday at 7:00 p.m.

BERRIEN vs. CARVER

By Tim Moore

After a 27-game winning streak, the Berrien High Rebels faced defeat Thursday evening in the quarter finals of the AA State Tournament in Atlanta.

Trailing 27-24 at the half, Carver Panthers came back in the second half, and the farther into the second half the Rebels went, the farther behind they fell. The Rebels were outscored 25-11 in the third quarter, and at one point early in the fourth they had fallen as far as 20 points behind.

Giving a strong last-minute fight the Rebels finally fell 60-70 to end their 1969-70 basketball season with a record of 27-2.

George Sorrell, for the Rebels, gave a tough final effort dumping in 14 of his 25 points in the final quarter. He also cleaned 17 rebounds off the boards. Bobby Taylor made ten points, Charles Wright put in seven, Richard Tucker and Wayne Taylor each had six, David Harnage four, and Karl Harrell two.

[Compiler's note: The article repeated the girls' team photo from the January 22, 1970 edition.]

The Tifton Gazette, page 3, March 19, 1970

Berrien Girls Battle

ATLANTA – Berrien County's girls entered the State AA Tournament here today at the Northside High arena hoping that fate would treat them kinder than the school's boys last week.

In State AA boys' Tournament action last week at Alexander Dome, Berrien dropped a quarter-final battle to defending champion Carver of Atlanta.

Ironically, the Berrien girls – who were scheduled to combat O'Keefe of Atlanta today at 4:30 p.m. – are playing in the first game at the same time and day of the week as their boys did while losing.

Other action today includes St. Pius X vs. Forsyth County, 6 p.m.; Franklin County vs. Wheeler (Marietta), 7:30 p.m.; East Atlanta vs. Waycross, 9 p.m.

If Coach Stanley Simpson's Rebelettes survive today, they would battle Friday night in the semi-finals against the St. Pius – Forsyth victor at 7 o'clock. The finals are scheduled Saturday night.

Berrien qualified for today's quarter-finals by defeating Lakeshore in a state sectional game Monday night at Vienna, 43-26.

The Tifton Gazette, page 3, March 19, 1970
Boys Take No. 6 Spot
ATLANTA – Berrien County has finished as the No. 6-rated State AA boys' basketball team.

The Tiftarea representative has gained the recognition in the Atlanta Journal's final rankings. East Rome is rated No. 1.

All the state champions were picked No. 1 for the five classifications, with the top 10 for each, including:

AA – 1. East Rome, 2. Newton Co., 3. Central of Newnan, 4. Carver of Atlanta, 5. East Atlanta, 6. Berrien Co., 7. Sandy Springs, 8. Burney-Harris, 9. Lakeshore, 10. North Springs.

AAA – 1. Decatur, 2. Savannah, 3. Carver (Columbus), 4. Ballard-Hudson, 5. Beach, 6. Howard, 7. Douglass, 8. Dalton, 9. Druid Hills, 10. Forest Park.

A – 1. Early Co., 2. Cairo, 3. East Hall, 4. Central of Carrollton, 5. Haralson Co., 6. Norcross, 7. Statesboro, 8. Murray Co., 9. Hancock Central, 10. Monroe Area.

B – 1. Hogansville, 2. Johnson Co., 3. Springfield Central, 4. East Laurens, 5. Fairburn, 6. Jefferson, 7. Blackshear, 8. Harris Co., 9. Roswell, 10. Vienna.

C – 1. Arlington, 2. Pike Co., 3. Ga. Industrial, 4. Stratford, 5. Ga. Christian, 6. Savannah Country Day, 7. Taylor Co., 8. Crawford Co., 9. Lanier Co., 10. Plains.

The Valdosta Daily Times, page 21, March 19, 1970
Area Teams in State Tourneys
By Times Staff Writer

Two girls basketball teams representing area high school are scheduled to see action in quarter-final round games in a pair of state tournaments today.

Coach Stanley Simpson's Berrien Rebelettes from Nashville, Ga., are to take on O'Keefe in Atlanta, while coach Angie Devivo's Lanier County Bulldogettes from Lakeland, Ga., meet Dacula, in Macon.

The Rebelettes will take an unblemished 27-0 record into their second-round battle of the Class AA tournament. They will be going against an 18-10 mark owned by coach Dick Dundan's O'Keefe Fighting Irish.

Berrien captured the Region 1-AA crown, while O'Keefe is the top team from region 6-AA. They were to see action at 4:30 p.m. at the Northside High school gym.

Meanwhile, at the Macon Coliseum, Devivo's Bulldogettes are scheduled to put their 13-11 record on the line at 8 p.m. against coach Myron Bulloch's Dacula Falcons, who will take a 17-9 mark in to a state Class C tournament duel.

Lanier is the runner-up from Region 1-C, while the Falcons won the title in Region 8-C.

The Tifton Gazette, page 2, March 20, 1970

Berrien Girls Demolish O'Keefe in AA Tourney

By John Futch

ATLANTA – O'Keefe's Fighting Irish forgot their Shamrocks, ran into a blitz called Berrien County, and watched Coach Stanley Simpson's Rebelettes gain the semi-finals of the State AA Girls' Tournament, 53-28, here Thursday afternoon.

Berrien Captain Marla Brown, hobbled with a painful back injury and counted out for the rest of the tournament, pumped in 20 points to lead the Rebelette deluge. Donna Jernigan with 17 and Grace Bailey with 14 rounded out the balanced Berrien attack.

In other action, Forsyth County dumped St. Pius X, 79-68, to earn a semi-final berth against Berrien tonight at 7 p.m.; Wheeler beat Franklin County 59-51, and Waycross buried East Atlanta, 47-19.

The Berrien attack faltered early, despite a 6-0 edge with 2:15 left in the opening period on a Bailey medium jumper. The Irish hit six quick points and Berrien led 13-6 at quarter's end.

Jernigan, rolling down the middle, hit three easy second quarter baskets as the Rebelette forwards began to shred the O'Keefe defense to hold a 25-13 halftime edge.

Irish eyes stopped smiling in the third quarter as guards, Lenna Carey, Peggy Barber and Andrea Carter shut down the O'Keefe offense and the Brown-Bailey-Jernigan combo contributed six points each to outscore the Atlantans 18-3 and blow O'Keefe out of the gym for a 43-16 margin.

Simpson's subs took it from there.

Carey and Barber hauled down eight rebounds each as Berrien dominated the boards, 38-20. The Rebelettes, the first Berrien girls team ever to get past the state quarter-finals. (seems to have missing print)

Berrien (53)	O'Keefe (28)	Berrien subs: Langford 2, McMillan,
Brown 20	Thompson 11	Williams, Rudeseal, Swain and Harrell.
Jernigan 17	Morgan 12	O'Keefe sub: Smith.
Bailey 14	Warlack 5	
Barber	Carey	
Carter	McCallum	
Carey	Peters	

Berrien	13	25	43	52
O'Keefe	6	13	16	28

The Valdosta Daily Times, page 12, March 20, 1970

Berrien Advances Into Semi-Finals

Special to the Times

ATLANTA – Berrien County's Rebelettes made basketball history here Thursday night by demolishing O'Keefe's fighting Irish, 53-28, in the quarter-finals of the state Class AA tournament.

The victory put the Berrien girls of coach Stanley Simpson into the semi-finals tonight for the first time in the school's history. They have reached the quarter-finals four times before.

Berrien is scheduled to meet at 7 p.m. today and Wheeler is scheduled to go against Waycross in the semi-finals at the Northside High gym. The winners are to meet in the championship round Saturday at 8:30 p.m. [Compiler's note: Typed as it appeared in newsprint. Berrien's opponent was left out of the first sentence.]

Simpson's sextet is still undefeated. The win over O'Keefe brought their record to 28-0.

The loss sent coach Dick Duncan's Fighting Irish to the sidelines. They leave with an 18-11 overall record.

In other action last night, Forsyth slipped past St. Pius X of Atlanta, 79-68; Wheeler trimmed Franklin County (Carnesville), 59-51, victory and Region 1-AA runners-up Waycross defeated East of Atlanta, 47-19.

Berrien's leading scorer and team captain Marla Brown is bothered by a back injury and was not expected to play. But she recovered long enough to chalk up 20 points for the Rebelettes. Donna Jernigan and Grace Bailey brought in 17 and 14 points respectively to balance the effort.

On defense Lenna Carey, Peggy Barber and Brenda Rudeseal stalled the Irish forwards. The trio allowed only six, seven and three points in the first three quarters respectively before retiring to the sidelines for the final stanza.

Joanna Margan was the only Irish forward in double figures.

The Rebelettes made field goals, twice that of O'Keefe's and sank 9 of 16 free throws against 6 of 19 for the Irish.

(Box Scores Omitted)

The Tifton Gazette, page 2, March 21, 1970
<u>**Face Waycross in Atlanta**</u>

Girls from Berrien Go for State Title

By Johnny Futch
Gazette Correspondent

ATLANTA – What was advertised as the State AA Girls' championship will be an instant replay as the Pine Flats' playoffs when Berrien County meets Waycross for the Georgia title here tonight at 8 o'clock. The site is the Northside High gym.

Coach Ramrod Simpson's Berrien Rebelettes destroyed Forsyth County Friday night in the semi-finals, 54-42. Waycross ended the evening with a 55-51 overtime victory over tough Wheeler High of Marietta to gain the finals.

The championship game will be the second meeting between Berrien and Waycross. The Rebelettes dumped Waycross, 41-25, for the South Georgia title three weeks ago.

Forsyth looked like championship material in following torrid shooting of Joyce Gravitt to a 12-10 first quarter lead. The lanky Bulldogette forward pumped in eight of the points as the Berrien defenders had difficulty adjusting to the attack.

The Rebelettes must have been playing cat and mouse because just when it appeared that Forsyth would run away with the bait, Berrien yanked out the rug.

Grace Bailey tied it at 14-14, and with 5:13 left in the half, Marla Brown connected to make it 16-14, the last time Forsyth was close.

Brown hit five, Bailey six and Donna Jernigan added 11 before halftime. This gave Berrien a decisive 11-point intermission bulge, 32-21.

After that the game belonged to the Rebelettes. Jernigan scored 24 and Bailey 21 to spearhead the attack.

Lenna Carey ignored a painful ankle injury to pace the guard corps with seven rebounds and a pair of steals. Brenda Rudeseal came off the bench and played one of her best games while claiming six rebounds.

Debbie Lummus scored 22 points to spark the losers. Gravitt contributed 17.

Waycross, the surprise team of the year, bombed Wheeler for three quarters, leading once by as much as 12.

However, the Bulldogettes had their troubles in the final quarter. They won the tilt in overtime with a field goal and free throw by Vicki Cason and pair of gratis tosses from Christine Gainer. Wheeler went scoreless during the extra session.

Cason bucketed 21 points to lead Waycross. Gail Baker found the range for 20.

Berrien puts the only perfect record in the tournament, 29-0, on the line against Waycross for all the marbles tonight at 8:30. Forsyth and Wheeler meet for the leftovers at 7 o'clock.

Berrien (54)	Forsyth (42)
Brown 9	Boling 3
Jernigan 24	Lummus 22
Bailey 21	Gravitt 17
Carey	Martin
Barber	Monroe
Carter	Linton

Berrien subs – Rudeseal. Forsyth subs – Holtzclaw, Wentz.

Berrien	10	32	40	54
Forsyth	12	21	28	42

The Valdosta Daily Times, page 6, March 21, 1970

Berrien's Girls in 'AA' Finals
Special to the Times

ATLANTA – Berrien's Rebelettes will be meeting a foe here tonight when they face Waycross' Bulldogettes in the championship game of the State Class AA girls high school basketball tournament.

Coach Stanley Simpson's Berrien Rebelettes kept their record unblemished and brought it to 29.0 by defeating Forsyth County (Cumming), 54-42, in the semi-finals Friday night.

In the other semi-final match, Waycross' Bulldogettes sank in four free throws while blanking their opponents in overtime to take a 55-51 victory over Wheeler of Marietta.

Berrien won the Region 1-AA title in an earlier tournament by defeating Waycross, 41-35, in the title match of that event. The Bulldogettes now have a 23-4 record. The title contest is set for 8:30 p.m. at the Northside High gym.

Simpson's Rebelettes have reached the quarter-finals four times before, but if they win tonight it will be their first state championship.

The Rebelettes exploded in the second quarter against Forsyth to come from two points behind the Cumming sextet and go 11 ahead to the tune of a 32-21 halftime score.

By the time the final quarter had rolled around the Berrien forwards had racked-up 40 points, while guards Lenna Carey, Peggy Barber and Andrea carter had allowed Forsyth only 28.

Donna Jernigan made 24 points to lead the way for the Rebelettes. Grace Bailey added 21 and Marla Brown totaled 9.

Debra Lummus scored 22 points for Forsyth, followed by Joyce Gravitt with 17 and Sue Bowling with 3.

The Nashville girls only outscored Forsyth 17 to 16 in field goals, but made up the difference in free throws, hitting 20 of 35 compared to 10 of 15 for their opponents. Berrien was charged with 13 fouls, while Forsyth made 25.

In the other semi-finals game, the Bulldogettes held the lead for three quarters, but found the score tied at 51-51 as Wheeler staged a last-minute rally.

In the two-minute overtime period the Waycross sextet got four more points while their guards kept Wheeler scoreless.

Vicky Cason and Gail Baker were the leading scorers for the Waycross sextet with 31 and 20 points respectively.

(Box Scores Omitted)

The Tifton Gazette, page 4, March 23, 1970

Berrien Girls Take State AA Title, Pace All-State

By Johnny Futch
Gazette Correspondent

ATLANTA – Berrien County High School's Rebelettes swept through the formality of beating Waycross, 37-32, here Saturday night for the State AA girls Basketball championship and in the process, Coach Ramrod Simpson's team left absolutely no doubt as to (who) had the best team in AA.

No team in recent years has so totally dominated a tournament like Berrien, the fact underscored by sportswriters and broadcasters when they named seven Rebelettes to All-State honors. Five Rebelettes – forwards Marla Brown, Donna Jernigan and Mary Grace Bailey and guards Lena Carey and Peggy Barber – were named to the first team All-State squad, while Brenda Rudeseal and Andrea Carter – who shared playing time at the other guard spot received Honorable Mention.

The All-Staters earned their honors. Despite the team effort which characterizes a Simpson squad, all were heroines in their own right.

Team captain Brown ignored a painful back injury that was supposed to have ended her playing career, scoring 41 points in three games and coolly quarterbacked the liquid Berrien offense. Bailey shredded opposing defenses with her driving ability and deadly medium jumper Jernigan, who at 5-4 was a lot closer to the floor than most players, drove, dribbled and shot like a tank-sized Pete Maravich, and with a total of 76 points, ran away with high-scoring honors in three of the four tournament games.

On the other end of the floor, Carey dominated the boards, setting a school record in the opener with Lakeshore by snaring 12 rebounds and shattering it in the final with 14 on the official books. Barber, who specialized all season in shutting off hot shooters, did just that against some of the best in the state. The Rudeseal-Carter duo kept opponents off balance with their harassing tactics.

Only the tournament heroics by Vicki Cason and little but mobile Gale Baker kept Waycross' Bulldogettes' close.

A Bailey layup and jumper game, and Waycross' title hopes lead in the opening moments. Cason and Baker hit a field goal apiece to tie matters at 4-4 but Brown retaliated from outside with 1:22 gone in the game, and Waycross' title hopes fell with the ball to the bottom of the basket. The remaining 26 minutes and 38 seconds just made things official. [Compiler's note. There seems to be missing or misplaced print in this paragraph.]

Waycross could manage only two more points in the opening period, and the Bulldogettes trailed, 6-4, at the quarter turn. By halftime, Berrien had a 23-12 margin.

The Rebelettes spent the rest of the game cooling it and watching Waycross shoot – and miss – hitting a miserable 26 per cent from the field.

Leading at times by as much as 12, Berrien let Waycross farm away while the partisan crowd roared the inevitable in the Northside High Gym "We're No. 1."

While Waycross was missing 38 of 51 shots from the field, the deliberate Berrien forwards hit 15 of 26 for 58 per cent. They also cashed in on 7 of 9 free throws in the game that saw only 16 fouls called, seven on Berrien and nine on Waycross.

Jernigan ended the evening with 15 points. Brown had 13 and Bailey nine.

Cason, used to hitting in the 30's was baffled by Barber and could hit only 16. Baker, named with Cason to the All-State first team, had 14.

The victory capped a perfect 30-0 season and was the fourth Rebelettes championship of the year. They won the Lowndes-Hahira Invitational, 1-AA West and the 1-AA title.

This was the first state championship ever collected by a Berrien County High athletic team.

Berrien had beaten Waycross earlier in the Region 1-AA championship, and the state win marked the 18th time in 21 years that the champion has come out of the present league area.

BOX SCORE

Berrien (37)		Waycross (32)	
Brown	13	Cason	16
Jernigan	15	G. Baker	14
Bailey	9	Garner	2
Carey		D. Baker	
Barber		Williams	
Carter		Miles	

Berrien subs – Rudeseal. Waycross subs – None.

Berrien	14	23	32	37
Waycross	6	12	22	32

Berrien: field goals, 15; free throws, 7-9; personal fouls, 7. Waycross: field goals, 13; free throws, 6-8; personal fouls, 9.

Coverage of Berrien's state title win from the Tifton Gazette.

The Valdosta Daily Times, page 11, March 23, 1970

Berrien's Girls Cop State Title

By Times Staff Writer

ATLANTA – Berrien's Rebelettes put the clincher on a super-successful season by defeating the Waycross Bulldogettes, 37-32, in the championship game of the state Class AA girls high school basketball tournament here Saturday night.

Coach Stanley Simpson's Rebelettes kept their record perfect throughout the campaign and finished with a 30-0 mark. The defeat left the Bulldogettes with a 23-5 record.

It was not the first time the Bulldogettes had to take a back seat to the rampaging Rebelettes.

After winning the Region 1-AA (West) sub-region championship, the Rebelettes went against 1-AA (East) champion Waycross for the region title and posted a 41-35 victory.

Then both teams advanced to the state playoffs and stayed in the running long enough to meet again in the finals.

"They were just fabulous, each and every one of them," Simpson said after the victory. "I'm proud of them all."

In the championship match Rebelette forward Marla Brown broke a 4-4 tie in the opening moments with a field goal and the Nashville girls never lost the lead after that.

The Rebelettes had racked up 14 points by the end of the first quarter while the Berrien guards, Lenna Carey, Peggy Barber, Andrea Carter and Brenda Rudeseal, held the Bulldogettes to only six in each of the first two quarters.

Donna Jernigan and Marla Brown scored 15 and 13 points respectively to lead Berrien, with Grace Bailey adding the other nine. Carey grabbed 14 rebounds.

Vickie Cason and Gail Baker led the Bulldogettes with 16 and 14 points respectively.

The Berrien sextet has advanced to the quarter-finals of the state tourney four times in the past, but this is the first time in history they got past that point.

They made an impression on everyone at the tourney because five of their starters were placed on the six-girl all-tournament team with their other two guards on the honorable mention team.

Brown, Jernigan and Bailey were picked as the all-tournament forwards, with Lenna Carey and Barber as guards. Carter and Rudeseal were honorable mention selectees.

(Box Scores Omitted)

Coverage of the undefeated season from the Valdosta Daily Times.

The Waycross Journal-Herald, March 23, 1970

Bulldogettes Defeated In "AA" Cage Finals

By Paul Robinson
Sports Editor

ATLANTA - The dramatic drive of the Waycross Bulldogettes toward a state "AA" girls basketball championship came to a heartbreaking end here in the Northside High School gym Saturday night as the Cinderella Six fell 37-32 to the Berrien County sextet in the tourney finals.

In the first state tournament championship match ever for a Waycross cage team and in what might be the final appearance of a Waycross High girls basketball squad, the Bulldogettes of Coach Bill Gowan were victims of a tourney-tested band of veterans.

Despite having their title hopes shattered by the 1-AA neighbors from Nashville, the Bulldogettes never lost their poise and displayed all the qualities of a champion right down to the final horn before a near-capacity crowd.

THE LOW-SCORING state tournament finale was a brilliant defensive battle from start to finish.

Though losing, the Waycross defense played perhaps its finest second half of the season. Ava Williams, Brenda Gail Miles, Dale Baker and Melissa Parker combined talents to allow Berrien but 24 shots from the field during the 28 minutes of action, seven in the last half.

But the sterling efforts of Berrien's Andrea Carter, Peggy Barber and Lenna Carey kept Waycross forwards off balance and shooting hurriedly to capture the defensive struggle.

Astounding accuracy from the field by Berrien saw the Rebelettes of Stanley Simpson hit 15 of 24 for a sizzling 62.5 per cent. Waycross had a cold night from the field, connecting on 13 of 45 for 28.8.

BERRIEN MADE it to the throne room of the state in its third consecutive try. Simpson's sparklers won the 1-AA title in 1968 and placed third in the state.

Repeating as 1-AA queens last year, Berrien lost in the state quarterfinals. But this year, the Rebelettes conquered 30 consecutive foes to bring home the top trophy.

Berrien dominated the All-tournament team chosen by sportswriters and sportscasters.

Marla Brown, Donna Jernigan, Peggy Barber, Mary Grace Bailey and Brenda Rudeseal getting honorable mention.

Waycross placed two on the top 12 or first team. Vicki Cason and Gale Baker were selected while Dale Baker received honorable mention.

Berrien's Simpson was named the All-Star Tournament team coach.

BAILEY HIT A field goal the first time Berrien had the ball in the championship match to send the Rebelettes to a 2-0 lead. Waycross missed its first four field attempts and Bailey scored again to make it 4-0.

Cason then hit a pair of fielders to knot the score at 4-4. Brown scored from the field and Bailey shot a free throw to put Berrien ahead 7-4 and Waycross could never get any closer.

Hitting six of nine from the field in the first quarter to three of 13 for Waycross, Berrien pulled into a 14-6 advantage at the first juncture.

Still unable to solve the Berrien defense in the second stanza, Waycross scored but two of seven field shots while Berrien was getting four of eight and the Rebelettes built up a 23-12 halftime margin.

BERRIEN maintained the edge in the third canto, getting four of five from the field while Waycross was slipping to three of 11 and the Rebelettes were ahead by 10 points, 32-22, at the start of the last seven minutes of action.

Waycross then made a strong bid to overtake the champions. The Bulldogettes outscored Berrien 10-5 in the last quarter but the rally fell short. Waycross made four of 12 field shots and held Berrien to one of two as the Rebelettes went into a stall.

Vicki Cason hit for 16 points to take game scoring honors and Gale Baker added 14. Christine Garner played her usual steady game in setting up plays and rebounding.

Donna Jernigan led Berrien with 15 points and Marla Brown had 13.

"I WAS pleased with the defense in the last half," Coach Gowan said. Berrien attempted only seven field shots during the last 14 minutes of play.

Gowan told the Journal-Herald last night "I appreciate the administration giving me the chance to coach these girls.

"I really enjoying [c]oaching them and I am proud of every one of them. They gave tremendous effort and were responsive to my coaching. Their acceptance of my philosophy was tremendous," Gowan said.

Citing the difficulty of players having to change coaches, Gowan said "they have to make many adjustments but this team accepted me better than any first-year team I have ever coached.

"I am not ashamed of them. I'm proud. We lost but we were defeated by a good ball club. Of the 79 class "AA" teams in the state, we were better than 77 of them," the Bulldogettes [coach] said.

EXPRESSING appreciation for support in the state tournament, Gowan said "the girls appreciate the telegrams from fans who followed us by radio and they went to the desk each day to check on them.

"I am grateful for the telegrams, the interest and support of parents and fans who made the long trip to Atlanta for the tournament. This meant so much to the team," Gowan pointed out.

The 2-1 record in the state tournament left the Waycross girls with a 23-5 record for the season, one of the best records ever posted by a Waycross basketball team.

Tourney Notes: Many acquaintances were renewed during the tourney in Atlanta. Former Waycrossans seen included the Don Hights, John Bankstons, Ed Rusk, the former Wacona coach, Earl Fales, a former Wacona athlete who was one of the referees, the former Sue Allen and her family, the former Delores Scruggs who was a Bulldogette luminary of years past ... The weatherman was against the city of Atlanta during the tournament. It rained the entire weekend. Waycross support at the state tournament, particularly Saturday, was the greatest ever witnessed for such a trek ... Wheeler won third place with a 64-56 victory over Forsyth County.

(Box Scores Omitted)

The Thomasville Times-Enterprise, page 9, March 24, 1970

Berrien Co. Wins AA Girls Crown

ATLANTA – Donna Jernigan and Marla Brown paced the Berrien County Rebelettes to a 37-32 basketball victory over Waycross for the AA Girls State Championships here Saturday night.

Berrien County was the Region 1AA champion and Waycross was the 1AA runnerup. Both teams reached the finals after easy victories Thursday and Friday.

Jernigan scored 15 points and Brown added 13. The Rebelettes led 23-12 at halftime.

The Tifton Gazette, Doug's Digest, page 2, March 24, 1970

State Champion Berrien Showed Great Dedication

Before the past high school basketball season kicked off, Berrien County girls' Coach Stanley Simpson had told the Gazette, "All indications are we should have another winning season, but in order to do so, we are going to have to get a much better effort out of the girls than we have been getting in the preceding practices."

It would appear that his Rebelettes came up with this "better effort." In fact, they responded by going unbeaten through 30 opponents en route to the State AA championship.

Talking with Simpson about his team which clinched the title Saturday night in Atlanta over Waycross, he praised, "The decided at the beginning of the year they were not going to be denied. They said practically every day of the season they were going to win the state championship."

The Berrien genius of the roundball added, "This group did everything possible that it takes to win a state championship. They had ability … They had the greatest degree of loyalty that you'll find in one group … This was from our first girl through the 12th."

Did the pressure of an unbeaten campaign ever get to his girls?

"I think the only time we felt any pressure was in the sub region tournament (Region 1-AA West at Thomasville)," he answered. "I thought in the state tournament they were as loose as any group I've had … loose as a goose."

Simpson praised, "They devoted themselves this season to two things: books and basketball."

On the books' aspect, five seniors were named recently to the Gazette's annual All Academic Tiftarea squad. All have posted 90 or better averages for their prep careers.

The devotion to basketball was evidence in the state championship which climaxed a grand season for the Rebelettes. Simpson cited "off-the-floor leadership" as one of the chief factors.

Eight Take June Walk

How about the leading Berrien girls?

"Defensively, the play of Lenna Carey, Peggy Barber, Andrea Carter and Brenda Rudeseal was just tremendous," Simpson lauded.

"On offense, Mary Grace Bailey played the best she's ever played (state tournament). Donna Jernigan gave her usual great effort. I can't say enough for the leadership of Marla Brown … Her great value to the ballclub was on the floor and also off-the-floor leadership."

Five-sixths of the starting team gained All-Tournament recognition. Included were Bailey, Jernigan, Brown, Carey and Barber.

Carter and Rudeseal, who alternated at the third guard spot, both gained Honorable Mention citations.

Providing depth were forwards Jo Ann Langford, Donna Bennett, Sandy McMillan and Pat Williams, together with guards Debra Swain and Debbie Harrell.

Opponents are happy to know that eight will be taking the graduation walk come June. They include Carey, Barber, Carter, Brown, Bailey, Jernigan, Langford, McMillan and Williams.

As Simpson warns about next year, though, "Going undefeated and winning the state championship will make it much easier."

Boys Are Overshadowed

When a boys' high school basketball team can win 27 consecutive games and finish 27-2 for overall play, you would hardly expect the group to be overshadowed by the girls.

Yet, that was the plight of the Berrien boys. They advanced to the State AA quarter-finals before elimination by defending titlist Carver of Atlanta.

Simpson, who also guided this team (f)or an incredible 57-2 record for the year, calls that defeat to Carver his boys' "worst game in four years." Turnovers for the most part killed the Rebels.

Surprisingly, he called Lakeshore – which fell to Berrien in first round play – "quicker than Carver" and a better overall team.

"If we had been ready to play," Simpson observed, "I think we could have handled anybody in the tournament with the exception of East Rome (eventual champion)."

Future Foes Shudder

While evaluating his most recent Rebels' edition, Simpson asserted, "Defensively, it was the best basketball team I've ever had … physically the strongest team I've coached."

There were two primary reasons why the Rebels were his "best" defensive team and "physically the strongest team." They came in the 6-5 forms of George Sorrell and Charles Wright, with the former making the All-State squad.

Berrien foes next year are hardly pleased to know that four-fifths of the starting lineup will return, including Sorrell and Wright. Roger Guess and Bobby Taylor are also due back.

Richard Tucker is the only starter departing. David Harnage and Jerry Slaughter saw backup duty.

Other varsity members slated for returns are David Bobo, Bobby Conway, Kim Carey, Wayne Taylor and Karl Harrell.

If these Rebels set their sights as the Rebelettes did this year, they just might not be "denied" that state championship a year hence.

The Valdosta Daily Times, page 14, March 24, 1970

Rebelettes Added Frosting to Cake

By Sammy Glassman
Times Sports Editor

It just wouldn't have been right for this area's most successful high school basketball season in more than a decade to end without a state championship being added to the list of honors.

Well, coach Stanley Simpson's amazing Berrien Rebelettes from Nashville, came through in sparkling fashion and added the frosting to the cake.

The Rebelettes, as most of you already know, now rule as Georgia's Class AA girls champions and they closed the book on their 1969-70 season with a perfect 30-0 record.

An undefeated season, topped off by a state crown, well, there just isn't any way you can improve that.

The Rebelettes have had seven who have carried most of the load this winter. They include forwards Marla Brown, Mary Grace Bailey and Donna Jernigan and guards Peggy Barber, Lenna Carey, Andrea Carter and Brenda Rudeseal.

On offense the girls from Nashville offered an attack which was well-balanced and very potent. As for the Berrien guards, they've got to be rated as one of the all-time great defensive combos to turn up on a girls team in this or any other part of the state.

Simpson, with many years of coaching success behind him, must be credited with doing another outstanding job.

We've talked about the success the quintets and sextets in the area had during the 1969-79 season before. But now that the last dribble has been made and the final shot taken let's recap it just one more time.

In all, eight teams from the area gained state tourney berths. We've already made note of the Berrien girls success. Now let's list, briefly, the others' accomplishments.

Long, Long List

In addition to his girls becoming state champions, Simpson's Berrien Rebels won the 1-AA (West) and 1-AA boys titles and gained the state "AA" quarter-finals. They finished with a 27-2 mark.

At the Class AAA level, coach Steve Kebler's Lowndes Vikettes copped the 1-AAA title and advanced to the state quarter-finals before closing with a 21-6 mark. Coach Joe Wilson's Valdosta Wildcats finished with a 16-9 record after becoming the 1-AAA boys champs and gaining the first round of the state "AAA" tourney.

Over at Homerville, coach Austin DeLoach's Clinch County Panthers went 16-9. They won the 2-B (West) crown, were runners-up in the 2-B playoffs and went as far as the first round of the state tourney.

Among the Class C entries in this section coach Jon Hazelip's Georgia Christian School Generals from Dasher chalked up a 21-5 record while winning the 1-C boys crown and advancing to the semi-finals in state tourney play.

Coach Angie Devivo's Lanier County (Lakeland, Ga.) Bulldogettes wound up with a 13-12 record. They were the 1-C girls runners-up and reached the quarter-finals before they bowed out of the state "C" tourney.

Super Year

Down at Hamilton County (Jasper, Fla.), coach Ray Rollyson's Rebels had a super year. Their final record was 24-4. They won the Suwannee Conference, District 5 and Region 2-B tourneys and then lost in overtime in the finals of their state tournament.

The eight who gained state tourney berths weren't the only teams in the area to finish well above .500. Three others who did it were coach Charles Cooper's Lowndes Vikings, 18-7; coach Billy Pafford's Lanier Bulldogs, 17-5, and coach Larry Prestridge's Brooks County (Quitman) Tigers, 12-9.

There can be no doubt. Prep basketball in this section is moving forward at a rapid pace, to the obvious delight of the many cage fans in the area.

The Tifton Gazette, page 4, March 25, 1970

Berrien's Brown, Sorrell Take All-Tiftarea MVP Cage Prizes

By Doug Hawley
Gazette Sports Editor

A pair of Berrien County stalwarts, who sparked their respective teams to marvelous seasons, have earned Most Valuable Player awards on the Gazette's seventh annual All-Tiftarea basketball teams.

Forward Marla Brown has the Most Valuable Player prize for the girls' elite team. George Sorrell, a forward, boasts the boys' honor.

Brown is joined on the girls' squad by three Berrien teammates. Included are guard Lenna Carey and Peggy Barber, together with forward Donna Jernigan.

Tift County boasts two selections for the girls, namely forward Juanita Dickens and guard Sherri Whittington. Atkinson County also has a pair, including forward Shelia Browning and guard Linda Sue Nugent.

Other girls tabbed include forward Lyn Futch, Cook County; forward Martha Woodward, Turner County.

On the boys' ledger, Tift and Berrien shared top honors in terms of numbers, with two each. Fitzgerald, Cook, Worth and Turner have one apiece.

Tift's duo includes center Edd Dorminey and guard Riley Cates. Guard Bobby Taylor joins Sorrell from Berrien.

Rounding out the elite boys' squad include Larry Barber, Fitzgerald; Robert Ray, Cook; Keith Bridges, Worth; Wayne Kennedy, Turner.

In the girls' division, Berrien's Brown was not the area's leading scorer (18.5 per game). However, the 5-9 senior provided the spark for a well balanced unbeaten team (30-0) which captured the State AA championship.

"She is the most dedicated ballplayer I have ever coached, Berrien Coach Stanley (Ramrod)

Simpson asserts of his girls' captain for the past two years. "Marla Brown has put in over 1,150 individual work hours on basketball during the past three years. Her leadership ability has been above and beyond the call of duty. Her on and off the floor leadership for the past two years has played one tremendous roll toward making our record what it is."

Despite playing most of the season with an ankle injury and nursing an ailing back in the State Tournament, Brown kept the Rebelettes going. She led the most recent edition in least number of floor mistakes.

Sorrell (6-5, 185), who is only a junior, spearheaded Berrien to easily the best boys' Tiftarea record, 27-2. The Rebels had a 27 game winning streak going before falling to defending champion Carver of Atlanta in the State AA quarterfinals.

The Berrien stalwart averaged 17.1 points per game in the Rebels' deliberate offense. He hit a fantastic 65 per cent of his field goal shots, a school record.

On the rebounding ledger, Sorrell averaged 15.4 each time out, marking another Berrien school mark. Defensively, the agile, big forward was downright intimidating.

It's small wonder that Simpson calls Sorrell "the most outstanding basketball player I have ever coached."

Both Most Valuable Player recipients will receive trophies from the Gazette in the near future.

Tift's contributions to the boys' team, Dorminey (19.3) and Cates (16.2) provided two-thirds of the Blue Devils' offense. The former, who missed the first part of the season due to an injury, was a demon on the boards with 17 per outing.

On the girls' ledger, Tift placed a pair of juniors in Dickens (18.0 scoring average) and Whittington. The latter was selected by her teammates as captain though she still has another year.

A torrid-shooting forward group also includes Browning (25.0), Woodward (25.0) and Futch (24.5). Jernigan's average (15.7) was deceiving in the disciplined Berrien attack.

Berrien's defensive contributions, Carey and Barber, shut off all offenses so unlucky as to face them. Nugent was a pillar of strength defensively for Atkinson's Region 2-B titlists.

On the boys' ledger, the individual average game marks read like Who's Who, such as Barber (19.2 points and 18 rebounds), Kennedy (18 points and 17 rebounds), Ray (16 points and 12 rebounds).

Bridges was Worth's leading scorer (13 points per outing) and an excellent rebounder. Taylor did not have the average of the others (8.6), but he rated Simpson's plaudits as his team's "best defensive man."

Four boys have repeated on the All-Tiftarea squad, including Sorrell, Dorminey, Kennedy, and Barber. Only one girl encored, namely Carey.

There were 10 girls picked this time, the group boasting six forwards. An unusual number of sharp-shooters existed this go-around.

Berrien (Region 1-AA) and Atkinson (Region 2-B) both claimed girls' league titles. Cook was a sub-region runnerup (1-A East), and fast-finishing Tift took fourth in its region (1-AAA).

Of the six forwards, only two are seniors, those being Brown and Woodward. Whittington is the only non-senior among the guard corps.

On the boys' scene, there were eight selected – three forwards, three centers and two guards. Only Berrien took a league title.

Five of the eight performers are seniors. Sorrell, Barber and Taylor all have junior status.

No boy picked is under 6-0. Dorminey (6-6), Sorrell (6-5) and Barber (6-5) all supply inside height and strength.

ALL-TIFTAREA BASKETBALL

Girls' Team
Marla Brown (5-9, sr., Berrien)....................... F
Juanita Dickens (5-6 ½, jr., Tift) .... F
Donna Jernigan (5-4, jr., Berrien) .... F
Lyn Futch (5-7, jr., Cook) .... F
Sheila Browning (5-5, soph., Atkinson)......... F
Martha Woodward (5-7, sr. Turner) .... F
Lenna Carey (5-10, sr., Berrien) .... G
Sherri Whittington (5-7, jr., Tift)................... G
Peggy Barber (5-7, sr., Berrien)..................... G
Linda Sue Nugent (5-8, sr., Atkinson)............G

Honorable Mention: Forwards – Gail James, Worth; Cheryl Griffin, Cook; Debra Hawkins, Tift; Mary Grace Bailey, Berrien; Jeannine Peterson, Atkinson. Guards – Andrea Carter, Berrien; Janice Ward, Cook; Linda McSwain and Margaret Ann Scott, Turner.

Boys' Team
George Sorrell (6-5, jr., Berrien) .... F
Wayne Kennedy (6-1, sr., Turner)................. F
Keith Bridges (6-3, sr., Worth) .... F
Edd Dorminey (6-6, sr., Tift) C
Larry Barber (6-5, jr., Fitzgerald C
Robert Ray (6-2 ½, sr., Cook) C
Riley Cates (6-0, sr., Tift)............................. G
Bobby Taylor (6-0, jr., Berrien .... G

Honorable Mention: Richard Tucker, Charles Wright and Roger Guess, Berrien; Bobby Tucker, Cook; Lindsey Napier, Worth; Billy Huffstuttler, Atkinson.

The Berrien Press, front page, March 26, 1970

Simpson Builds Character Along With Champions

Folks in Berrien County didn't know what an asset they had acquired when Stanley Simpson came to town 10 years ago.

When Simpson moved to the place known to upstaters as "Nashville – that's in Tennessee, isn't it," Berrien High School had a basketball program that had very average material, no tradition and, possibly worst of all, no gym.

Simpson didn't make any miracle-man claims – he knew that to build a successful program he had to start at the bottom and, at the time, Berrien County basketball was about as bottom as he could get.

That first year was rough for Simpson and his homeless traveling circus – his Rebels won only two games while losing 20 – but he carried the Rebelettes to a 16-5 record and the quarterfinals of the state tournament.

Since that hectic first year, Berrien County has become a name that gives opposing coaches white-knuckle-itis.

The Simpson teams moved into their new gym for the 1962-63 season and since then have put 19 first place trophies and eight runners-up trophies in the Berrien trophy case.

The Rebelettes have won 11 firsts including five sub-region championships and two region championships, three straight Lowndes Invitational titles, three trips to the state quarterfinals and the most recent addition, the first state championship ever won by a Berrien High team.

The Rebels won three subregion crowns, two region titles, three Lowndes Invitational titles and finish third in the state in 1968 and advanced to the quarterfinals this year.

Nowadays, those same upstaters know Nashville as "That's basketball country!"

Simpson's court wizardry is well known but there is another side to the personable athletic director that in the long run will have a more far-reaching effect on Berrien County.

A demanding task-master, he does more than produce basketball players. Simpson builds character.

In an era of permissiveness, Simpson requires self-discipline from his players and he gets it. His priorities place a player's religion and family first, school work next—then basketball.

The other diversions that take most high schoolers' time come way down the line.

On this foundation of self-discipline and priorities, Simpson teaches his charges to strive for the highest attainable goal – be it in basketball, school or life.

Simpson players can't reconcile themselves to finishing last in a two-horse race, and that's how leaders are made.

Folks in Berrien County didn't know what an asset they had acquired when Stanley Simpson came to town 10 years ago.

The world needs more teachers like him.

The Berrien Press, front page, March 26, 1970

BERRIEN HIGH REBELETTES WIN STATE AA BASKETBALL TITLE

By Johnny Futch

Berrien High School's Rebelettes went through the formality of beating Waycross, 37-32, in Atlanta Saturday night for the state AA girls basketball championship and in the process left absolutely no doubt as to who has the best team in AA.

No team in recent years has so totally dominated a tournament like Berrien, a fact underscored by sportswriters and broadcasters when they named seven Rebelettes for All-State honors. Five Rebelettes – forwards Marla Brown, Donna Jernigan and Mary Grace Bailey, and guards Lenna Carey and Peggy Barber – were named to the first team All-State squad while Brenda Rudeseal and Andrea Carter, who shared playing time at the other guard slot, earned honorable mention.

The All-Staters earned their honors. The massive team effort was typical of a Ramrod Simpson team but each was a heroine in her own right. Team captain Brown ignored a painful back injury that was supposed to have ended her playing career, scoring 41 points in three games and coolly quarterbacked the liquid Berrien offense; Bailey shredded opposition defenses with her driving ability and deadly medium jumper, scoring 54 points in the last four games; and Jernigan, who at 5-4 was a lot closer to the ground than most players, drove, dribbled and shot like a pint-sized Pete Maravich and, with a total 76 points, ran away with high scoring honors in three of the four tournament games.

On the other end of the floor, Carey dominated the boards despite an ankle injury, setting a school record in the opener with Lakeshore with 12 rebounds and shattering it in the finale with 14 rebounds on the official book; Barber, who specialized all season in shutting off hot shooters, did just that in the tournament against some of the best in the state; and the Rudeseal-Carter duo kept opponents off balance with their harassing tactics.

Simpson's charges blitzed through the field beating Lakeshore early in the week, 43-26, to move on to Atlanta where they buried O'Keefe 53-28 and dumped tough Forsyth County 54-42 in the semi-finals.

Only the determined heroics of Vicki Cason and little but mobile Gale Baker kept Waycross Bulldogettes close in the title showdown.

A Bailey layup and jumper gave the Rebelettes a quick 4-0 lead in the opening minute. Cason and Baker hit a field goal each to tie things at 4-4, but Brown retaliated from the outside with 1:22 gone in the game and the Waycross title hopes fell through the bottom of the basket with the ball. The remaining 26 minutes and 38 seconds just made things official.

Waycross could manage only two more points in the opening period and the Bulldogettes trailed 14-6 at the end of the quarter. By halftime Berrien had a 23-12 margin.

The Rebelettes spent the rest of the game cooling it and watching Waycross shoot – and miss – for a miserable 26 percent from the field.

Leading at times by as much as 15, Berrien let Waycross fram away while the partisan crowd roared the inevitable "We're Number One" chant.

While the Waycross forwards were missing 38 of 51 shots from the field, the deliberate Berrien offense hit 15 of 26 for 58 percent. They also cashed in on seven of nine free throws in a game that saw only 16 fouls called, seven on Berrien and nine on Waycross.

Jernigan ended the evening with 15 points, Brown had 13 and Bailey nine. Cason, used to hitting around 30, was baffled by Barber and managed only 16. Baker, named with Cason to the All-State first team, had 14.

O'Keefe didn't provide much competition in the Atlanta opener, the quarterfinals.

Berrien vaulted to a 13-6 lead at the end of the first quarter and coasted, while widening the margin, the rest of the way. Simpson cleaned the bench after running out a 27-point edge at the end of the third quarter.

Captain Brown, a doubtful starter at gametime, scored 20 points while Jernigan added 17 and Bailey 14. The starting guards, Carey, Barber and Carter, allowed O'Keefe only 16 points in three quarters.

Forsyth County promised to be a tougher test in the semifinals but a whirlwind scoring binge in the second quarter smashed the Bulldogettes from Cumming.

Forsyth actually led at the end of the first quarter, 12-10 but Berrien exploded for 22 points while allowing the Bulldogettes only nine and the Rebelettes went ahead, 32-21 at intermission.

Jernigan poured in 24 points, Bailey scored 21 and Brown nine in the romp.

The state championship capped a perfect 30-0 season and was the fourth Rebelette title of the year. They won the Lowndes-Hahira Invitational title, the 1 AA-West crown and beat Waycross 41-35 for the 1 AA championship. The win marked the 18th time in 21 years that AA champions have come from the present region 1AA area.

BERRIEN (53): Brown 20, Jernigan 17, Bailey 14, Carey, Barber, Carter, Langford 2, McMillan, Williams, Rudeseal, Swain, Harrell.
Team Totals: field goals – 22; free throws – 9 of 16; fouls – 17.
O'KEEFE (28): Thompson 7, Morgan 12, Warlick 5, Carey, McCullums, Peters, Nichols 2.
Team Totals: field goals – 11; free throws – 6 of 19; fouls – 15.

BERRIEN (54): Brown 9, Jernigan 24, Bailey 21, Carey, Barber, Carter, Rudeseal.
Team Totals: field goals – 17; free throws – 20 of 35; fouls – 13.
FORSYTH CO. (42): Boling 3, Lummus 22, Gravitt 17, Martin, Monroe, Linton, Holtzclaw, Wentz.
Team Totals: field goals – 16; free throws – 10 of 15; fouls – 25.

BERRIEN (37): Brown 13, Jernigan 15, Bailey 9, Carey, Barber, Carter, Rudeseal.
Team Totals: field goals – 15; free throws – 7 of 9; fouls – 7.
WAYCROSS (32): Cason 16, Gale Baker 14, Garner 2, Dale Baker, Williams, Miles.
Team Totals: field goals – 13; free throws – 6 of 8; fouls – 9.

April 1970

The Berrien Press, front page, April 2, 1970
We Are Proud
Readers may note on this front page the many good things about Berrien County for which everyone can be thankful:

Girls State AA Basketball Champs . . . national 4-H Club recognition . . . state social studies recognition . . . increased emphasis on manufacturing a diversified economy . . . the beauty of nature in the trees and flowers . . . and more young people who are starting young on right path.

The accent is on youth and the leadership they provide. We are proud of them and what they do – and just couldn't help reminding the rest of the world of what a good place Berrien County is.

The Berrien Press, page 3, April 2, 1970

Rebelettes Add Frosting to Cake in Sports

It just wouldn't have been right for this area's most successful high school basketball season in more than a decade to end without a state championship being added to the list of honors.

Well, coach Stanley Simpson's amazing Berrien Rebelettes from Nashville, came through in sparkling fashion and added the frosting to the cake.

The Rebelettes, as most of you already know, now rule as Georgia's Class AA girls champions and they closed the book on their 1969-70 season with a perfect 30-0 record.

An undefeated season, topped off by a state crown, well, there just isn't any way you can improve that.

The Rebelettes have had seven who have carried most of the load this winter. They include forwards Marla Brown, Mary Grace Bailey and Donna Jernigan and guards Peggy Barber, Lenna Carey, Andrea Carter and Brenda Rudeseal.

On offense the girls from Nashville offered an attack which was well-balanced and very potent. As for the Berrien guards, they've got to be rated as one of the all-time great defensive combos to turn up on a girls team in this or any other part of the state.

Simpson, with many years of coaching success behind him, must be credited with doing another outstanding job.

In addition to his girls becoming state champions, Simpson's Berrien Rebels won the 1-AA (West) and 1-AA boys titles and gained the state "AA" quarter-finals. They finished with a 27-2 mark. – Sammy Glassman, Valdosta Times.

The Berrien Press, page 6, April 9, 1970

Photo captions:

PREPARATIONS – Busy cooking and serving steaks and all the trimmings to the Berrien High basketball teams last week, left to right were: Charles Tomberlin, W.R. Roberts, Mrs. Dumps Futch, S.T. Hamilton, Wilson Connell, Roy Harrell, Virgil Jones, Curtis Giddens, Marcus Hughes and Julian Baldree.

STEAK SUPPER – Thomas G. (Pig) Futch, center foreground, and other members of the VFW served a steak supper to members of the winningest teams of the Berrien High School last week at the VFW home. The Rebelettes returned from the State AA tournament with the championship trophy and a 30-0 record and the Rebels advanced to the quarterfinals of the State AA tournament with a 26-1 record.

The Berrien Press, front page, April 16, 1970

Coach Stanley Simpson Expresses Appreciation

We have just completed the most successful season in the history of Berrien High School, and I would like to take this opportunity to express to our fans my sincere appreciation for a number of things that have made this past season a most enjoyable one for a coach.

First of all, the Berrien High Rebelettes accomplished the ultimate goal of all athletic teams, an unbeaten season of 30-0 and a state championship. No one will ever realize what all it takes for a team to reach this goal, but this group of young ladies put it all together and with the help of some wonderful fans, they came away perched atop the basketball world. I take this opportunity to give a public "thank-you" and a special word of praise to all members of the Berrien High Rebelettes.

The Berrien High Rebels had a most successful season, winning three championships and finishing with a record of 27-2. When we stop to consider the fact that we only started one senior, this group really did a great job. I am especially thankful for this group of young men who represented themselves in such an outstanding manner.

To the fans who showed their appreciation to the teams by recognizing them in various manners we are very grateful. To the people who saw fit to contribute certain gifts to myself, especially the big one, I offer my sincere appreciation. The $1,000 gift was the nicest thing to happen in my life. No coaching situation is a perfect one and neither is any coach a perfect coach, but our program at Berrien is now set under pretty strong conditions and with continued hours of work, dedication, understanding parents, and above all – sincere loyalty, the basketball program will continue to prosper. I would not trade jobs with any high school coach in Georgia, and I just hope I can make you happy with our program. I do have a personal ambition to enter college coaching in the future, but for now my "moments" at Berrien make me very happy.

Yours truly,
Coach W. Stanley Simpson
Head Basketball Coach
Berrien High School

May 1970

The Berrien Press, front page, May 7, 1970
Rebelettes Battle BHS Faculty Men May 12
By Johnny Futch

The eight senior girls who made up the Berrien High Rebelette basketball team this past season will play the men's faculty of Berrien High on Tuesday, May 12, at 8 p.m. at the Berrien High gym.

The Rebelettes, who finished the past season with a terrific 30-0 record enroute to the state AA championship, have already downed the faculty team one time before the entire student body, but the faculty team claimed they were tired from teaching during the day and that the officials (Sizemore and Futch) made several calls that turned things in favor of the girls.

The Rebelettes, after listening to such charges, are giving the faculty team another shot at them, and this time the public is invited to attend. All proceeds will go to the letter club of B.H.S. Admission will be 25 and 50 cents.

The Rebelettes will feature Andrea Carter, Peggy Barber, Lenna Carey, Joann Langford, Pat Williams, Sandy McMillan, Mary Grace Bailey and Marla Brown.

The faculty team will be composed of such greats as: Wayne Harris, Don Bridges, Johnny Rutland, Fred Tucker, Henry Patten, Jimmy Lane, Freddie Lawrence, Gene Sellars and Stanley "SOCKS" Simpson.

Everyone is invited to come see the best team in the history of B.H.S. perform once again as they battle the Berrien High Men's Faculty "Faults."

The Berrien Press, page 3, May 21, 1970
Rover Rules Prevail for Final Basketball Encounter
Berrien basketball coach, Stanley Simpson, announces that the annual spring basketball games will be held on Saturday, May 23 at 7 and 8 p.m. to conclude this year's spring practice.

The girl's game will feature this past season's seniors versus next season's probable team. It will be the last time the seniors will perform as a unit. The game will be played under the new "rover rules" which will go into effect next season. At this time, it looks as if the Rebelettes will be short and young for next year, but very quick. "We have a long, long way to go," is about the only comment you can get from Simpson concerning next year's team.

The boy's encounter will feature next year's team versus a group of seniors. The Rebels lost only three members off this year's team. The Rebels of next year should be tough if they all stay together. Simpson has installed a high-flying running offense to add to the attack. "We will not leave the set-up-disciplined type of offense, but we are simply adding something more to our attack," stated Simpson.

The public is invited to these games and there will be no charge for admission.

PART 4

Statistics

1969-70 Berrien High Rebelettes
State AA Basketball Champions

1969-1970
30-0 overall
Home: 10-0   Away: 10-0   Neutral: 10-0
Head Coach: Stanley Simpson
STATE AA CHAMPION
Region 1-AA Champion
Region 1-AA-W Champion
Lowndes Christmas Tournament Champion

				Leading Scorer
Dec. 3	40	at Tift County	16	Jernigan, 19
Dec. 5	51	Lowndes	30	Jernigan, 29
Dec. 6	63	Bainbridge	32	Jernigan, 31
Dec. 9	59	at Lanier County	27	Bailey, 27
Dec. 16	63	at Cook County	33	Brown, 26
Dec. 19	56	Worth County	15	Jernigan, 21

Lowndes Christmas Tournament

Dec. 29	57	Tift County	36	Bailey, 24
Dec. 30	44	Lowndes	37	Jernigan, 26
Jan. 2	55	Cairo	28	Brown, 29
Jan. 3	37	at Lowndes	29	Brown, 14
Jan. 6	42	Valdosta	20	Brown, 21
Jan. 9	42	at Crisp County	26	Jernigan, 17
Jan. 10	32	Tift County	27	Jernigan, 14
Jan. 16	49	Thomasville	47	Brown, 21; Jernigan 21
Jan. 17	48	at Cairo	47	Brown, 26
Jan. 20	56	Cook County	21	Jernigan, 20
Jan. 24	55	at Thomasville Central	23	Brown, 16
Jan. 27	54	Lanier County	46	Brown, 28
Jan. 30	48	Crisp County	27	Brown, 15; Jernigan 15
Jan. 31	42	at Bainbridge	26	Brown, 17
Feb. 6	50	at Thomasville	38	Jernigan, 25
Feb. 10	26	at Valdosta	21	Brown, 15

Region 1-AA-W Tournament at Thomasville

Feb. 19	63	Bainbridge	46	Brown, 26
Feb. 21	53	Thomasville	27	Brown, 29

Region 1-AA Tournament at Crisp County

Feb. 26	46	Appling County	28	Jernigan, 20
Feb. 28	41	Waycross	35	Bailey, 24

State AA Tournament at Vienna

March 16	43	Lakeshore	26	Jernigan, 20

State AA Tournament at Northside-Atlanta

March 19	53	O'Keefe	28	Brown, 20
March 20	54	Forsyth County	42	Jernigan, 24
March 21	37	Waycross	32	Jernigan, 15

1969-70 TEAM STATISTICS
(Information from chart in back of team scorebook)

Player	FG	FTM	Rebounds	Points
Marla Brown	181	141	70	503
Mary Grace Bailey	133	51	68	317
Donna Jernigan	198	115	93	511
Jo Ann Langford	30	11	25	71
Donna Bennett	2	3	3	7
Sandy McMillan	9	23	11	41
Pat Williams	3	2	1	8
Lenna Carey			198	
Peggy Barber			139	
Andrea Carter			47	
Brenda Rudeseal			85	
Debra Swain			14	
Debbie Harrell			4	

Awards and Honors

Atlanta Journal-Constitution All-State AA Basketball, 1969-1970
Coach of the Year: Stanley Simpson
Mary Grace Bailey
Peggy Barber
Marla Brown
Lenna Carey
Donna Jernigan
<u>Honorable Mention</u>
Andrea Carter
Brenda Rudeseal

The Tifton Gazette All-Tiftarea Basketball Team, 1969-1970
Most Valuable Player: Marla Brown
Peggy Barber   Guard
Lenna Carey   Guard
Donna Jernigan   Forward
<u>Honorable Mention</u>
Mary Grace Bailey   Forward
Andrea Carter   Guard

The Tifton Gazette Academic All-Tiftarea Basketball Team, 1969-1970
Peggy Barber
Andrea Carter
Jo Ann Langford
Sandra McMillan
Pat Williams (co-captain)
<u>Honorable Mention</u>
Mary Grace Bailey
Marla Brown
Lenna Carey

<u>Team Banquet Awards, 1969-1970</u>
Most Outstanding
    Peggy Barber
    Lenna Carey
    Andrea Carter
    Brenda Rudeseal
    Marla Brown
    Donna Jernigan
    Grace Bailey
    Jo Ann Langford

GAME OFFICIALS FOR 1969-1970 SEASON
(Information as available from BHS basketball scorebook)

	Timer	Scorer	Referee	Referee
Dec. 3 at Tift County		M. Sizemore		
Dec. 5 Lowndes	W. Hancock	M. Sizemore	Alton N. Sparks	799
Dec. 6 Bainbridge	W. Hancock	M. Sizemore	Allen Jewett	C. Bettiere
Dec. 9 at Lanier County		M. Sizemore		
Dec. 16 at Cook County		M. Sizemore		
Dec. 19 Worth County	W. Hancock	M. Sizemore	Allen Jewett	780
Lowndes Christmas Tournament				
Dec. 29 Tift County		M. Sizemore		
Dec. 30 Lowndes		M. Sizemore		
Jan. 2 Cairo	W. Hancock	M. Sizemore	1292	Jewett
Jan. 3 at Lowndes		M. Sizemore		
Jan. 6 Valdosta	W. Hancock	M. Sizemore	Don Morrow (780)	Jim Daniels
Jan. 9 at Crisp County		M. Sizemore		
Jan. 10 Tift County		M. Sizemore	1292	D. Arnold
Jan. 16 Thomasville	W. Hancock	M. Sizemore	Jim Daniels	Joe Gore (1228)
Jan. 17 at Cairo		M. Sizemore		
Jan. 20 Cook County	W. Hancock	M. Sizemore	Arnold (1478)	Gore (1228)
Jan. 24 at Thomasville Central		M. Sizemore		
Jan. 27 Lanier County	W. Hancock	M. Sizemore	Joe Gore	Jim Daniels
Jan. 30 Crisp County	W. Hancock	M. Sizemore	Allen Jewett	Walt Carter
Jan. 31 at Bainbridge				
Feb. 6 at Thomasville		M. Sizemore	Don Morrow	Crozier (799)
Feb. 10 at Valdosta				
Region 1-AA-W Tournament at Thomasville				
Feb. 19 Bainbridge				
Feb. 21 Thomasville				
Region 1-AA Tournament at Crisp County				
Feb. 26 Appling County				
Feb. 28 Waycross		Beach		
State AA Tournament at Vienna				
March 16 Lakeshore				
State AA Tournament at Northside-Atlanta				
March 19 O'Keefe				
March 20 Forsyth County				
March 21 Waycross				

CLASS AA SCHOOLS, 1969-70
(From pages 115-116 of the 1969-70 GHSA Constitution and By-Laws)

CLASS AA – Adjusted ADA (average daily attendance) 650 to 925

Region 1 – Appling County, Bainbridge, Berrien, Crisp County, Dodge County, Dublin, Dudley Hughes (Macon), Thomasville, Waycross.

Region 2 – Briarwood (East Point), Campbell (Fairburn), Central (Newnan), College Park, Hapeville, Headland (East Point), LaGrange, Lakeshore (College Park), Newnan, North Clayton (College Park), Ridgeview (Atlanta), Russell (East Point), South Fulton (East Point), Troup (LaGrange).

Region 3 – Campbell (Smyrna), North Springs (Atlanta), Sandy Springs (Atlanta), Wheeler (Marietta), Wills (Smyrna).

Region 4 – Henderson (Chamblee), Marist (Atlanta), St. Pius X (Atlanta), Shamrock (Decatur), Westminster (Atlanta), Woodward Academy (College Park).

Region 5 – Bass (Atlanta), George (Atlanta), Murphy (Atlanta), Roosevelt (Atlanta), Southwest (Atlanta), Sylvan (Atlanta).

Region 6 – Brown (Atlanta), Carver (Atlanta), East (Atlanta), Fulton (Atlanta), Grady (Atlanta), O'Keefe (Atlanta), Smith (Atlanta).

Region 7 – Calhoun, Cartersville, Cass (Cassville), Cedartown, Chattooga (Summerville), East Rome, Lafayette, Lakeview (Rossville), North Whitfield (Dalton), Pepperell (Lindale), Ringgold, West Fannin (Blue Ridge), West Rome.

Region 8 – Baldwin (Milledgeville), Blakeney (Waynesboro), Burney-Harris (Athens), Elbert County, Franklin County, Gainesville, Hart County, Newton County, South Hall (Gainesville), Stephens County, Winder-Barrow.

ABOUT THE AUTHORS

Jim Barber grew up in South Georgia, helping his family raise hogs and working on his uncles' tobacco farms while pursuing his dream to become a newspaper reporter. His first "public job" came at age 16, covering sports for his county newspaper, *The Berrien Press*. After graduating from the University of Georgia with a degree in Journalism-Newspapers, Jim worked for a number of media outlets, including United Press International and the *New York Daily News*. He eventually made his way to the world of corporate journalism and a 25-year career with Georgia Power and Southern Company, one of the nation's largest utilities. A state and national award winner for his writing, Jim is the author of *Plowed Fields*, a novel about life on a South Georgia tobacco farm in the 1960s. He also co-edited three previous nonfiction works, including *Atlanta Women Speak*, a collection of speeches from notable women such as Jane Fonda, Atlanta Mayor Shirley Franklin and author Pearl Cleage, as well as *Journey of Faith* and *Art From Our Hearts*, both church histories. While his work on the family farms is a distant memory, Jim does enjoy raising gardens in his backyard, especially tomatoes for his wife of 35 years. Jim doesn't eat tomatoes, but he does play a lot of tennis and works part-time as the administrator of his church. He and Becky live in Atlanta near Stone Mountain, which he climbs faithfully almost every day. They have three grown daughters, two sons-in-law and three grand dogs. Visit the author's website at www.jimbarber.me.

Skeeter Parker was born January 15, 1967—the day Super Bowl I was played—in Hahira, Georgia, and is a lifelong resident of Nashville. He earned a bachelor's degree in Business Management and a master's degree in Secondary Education from Valdosta State University, as well as an Education Specialist degree from Georgia Southern University in 2008. A 29-year veteran teacher, Skeeter has spent 27 of those years in the Berrien County Schools—nine at Berrien Middle School and the last 18 at Berrien High School where he teaches math. He has been named STAR Teacher three times and was Berrien High's Teacher of the Year for the 2016-17 school year.

Skeeter has spent over 30 years researching the history of various entities and events in Nashville and Berrien County. Starting in 1985, he began compiling sports histories of high school teams in the county. With the revival of the Berrien Historical Foundation (BHF) at the time of Berrien County's sesquicentennial in 2006, his attention turned toward researching the people, places and events of the county. The BHF has hosted two Smithsonian traveling exhibits, the first being *New Harmonies*, a music heritage exhibit, and in 2016, *Hometown Teams*, a sports heritage exhibit. Skeeter was the chief researcher for the local exhibits that served as companion pieces to the Smithsonian exhibits. His compilations have covered topics from the serious (murder and mayhem) to the whimsical (Christmas in Nashville) and all points in between.

Skeeter serves on the board of directors for the Berrien Historical Foundation and is chairman of the Berrien County Library Board. He is an occasional writer for the local newspaper, *The Berrien Press*, where he currently does a column on buildings that are "Gone But Not Forgotten." He and his wife, Judy, are members at First Baptist Church in Nashville where they are both actively involved in the church music ministry.

www.ingramcontent.com/pod-product-compliance
Lightning Source LLC
Chambersburg PA
CBHW050636150426

42811CB00052B/851